Worlding Women

Worlding Women

A Feminist International Politics

Jan Jindy Pettman

London and New York

First published 1996
by Allen & Unwin
9 Atchison Street, St Leonards, Sydney, NSW 2065

Published and distributed outside Australasia
by Routledge
11 New Fetter Lane, London EC4P 4EE

and in the USA and Canada
by Routledge
29 West 35th Street, New York, NY 10001

Routledge is an International Thomson Publishing company

Typeset in 10/11.5pt Garamond by DOCUPRO, Sydney

Printed and bound in Singapore by KHL Printing
Company (Pte) Ltd

British Library Cataloguing in Publication Data

A catalogue record for this book is available from the
British Library

Library of Congress Cataloging in Publication Data

A catalogue record for this book has been requested

ISBN   0–415–15201–1
          0–415–15202–X (pbk)

Contents

Introduction

Several years ago, when this book began, no single–authored feminist overview had yet emerged from within International Relations (IR). To make a place for myself to write, I began by introducing different players—'IR', 'feminism/s', 'gender'—to see what might happen when these were brought together. My aim was to reveal that IR *is* gendered, and gendered *male*, in its theory and practice, and that women *are* players in the world that IR seeks to explain.

IR is one of the most masculinist of disciplines, in its personnel and in its understandings of states, wars and markets. It is, not coincidentally, one of the most resistant to feminist scholarship. It proceeds, largely, as if women aren't in world politics. This suggests that 'the international' is literally men's business; or possibly that women and men play similar roles and are similarly affected by international relations and processes. IR has been reluctant to attend to the politics of its own knowledge–making, including its own gender politics. It has, until very recently, and still, in many places, kept feminist scholarship—and feminists—out.

The first IR journal special issue on women and International Relations appeared in *Millennium* in 1988. From alongside IR, Cynthia Enloe's pathbreaking *Bananas, Bases and Beaches: Making Feminist Sense of International Politics* appeared in 1990. Since then, feminist IR books have proliferated, written or edited by Rebecca Grant and Kathleen Newland (1991), Ann Tickner (1992), Spike Peterson (1992a), Spike Peterson and Anne Sisson Runyan (1993), Christine Sylvester (1994a), Francine D'Amico and Peter Beckman

(1994), for example. There are more articles, mainly in *Millennium* or *Alternatives*, or in non–IR feminist journals; and an active Feminist Theory/Gender Studies section in the International Studies Association (ISA).

Now we can talk of a feminist IR community, or maybe of feminist IR, while recognising both its marginal and beseiged status within the discipline and the differences within the community. Feminist IR projects can be identified as deconstructing, revealing the discipline and its key concepts and categories as male; and as reconstructing, making women and gender relations visible (Peterson, 1992a; Hall, 1994). These reconstructions in turn disrupt the discipline. Women cannot simply be added in, for 'IR' has been constructed on the exclusion of women from 'high politics'. Peopling IR is especially difficult, for traditionally IR takes states as its central unit. As IR makes states into international persons, most men and all women are erased from its view.

The feminist deconstructionist project is now well advanced, critiquing foundation texts and current presumptions (Grant, 1991; Peterson, 1992a; Tickner, 1992; Sylvester, 1994a; Whitworth, 1994). It reveals IR encoded as masculine territory, and the ways that 'women' have been rendered homeless in IR (Sylvester, 1994b). The soldier, the citizen, the political subject, and the state are gendered male.

Some critics question whether IR is or can be a place from which to do gender and feminist work. Given the traditional constitution of the discipline, and its current politics, feminism and IR might indeed be incompatible (Smith, 1993; Walker, 1993). But such a conclusion concedes IR to those who currently occupy its territory and determine its boundaries.

Now IR is much pressed upon by critics within its borders, including—but not only—feminists, and by changes in the world, especially the end of the Cold War—the chief organising device for many in the discipline. With its particular Anglo–American, especially United States of America, looking positions, its western and great-power focus, IR was badly caught out by international changes, and especially by newly visible (but not new) identity conflicts, nationalisms and other boundary wars. It is under challenge, too, from intensifying globalisation and the restructuring of the world economy. These processes sit oddly with IR notions of state sovereignty and its clear distinction between the inside and the outside of states, the latter its particular reserve.

Is there room for a more inclusive—and more internationalist—

IR? Can the discipline be 'worlded', and the different worlds of those outside the powerful centres and classes be included in our understandings of international politics?

A dramatic attempt at reconstructing comes from feminist scholars who seek to make visible both 'women' and the different kinds of masculinity and femininity necessary to 'make the world go round'. Cynthia Enloe began by asking the subversive question: 'Where are the women?' (1990a). She revealed women as active players in and gender relations as constitutive of international politics. Feminist IR scholars are reworking war (Elshtain, 1987, 1992a), security (Tickner, 1992), revolution (Tetreault, 1994), productive relations (Peterson and Runyan, 1993; Marchant and Parpart, 1995) and international organisations (Whitworth, 1994) to name a few. There are studies, too, that refocus on men and masculinities in IR, involving collaboration among feminist IR women and pro-feminist men (Zalewski and Parpart, 1995).

Such rich writings, swiftly building, relieve the pressure on feminist IR writers to try to cover everything in a single book. (The fewer you are, the more representative you are expected to be, and feel you should be). Reaching 'critical mass', it is no longer an easy task to map the beginnings and growth of feminist IR in a short introductory section. Now we have much to draw on, and I, along with other feminist IR writers, can focus on my own particular project.

This project is enormously strengthened by the extensive writings in English by third-world feminists and others outside the white northern IR heartlands, helping to 'world' the account (for example, Afshar, 1987; Mohanty et al., 1991; Kandiyoti, 1991a; Moghadam, 1994a). The feminist IR project draws from and hopefully contributes to the growing visibility of women and feminist transnational organising on the world stage. Because women, gender relations and feminist scholarship have so effectively been excluded from IR until very recently, and still are in many places, the reconstructionist project in particular searches far beyond the discipline's boundaries for writings on, and by, women in the international, and for feminist critiques of identities and relations which are a part of that international. There are by now many feminisms (Tong, 1989; Humm, 1992). Alongside and often overlapping with older-identified distinctions between liberal, socialist, radical and cultural feminisms, for example (important as they are in their different accounts of sexual difference and gender power), are variously named black, third-world and ethnic-minority feminisms, themselves far from homogenous. They have prompted increasing feminist attention to difference as an issue between women, as well as between men and women. They are in shifting alliance or contest with postmodern critiques, which at times seem to threaten the very category 'women' and its possibilities for a feminist politics. These debates inform this attempt at worlding women—moving beyond white western power centres and their dominant knowledges (cf. Spivak, 1985), while recognising that I, as a white settler-state woman, need to attend to differences between women, too.

Worlding women

This book, then, is *a* feminist international politics. While drawing on feminist deconstructions of the field of IR, it is primarily an exercise in reconstruction, of writing women, gender relations and feminist scholarship into 'the international', perceived rather more widely than traditional IR. At the same time, it argues that gender relations never exist apart from other power relations, and so pursues intersections of gender, race, nationality and class in the international.

The book is organised into three parts. The first addresses international political identities, and the role of international processes in constructing political identities within states, too. It explores the gendered makings of states, citizenship, colonial relations and racism, nationalisms, migration and postcolonial identities, and women's experiences of these identity politics. The second part focuses on war and peace, exploring popular associations of men with war, and women with peace. It asks What do women have to do with war? and looks at women warriors, and sexual politics in state militaries. The third part looks at the international sexual division of labour, including the growing feminisation of the global assembly line, and the gendered politics of development, environment and population debates. It analyses contemporary kinds of international traffic in women, and suggests the notion of an international political economy of sex. The book concludes with a review of women's organising internationally, and with the possibilities and problems of transnational feminisms.

The term 'Worlding women' means taking women's experiences of the international seriously, while not assuming that any experiences are transparent or politically innocent. It assumes that all social relations are gendered, and rely on and reproduce certain kinds of masculinity and femininity, though not without contest or change. It critiques the profoundly gendered nature of IR as text and territory, discipline and practice. Here, too, relations are often sexualised, as women's bodies become markers of identity boundaries, and of forms of work that might endanger them. A different 'body politics' makes sexuality, and women's and men's bodies a part of 'international relations'.

Worlding Women seeks to make visible places and ways that women are in the world. I argue the central significance of the international in the everyday lives of women and men, and in gender relations, and ask what feminist scholarship has to tell us about these lives and relations. I ask, too, what feminism can learn about women, and gender relations, by interrogating the international, and by recognising the global and powerful structuring effects of 'difference', along gender, class, nationality and other axes.

But 'the world' is no more singular than gender is, or than women and men are. Different women, and men, experience the world/their worlds differently. These differences are powerful markers of location and interest. Beyond gender relations as power relations between men and women, 'worlding women' means exploring differences among and between women, too.

A (personal) politics of location

My shifting academic lives have taken me through territories labelled African studies, development studies and Australian studies. My work across boundaries of Aboriginal studies, multicultural studies and women's studies taught me the art of multidisciplinary learnings, and prompted my recent book *Living in Margins: Racism, Sexism and Feminism in Australia* (1992a).

In the late 1980s, as feminist subversions were just beginning in IR, I joined the Peace Research Centre at the Australian National University. Next-door was the (Realist) Department of International Relations, and next-door but one the Defence and Strategic Studies Centre. The corridor geography indicated a continuum of politics and studies from 'soft' to 'hard'. I was seen as even softer, 'down the wimpy end of peace research', as a male peace-research colleague reminded me. I was also, for some of that time, the only woman academic in those corridors.

My brief was wide; it included racism and community conflicts, women, war and peace, and the gendered politics of nationalism in Australia and internationally. Initially these concerns were seen as marginal to or outside the IR agenda, though they were soon to become painfully topical. While at the Centre, I organised a workshop on women, ethnicity and the state, which marked the beginning of close collaboration with Nira Yuval–Davis in conferences and networks exploring issues related to women and citizenship, migration and ethnicity. I also organised a conference on women and militarisation in the Asia–Pacific region, whose keynote speaker, Cynthia Enloe, had just published *Bananas, Bases and Beaches*. So when I returned to IR in 1991, I did so with a widening agenda that reflected the coming-together of my own interests and the newly emerging post-Cold War dis-order, and a determination to pursue questions around 'women' and gender as power relations in IR.

Acknowledgements

I owe many thanks to the students of my gender and international politics course, who provided me with practice runs through the material for this book. Parts, too, were rehearsed through various conferences and book collections, and with colleagues and friends. (An earlier version of Chapter 9 appears in Kofman and Youngs, 1996.) Cynthia Enloe's boundless enthusiasm and generosity, and her own searchings, have lightened my way. Spike Peterson shared bibliographies and conference panels early on, and her recent stay in Canberra enabled an everyday sharing of ideas and writing projects. Members of the Feminist Theory/Gender Studies section make ISA conferences adventures of intellect and friendship.

Elizabeth Weiss at Allen & Unwin had faith in me and in the book when I doubted it, and combined patience and pressure in just the right proportion. My thanks, too, to others at Allen & Unwin; and to Brenda Fajardo for the beautiful covers. Colleagues and friends who did good critical reading for me include Cynthia Enloe, David Hollinsworth, Carolyn Nordstrom, Spike Peterson, Steve Smith, Christine Sylvester and Tasha Sudan, who also suggested images used in the postscript. Sue Fraser, Jackie Lipsham and Sharon Merten worked on the Bibliography and supported me warmly at work, as Frances and Jude did outside work. Dominic sent me choice finds from Melbourne bookshops and libraries as he pursued his own postcolonial projects, and he and Merritt entertained me during my work there. Tasha and Saul kept me supplied with classy coffee at the Currockbilly Mountain Cafe on my way to and from the coast, where this book was written. It was reworked in large part at the Ulladulla Harbourside Cafe, whose fabulous water views encouraged my labours. Much within the book, and in my everyday, was explored in close conversations with Mike, whose company and wise counsel have helped carry me through.

PART 1

THE GENDERED POLITICS OF IDENTITIES

1

Women, gender and the state

States and sovereignty are at the centre of the practice and study of international relations. 'States continue to monopolise our understanding of how we organise ourselves politically, how political identity is constituted, and where the boundaries of political community are drawn' (Peterson, 1992a: 31). This is seen in the many who identify themselves as 'Australian', 'Japanese' or 'Chilean', for example, and in the widespread rallying behind a state in times of war.

Feminist critiques reveal the state, and citizenship, to be gendered. This chapter asks how the 'body politic' comes to be associated with male bodies, and why women find it so difficult to become full citizens of their state. This is especially so with regard to the IR state in its foreign policy, and in its military and security concerns. This warfare state is highly problematic for women, and for many men (Peterson, 1992a; Tickner, 1992).

IR has long taken the state for granted. Yet women's and men's experiences of states and citizenship vary enormously, within and between states. And states are changing, as intensifying processes of globalisation and fragmentation undermine states from above and below. States, sovereignty, and so IR, require rethinking, in ways that take both global dynamics and gender relations seriously (Peterson, 1995).

Sovereign states

State sovereignty makes a place for IR, as the discipline carves out territory for itself in the space between states. It does so by drawing

3

a distinction between the inside of states, which it relegates to other disciplines, such as sociology and political science; and the outside of states, misnamed international, but usually meaning interstate relations. This distinction between the 'domestic' and the 'international' is used to construct a particular understanding of the world. The inside of states is imagined as a place where order reigns, while the outside is seen as beyond community, a place of anarchy, danger and foreigners.

The linked ideas of 'states and sovereignty' encourage a conflation of space, territory and identity (Walker, 1993). Sovereignty declares the supreme political authority of the state against both internal and external competition. Sovereignty is an assumption about authority (R. Pettman, 1991), a right of command and an expectation of obedience and loyalty. It is backed up by the state's claim to a monopoly of the legitimate use of violence, and by its readiness to use force in pursuit of national interests. This is the special form of the IR state, where security becomes national security, the security of the state; hence IR's focus on wars and violence between states, despite the overwhelming experience of violence within states.

'States and sovereignty' privilege the particular over the universal, placing loyalty to the state above loyalty to humankind. It allows for the fictive 'state as person' of IR, so that we speak of 'Iraq' invading Kuwait, or 'Australia' protesting against French nuclear testing in the Pacific. Sovereignty refers to a set of rules or social practices, to 'what a state must do to be (recognised as) a state' (Weber, 1992: 200). These include consolidating dominant authority within the state, and representing the people of the state in the international, even though many states do not have effective control over all their territory or population. Sovereignty allows the state to speak for its people, regardless of how many of those people recognise its legitimacy. In this sense, it becomes a substitute or an alibi for a 'domestic community' (Weber, 1992: 215).

'States and sovereignty' territorialise political identity, so the people within the territorial boundaries of the state are expected to give their primary loyalty to the state. States also homogenise political identities in ways that disguise differences within the state—including gender differences—and create differences between states. They draw border lines along bounded space containing people, and charge the state with policing the boundaries, to keep the right people in and the wrong people out. To do this, the state requires a bureaucracy and centralised authority, the means of organised violence and of manufacturing consent, and a citizenry that it both disciplines and represents. 'The state's construction of "security" and "sovereignty" and its mobilisation of militarism and nationalist ideologies are particularly significant factors in consolidating and effectively reproducing centralised authority' (Peterson, 1992a: 4–5).

There is a close connection between state-making and war-making. States claim a monopoly of legitimate use of force, and the power to determine what force is legitimate. States have been described as protection rackets (Tilly, 1985), assuming rights, control and reward for 'protecting' citizens, while their own behaviour is often what most threatens those it supposedly protects. Ken Booth suggests that many states resemble mafia neighbourhoods.

> To countless millions of people in the world it is their own state, and not 'the Enemy', that is the primary security threat. In addition, the security threat to the regimes running states is often internal rather than external. It is almost certainly true that more governments around the world at this moment are more likely to be toppled by their own armed forces than by those of their neighbours (Booth, 1991: 318).

The narrowness of IR's focus, on wars and violence between states, was one reason the discipline was so taken by surprise by the end of the Cold War, and the dramatic conflicts around national identities and contestations for state power in the contemporary world.

Making the state

Gendered and feminist analyses reveal that the state is in almost all cases male dominated, and is in different ways a masculinist construct. It is simply not possible to explain state power without explaining women's systematic exclusion from it (Runyan and Peterson, 1991).

There is now much debate about the nature of politics and society, about the origin and development of states, and their relation to patriarchy. Feminist IR has reexamined foundation texts in western liberal political theory. It has tracked women's exclusion from public power, revealing the citizen who is presumed to be male (Elshtain, 1981; 1990; Grant, 1991). Indeed, it has revealed *gendered states* (Peterson, 1992a).

Feminist tracings of early state formation focus on the emergence and consolidation of public political power and the centralisation of authority, which simultaneously (though in different forms in different times and places) displaced autonomous kin communities, and constituted a separate domestic or private sphere that came to be associated with women and the feminine. Myths of the origins of Greek city-states inform western political theory, now incorporated into IR. The transition to institutionalised forms of domination and control were gendered. The Athenian polis marks the emergence of the (free) male citizen, and the construction of public space as male. Politics involved performance and appearance in the public space. In the private space of the home, women, children and slaves lived and worked to provide for the physical and emotional needs of men thus freed to go about their public and citizen duties.

In many non-western political economies, too, there was a long historical process of state formation, through which patriarchal norms became so extensive and entrenched as to become invisible (Lerner in Silverblatt, 1988: 445). Gradually and unevenly, states developed over the period 3100 to 600 BC in the ancient Near East. In Asia, for example in China, patriarchal states also developed. In many places regional or local authorities were rather less centralised or formalised, while in other places autonomous kin communities remained the basis of political and social order, at least until colonisation disrupted local power relations.

The modern state system dates from the Treaty of Westphalia in 1648, marking the end of the European religious wars. European state forms were imposed through wars and globally through colonisation. European settler states emerged in the late eighteenth and early nineteenth century in the Americas, and later in Australia, New Zealand and South Africa for example. The modern state was globalised through decolonisation after World War 2, so that now almost everyone lives in an internationally recognised sovereign state.

Under colonisation, European state-making processes were reproduced in other parts of the world, through the consolidation of centralised government and power. Colonised elites mobilised against foreign control but rarely against the introduced forms of political authority, seeking to take over the state rather than to remove it. Beginning in colonial rule and often intensifying since decolonisation, state-making included the conceding of local political power and resources to the state by some men, in return for men's increased control over their families (Charlton et al., 1989: 180). These processes strengthened the public/private divide, and increasingly subordinated women within the private—though the location and meaning of this divide was never fixed or uncontested.

States are historical and contingent. They are ongoing projects and a lot of work goes into keeping them going. State-making is a process that is neither inevitable nor unilinear. States themselves, or those who control and administer them, define boundaries of belonging and authority. The state itself becomes a player in politics; it plays in its own interests.

Gendered states

Classical western political thinkers, such as Plato and Aristotle, and those theorising the development and meaning of the modern state system, such as Hobbes and Locke, didn't ignore gender in the ways that contemporary theorists often do. Instead they incorporated notions of difference, of biology or culture, as reasons for excluding women from the political. Carole Pateman's retelling of the myth of origin (1988) sees the overthrow of the despotic fathers through a fraternal contract establishing the political rule of (elite) men and the gender rule of men as a group over women as a group. This contract did not simply overlook women, but was constituted on the basis of their exclusion. It established men's sex right to women's bodies and labour, and was a contract of citizenship, a political fraternity or brotherhood. Not all men were admitted to public power, but all men were admitted to sex right, to women's unpaid labour, sexual services and reproductive powers—to women's bodies.

The enlightenment's man turns out, indeed, to be a man. The state subject becomes an individual male—citizen, soldier, worker—a reasonable man. Women are not only different, but constructed in relation to men, and given inferior value. This gender dichotomy includes men as active, women as passive; men as heads of households and breadwinners, and women as their dependents (Peterson and Runyan, 1993).

Men move from public to private and back again. They are in positions of authority over unequals in the domestic sphere and recognised as individuals and citizens in the public sphere (or elite men are). Women are contained and constrained in the home and in their sexed bodies. Because public space is male, and women are seen as belonging in the private, women appearing in public space appear 'out of place'. '"The body politic" is masculinised, and a conflict is set up between female bodies and public space' (Jones, 1993: 78). There is a complex, shifting and contested association of

7

women with the domestic, but also with sexuality and danger, which makes women especially vulnerable to attack if they are seen as beyond protection, or out of control (Afshar, 1987).

'In the history of political theory, sex and woman go together like man and the polis' (Brown, 1987: 5). What has it meant to displace sex onto woman, and to see sex as not political? Men's disembodied political sphere and women's sexualised domestic one reflects the saturation of the female but not the male body with sex. Women are then constructed as needing disciplining; for female passions can ensnare or distract men, or set them up in competition with each other.

Adriana Cavarero (1992) critiques the forgetting, the radical erasure of the feminine and the domestic in the construction of politics and political theory, through the 'universalization of masculinity' in modern political thinking. The female and the domestic sphere in which she belongs 'naturally' is obscured, although the female labour and sexual services within it support and allow the male/public/political to function. A failure to 'see' women makes possible the transformation of 'man' into a supposedly neutral and universal being. This repression that excludes female difference can only allow female inclusion at the cost of homologising them—of making women become or be seen as being like men.

Through the work of many a male political theorist, the public/political of the individual citizen takes on the characteristics of the masculine, associating manhood with ruling. Independence is a quality of the political man, disconnected, impartial, unlike the private female, who is connected, dependent, nurturing, or—alternatively—unruly, sexual, disorderly. In either case, she needs to be under the protection/control of a man (to protect her—or to protect the polis/the man from her?). The relegation of women away from the public sphere facilitates the definition of the political as that where the female and femininity are absent, and constitutes the male citizen and masculine authority. This heritage informs IR's construction of states and international politics. 'Men, states and wars were the bases of theory, not women' (Grant, 1991: 21).

Women and the state

Feminists theorising the state and women's relations with it frequently focus on the welfare state in the west, the effects of transition to a market economy in Eastern Europe, and on women and development in 'the third world'. Even within states, generalisations about women and the state are difficult.

'The state' is an abstraction that refers to a set of relations, practices and institutions. States are not monolithic, uniform or unitary. Each state consists of a variety of sites, institutions, operations and functions, ranging in western states, for example, through warfare, policing, welfare and state funding for community organisations. States try to maintain conditions for capital accumulation, and manage productive relations and the labour market. States also attempt to contain different groups' claims in the face of political mobilisation, including claims by those who seek to escape from state power or to renegotiate their relations with the state.

Western liberal democratic states are interventionist states (Yeatman, 1990). They are highly bureaucratised, with a huge information gathering capacity, and a reach that affects almost everyone in every aspect of life (Sassoon, 1987). They are male states, in terms of those who 'man' them, although, especially in the Scandinavian states, there are significant numbers of women in higher positions. The state is still largely masculinist, in its assumption of (elite) male interests and characteristics as the norm, though in some states there is now a feminist presence, often marginalised and contained. What the state does is heavily gendered. The state is 'the main organiser of the power relations of gender' (Connell, 1990: 520) through its legislation and policies, and the ways it is implicated in the construction of the public/private.

The impact of state action and inaction is gendered, affecting men as a group and women as a group differently. Even within any one state, it is very difficult to generalise 'an entire range of relationships between groups of women in particular locations and a variety of state policies, agencies and processes' (Randall, 1987: 14). But we can say that women as a group are more dependent on the state than men. Much of the provisioning that is directed at women as women or as mothers comes as a result of long decades of struggle. There is a very complex politics here, as women's organisations and feminists direct demands at the state, for more services or protection, while many are profoundly suspicious of the state and its implication in the reproduction of unequal gender relations.

Different feminists conceive of the state and of women's actual and potential relations with it differently. While the labels that emerged from experiences with western states are now often inadequate even in the west, we can identify tendencies or associations (Humm, 1992). Liberal or equality femininists seek to end state-directed or -sanctioned discrimination against women, and urge state action for women's equal rights. The state is dominated by men, but increasing women's access and power can alleviate gender inequalities. Socialist feminists see the state as propagating dominant class as well as gender interests, and often race and ethnic interests as well. They are therefore more ambivalent towards the state and the possibilities of using the state for feminist goals. While seeking state transformation, many also recognise the need to engage with the state in defence of women's practical gender interests now (Molyneux, 1985). Radical feminists who prioritise women's oppression and see the male state as part of that oppression are often hostile to any further intrusion of the state into women's lives; yet many also urge state action in defence of women's rights. Feminist commentators remark upon the ironies of appealing to a masculinist state for protection against the violence of individual men (Brown, 1992; Alvarez, 1990).

Individual feminists also find themselves taking up different positions in relation to the state at different times. This reflects the complexity of women's different relations with the state (Pettman, 1992a). States' construction of women as mothers, for example, helps constitute women's unpaid work, an enormous subsidy to the state and to employers. States have long resisted any responsibility for women's security from male violence, and become complicit by not taking violence against women seriously. As well, it is often agents of the state, especially police and military, who are major abusers of women's rights. At the same time, state legislation and provision can make a profound difference to women's survival and choices.

Often, women are treated by the state in ways officially ungendered, as citizens or workers; and yet we know that women's experiences of citizenship and the labour market are radically different from men's. Women also organise and approach the state as claimants and as political activists, where they may or may not constitute themselves as women. They are often dependents of the state, as the vast majority of old-age pensioners or single supporting mothers, for example. Many women are also state workers—in a gendered division of labour—mainly in teaching, nursing, social work, or helping, service and clerical roles. They are rarely in positions of policy or power. Women's work compensates for states' inadequate or inappropriate services, and makes invisible adjustments in the face of economic crises and cutbacks, in family and community care. Women also mediate between the state and other family members. The state depends for its survival on the labour of women, as obligatory unpaid service. 'To eliminate this exploitation would be to bring the whole system into crisis' (Cavarero, 1992: 44). No understanding of the state is possible without interrogating its own gender politics, and its gendered effects.

Or is this the western state? States differ radically from each other. There is now much material on states, and significant writings on the gender of states. While still preponderantly on western states, there are now numerous studies on, and often by, women in third-world states, and minority women in western states (Afshar, 1987; Parpart and Staudt, 1989; Charlton et al., 1989; Kandiyoti, 1991a; Moghadam, 1994a).

The shape and frame of women's relations with different states vary widely, although women everywhere are overwhelmingly responsible for reproductive, domestic and caring work, within a sexual division of labour that constructs certain kinds of work as women's work. All states are engaged in the construction of the public/private divide. Those with the capacity to do so intervene in the private, to regulate gender relations among other things. But the boundaries and the particular ideologies around the private vary, between states and within them over time.

The growth of the welfare state in the west and the provision of particular kinds of support to women, especially to mothers, has been characterised as a shift from private to public patriarchy. The state replaces individual men, though still with conditions for its 'protection', including, often, the surveillance of women's sexual relations. Women in the United Kingdom and the United States have been described as client–citizens (Jones, 1988: 25), in a dichotomy that sees men treated as workers and women as mothers, despite the large numbers of women who are both. In the Scandinavian countries, women are constructed more as citizen–workers, winning rights such as childcare and maternity leave as supports for this role. This rather different relationship between women and the state leads one writer to describe herself as a 'state-friendly feminist in search of the women-friendly state and as part of the rather optimistic, pragmatic, social-democratic tradition of Scandinavian welfare state analysis' (Hernes, 1988: 188; see also Siim, 1994).

Maxine Molyneux (1989), analysing socialist states before the fall, noted the ways in which their policies towards women were conditioned by international factors. States as diverse as those of Eastern Europe, the Soviet Union, China, Cuba and Vietnam were officially committed to equality for women and men, and treated both primarily as workers. These policies reflected the prioritising of class oppression and also Soviet dominance in post-World War 2 Eastern Europe, leading to the imposition of a Soviet model. Talk of feminism and women's organisations from the late 1970s stemmed partly from transnational and international processes, including the rise of third-world and national-liberation feminists who were also socialists. Meetings of different women through the UN Decade for Women, prompting the collection of extensive information on women's lives, documented the double shift in socialist countries, too.

Dramatic changes in the organisation of state power and productive relations, and in some cases changing state borders in the wake of Soviet collapse, have had mixed results for women. In Poland, for example, the rise of Solidarity and the renewed influence of the Catholic Church have limited women's earlier rights to abortion. Understandings about who is a citizen and who should have what rights, and reorganisation of productive relations in transition to market economies all have profound effects on different women (*Feminist Review*, 1991; Ward, 1993; Einhorn, 1993). Women's social rights are under attack, as are workers' rights generally in the face of growing unemployment and the radical removal of the socialist right to work. But pressure to push women back into the home also reflects the costs of women's rights as workers, which made women more expensive, rather than cheaper, workers (Moghadam, 1995). One result is a reassertion of the private sphere and the worker/mother dichotomy in ideologies of housewifisation, familiar elsewhere. Dramatic too is the drop in the numbers and visibility of women in many ex-socialist states' politics, and the difficulties of talking about feminist goals where official gender equality is identified with the now discredited former regimes. At the same time, the lifting of institutionalised repression and, in places, political terror enables a proliferation in women's groups and organisations, and growing contacts across the old iron curtain.

Generalising about the many states outside Europe and North America is a dangerous affair; though the incorporation of 'the rest of the world' into a European- and later western-dominated international structure was carried into its contemporary mode through decolonisation along colonially imposed borders. The impact of colonial power and the spread of capitalist productive relations on indigenous and precolonial political forms varied widely. Both precolonial and colonial forms of authority were gendered, and both colonial and anticolonial organisation often explicitly aligned with or opposed particular gendered practices, especially concerning the status of women (see chapters 2 and 3).

Processes of decolonisation were more or less violent, involving different levels of mobilisation and militarisation in different states. When state sovereignty or the regime controlling the state was not secure, political violence often saw women especially vulnerable to sexual attack. Attempts to consolidate and nationalise the state intensified the impact of states on population and territory. State management of productive relations and their internationally directed development policies impacted upon men and women differently (see chapter 8). These in turn generated women's and feminist organising, seeking access to, transformation of, or escape from the state or from particular policies or agents. In some cases, in Africa especially, states were so weak that some women could operate as an 'uncaptured element' (Chazan, 1989: 197), disengaging from state control; although this does not necessarily protect them from state harassment or attack.

In most cases since independence, third-world states have become increasingly centralised and bureaucratised, and increasingly important in women's lives (Afshar, 1987). Almost all states have been concerned to control women's sexuality and fertility, and 'the status of women' often signals priorities in state and nation building projects. Difficulties in generalising about women's relations with states is demonstrated by the variety of experiences of women in Muslim-majority states. The position of women in these states cannot be understood apart from the political projects of contemporary states and their struggles to legitimise their authority relations (Kandiyoti, 1991a). These may take the form of secularising states, as in Turkey, Egypt and earlier Iran, or the consolidation of communal control over women, as in Pakistan and post-1979 Iran. In each, different women respond differently. The central role of women and gender relations in times of national mobilisation and conflict is pursued in chapters 4 and 7.

Despite the variety of state projects and women's responses to them, we can make some generalisations about women and the state, which appear to be universal.

- Much state discourse renders women invisible, as if citizens and workers are gender neutral, or assuming they are men.
- All state policies affect women, often in different ways from the ways they affect men. Women's experiences of citizenship, the labour market and state violence are different from men's. Only through feminist analysis or a 'gender sensitive lens' (Peterson

and Runyan, 1993) do these differences and therefore the full meaning of these institutions become clear.

- All states rely on women's unpaid domestic and reproductive labour. No state could seriously attempt equality in work, or to pay fairly for women's work, without profound transformation of all social and power relations. The domestication of women means naturalising women's work as a labour of love, and so perpetuates the 'double load' and the containment of women.

- Many states exclude women from state rights as private or dependent, or as communal property. Women have great difficulties in becoming state subjects and citizens. State legislation regarding marriage, divorce, legitimacy of children and the status of women, profoundly affect women's rights and their access to resources and choices.

- States often attend to women as women, and especially as mothers. Despite historical, cultural and national specificity, there are remarkable similarities in the construction of women as mothers, and of motherhood as of political concern to states.

- Especially since 1975, states have developed women's sections, desks and policies. The UN Decade for Women placed women's issues on the international agenda and generated a huge amount of information that documented women's inequality internationally. Since then, international networks of feminists and women's non-governmental organisations (NGOs) have created a language around women's oppression or subordination, and have asserted the profoundly gendered nature of all politics, within and between states. Now more than 140 states have 'women's machinery' in bureaucracy and government (Lycklama à Nijeholt, 1991). Most states still translate women's issues into welfare issues, and contain women as a category or special-needs group, rather than analysing the gendered impact of state policies and the impact of gender power on people's lives. Some states have incorporated feminist inputs into policy making, creating 'femocrats' whose relations with other feminists are not always easy (Watson, 1990; Alvarez, 1990). Elsewhere, 'state feminists' appointed to run state policies of gender equity may have few relations with feminists or women's organisations outside the bureaucracy.

- While states treat women differently from men, states also treat different women differently, as citizens or not, or as members of dominant or minority groups, for example. Nira Yuval-Davis and Floya Anthias (1989) suggest a framework for understanding

14

the relations of women/nation/state internationally, in terms of how states attend to women, for example, as biological reproducers of citizens and workers of the state; as reproducers of the boundaries of national and ethnic groups; as culture carriers, responsible for socialising children and transmitting culture; as signifiers of national and ethnic differences; and as contributors to national and state struggles.

So not all citizens, and not all women, experience the state in the same ways. Differences within states push us to ask: Who does the state represent internationally? Who does it speak for? Who is not represented by the state?

Citizenship

The state can be thought of as a form of political community, with citizenship as membership in it (Jones, 1990). If women are overwhelmingly absent from state power, and state political constructs are masculinist, where are women in relation to citizenship? How do women experience citizenship?

Governments of states are in the business of 'citizen manufacture', making 'the people' (Wickham and Kendall, 1992: 22). In Western and Eastern Europe, citizenship debates have flared recently around issues of migration and racism. In different states globally ethnonationalist and communalist conflicts and the rise of fundamentalisms generate debates over who belongs and who doesn't. So it is necessary to ask what, or who, is a citizen? Who belongs, and what does belonging mean in practice?

There are many different ways of thinking about citizenship. It is useful to distinguish between membership, rights and participation (Hall and Held, 1989). Membership refers to legal citizenship—who is born a citizen, and who has the right to become one. This is a crucial right related to who is allowed to enter the state, reside and claim rights; and to the state's exercise of sovereignty. There are always non-citizens, legally and illegally in states, and debate about which rights should be restricted to citizens only. States determine who automatically acquires citizenship rights and who may become citizens, with those 'of the land' recognising birthrights to citizenship, while those 'of the people' privileging, for example, German or Saudi descent, so many locally born children of long-term residents are not recognised as citizens.

Citizens' rights in western liberal states were first claimed as civil and political, rights against the state and to vote. In more communitarian political traditions, but also in social-democratic and welfare states, social rights are important. In many states, the numbers and categories of people who are both formal citizens and have equal legal rights has increased over the last century and especially in the last few decades. Arguments over what rights citizens should have become ways of arguing about what the good society looks like, and about ways of organising authority relations within states.

Participation is one way of asking whether formally enjoyed rights are actually available to different people. Legal citizenship and 'paper' rights mark a person's admission to the state, but not necessarily to its resources, nor to the national community. Naturalised immigrants or their locally born children may still be seen as migrants and foreigners, and denied their entitlements through discriminatory or shoddy treatment. Racialised minorities, even after generations, may experience similar treatment. Particular groups are suddenly 'denationalised' by political events. Japanese-Americans became enemy aliens overnight after Pearl Harbor, and Muslim and Arab-Australians experienced racist attacks in the wake of the Gulf War.

The politics of citizenship is a politics of exclusion, where belonging for some is marked apart from and depends on others' not belonging. Early citizenship in western states was restricted to property-owning or head-of-household white males. Long struggles by different groups for inclusion as citizens took different forms. In the UK, for example, working men gained the vote, then all men in 1919; women over 30 in 1918, and all women in 1928. In the United States, African-Americans and white women struggled, sometimes together and sometimes against each other, for the vote (Shklar, 1991). State socialism usually enfranchised both men and women, even where the right to vote meant little. Many third-world states granted universal franchise on independence, contradicted in some Middle Eastern and Asian states in the privileging of religious or personal law, which subsumed women within family or communal boundaries. In European and South American states older civil codes often restricted women's legal rights, effectively jeopardising their autonomy. There is no clear geographic pattern in formal suffrage. Turkey granted women voting rights in 1934, well before France in 1946, Greece in 1949 and Switzerland only in 1971. The first women legislators in the Gulf states took their seats in Oman in 1994. Women are still unable to vote in Kuwait or Saudi Arabia. There is no inevitable progress in women's journeys towards a citizen identity—indeed, in a number of states their rights and status have recently deteriorated (Moghadam, 1994a). Many groups are effectively inside the state but outside the nation. These contradictions and ambiguities are summed up in the notion of 'second-class citizenship'. This points to struggles where claimants use their formal citizenship to protest informal exclusions and discriminations, as in US civil-rights movements and international second-wave women's movements, for example. Social movements mobilise to actualise citizenship and rights for those whose group or category identity has been the grounds for exclusion (Staeheli, 1994; Pettman, 1995c).

Citizenship is conventionally understood as the individual's relationship with the state, and as an association of equals in its political community. For this reason, citizenship has trouble accomodating those who claim inclusion as category-group members, on the basis of difference rather than of equality with already-citizens, dominant-group men. Citizenship's construction of the individual citizen making up 'the people' can silence or marginalise minorities and those whose interests or beliefs are different (Hall and Held, 1989). This is especially so where the state itself is engaged in the definition of 'the community' and in international relations where the state speaks for 'the people'. This fiction allows the state to construct 'the national interest' regardless of dissent, and of exclusions from the national community and from state power.

Women and citizenship

Women were long excluded from citizenship through the particular and masculinist constructions of politics and the citizen referred to earlier. They are caught between denial and exaggeration—overlooked, or attended to as different (Rhode, 1992: 149). Where noticed, women were excluded from full citizenship on the grounds of unsuitability, as not male and not reasonable; as emotional; as sexual, and so disruptive, or dangerous; as having particular family attachments that precluded the disinterested work of citizenship. They were excluded through their construction as dependents, where the notion of citizen included an independent and autonomous person. They were further excluded through the close associations of citizenship with bearing arms and being prepared to kill or die for the state. This militarisation of citizenship (Elshtain, 1985: 42) saw women caught in another dichotomy, with men as protectors and women as protected. This further compromised notions of women's independence and of their suitability for the guarding of the state.

There are tensions in women's citizenship, where they have been both excluded and included on the same grounds, as mothers, and the difficulties they face becoming subjects and citizens in their own right (Jones, 1990; Braidotti, 1992: 184). The maternal is located in the private and the family, away from the political. Yet the maternal is also claimed by the state, to give (the right kinds of women) particular civic duties; to give birth to, bring up, and offer to the state future citizens, soldiers, workers. So France, like other European and settler states in the early decades of this century fearing declining population and 'race suicide', awarded medals with ribbons to women with large families. More recently Ceausescu banned contraception and abortions in an attempt to achieve a Romanian population of 30 million by the year 2000 (Pateman, 1992).

Women seeking admission to the club of the state have been trapped in what Carole Pateman calls Wollstonecraft's dilemma. Mary Wollstonecraft's *Vindication of the Rights of Women*, published in 1792 in the radical excitement of the French Revolution, argued that women, too, should be included in the rights of man. Seeking to extend and ultimately to universalise citizenship, the 'equality' argument looks to a politics where gender does not matter. But arguments to include women as citizens often also assert the special work that women do as women. Earlier suffrage and women's-rights advocates claimed maternal citizenship, constructing mothering as an essential service to the state, and pointed out that women birthing future citizens did often die 'for their country'. They also argued for the particular contributions that women could make, as women, to civic politics, valorising womanly virtues of caring, nurturing, and hoping to 'humanise' and heal the masculinist politics of competition, greed and violence.

Feminist citizenship?

These debates over the meanings given to citizenship recur in contemporary form (Snitnow, 1989; Bock and James, 1992). Liberal feminists 'call the bluff' of liberal discourses, by appropriating their universalist rhetoric, and reveal that particular interests and rights are preserved here. They have had some successes in states where

18

equal-opportunity and positive state policies have encouraged women's entry into politics and public life (Sawer, 1994). Feminist critics assert that they smooth some women's entry into state politics under the current masculinist arrangements, on men's terms, and so women must behave like men to have a chance of succeeding. Some feminists urge new forms of participation that take account of many women's more relational and care-giving experiences (Elshtain, 1990; Ruddick, 1992). Other feminists are wary of using notions of women's difference to stake a claim, especially where those differences connect with qualities or roles which have long been used to keep women out (Dietz, 1989). They suggest, too, that using 'women's experiences' and moral reasoning might make for a new ethics, rather than a new citizenship (Voet, 1994). They question whether private care is translatable into public politics, and whether the mother–child relationship is a useful model for the equal relationship that citizenship is supposed to be. A distinction here suggests that it is not women's interests as women, but feminist goals that should guide us (Mouffe, 1992). But for many feminists, there should be a close, if never opaque or easy, relationship between the two.

These different positions relate to different understandings of the political, and of the causes of women's oppression. They generate sometimes bitter contest over the category 'women'. They are played out in different feminist positions on women's roles in the military, pivotal for citizenship claims and responsibilities, which I will take up in chapter 7.

Getting equal

Nowadays in most states women are enfranchised and their states declare men and women equal citizens in some form or other. The last century has seen a gradual extension of formal citizenship and political rights. But equal legal rights have not led to equal participation or representation (Phillips, 1993). This is of concern only if it matters who represents you. This is not to argue that only women can represent women (though some might). But we should suspect a system of representation that routinely restricts power to a particular group, usually dominant-group middle-aged and older men (Voet, 1994: 62).

What is it about citizenship, or about women, that makes it so hard for women to become full citizens? Women's formal rights and, in a number of states, their growing access to some parts of the state raise the possibility of public equality and private inequality (Bock and James, 1992: 7). But women are still far short of public equality, despite significant gains in Finland, Norway and Sweden, for example, where over one-third of elected parliamentarians are women. The double shift is still in place, and women's responsibilities in terms of family, domestic labour and care undermine the choice, mobility, independence and energy needed for sustained public presence. Everywhere many women are still dependants of men or states, and conditions may be attached to that. Women in a number of states are caught between formal or constitutional equality declarations, and the relegation of issues of women's status and rights to personal or religious law, which makes them family or community property. Women are frequently victims of violence—in their homes and outside them—aimed, often, at keeping women in their place. As long as the state cannot guarantee women's security, and does not seriously attempt to do so, the citizenship bargain whereby (elite) men give up unrestricted freedom in return for personal security holds little reward for women.

How then do we argue women's equal citizenship in the knowledge of many women's dependence (O'Connor, 1993) and their continued construction, often, as mothers of citizens rather than as subjects and citizens themselves? A flashpoint here is abortion rights, so densely symbolic of women's claims for control over their own bodies. Some see abortion as *the* basic female civil right, to establish autonomy over body and self, which is especially controversial given the different political, including state, investments in motherhood (Evans, 1993: 257; Hoff, 1994). While often dismissed as a white, middle-class, western rights claim, most women who die as a result of illegal abortions or who are forced into abortion through lack of contraception or the means to support more children are in poor states or racialised minorities in rich states.

The state's attention to motherhood also gives it an investment in family, charged with reproduction of the community. Different states have long supported or recognised certain kinds of family, and heterosexual sex. This is part of the state disciplining its citizen body, constructing 'deviant' forms of sexuality and regarding sexual minorities, and 'unruly' women, as a threat and as somehow disloyal (Alexander, 1994). These security threats materialise around debates about women—and gay men—in the military.

The complex and at times lethal connections between bodies, sex, difference and danger also materialise in a body politics that promotes threats and physical attacks against women, gay men and racialised-minority men. These threats contain or deny their rights and endanger their security. They mark the boundaries of power and belonging, and demonstrate the conditions of entry into full citizenship. Women, gay men and racialised-minority men suffer both from invisibility, where they and their interests are routinely ignored, and from hypervisibility, which places them in danger when they appear in public space. In these circumstances, some people restrict their own movements and claims. They cannot exercise full citizenship rights, even where they are legally entitled to them. Their insecurities demonstrate something that political theory often ignores—that identities are embodied, and bodies are inscribed in ways that are 'read' to grant or deny their rights (Grosz, 1994). While women and minority men are seen as threatening the body politic, it is the construction and imposition of a dominant or hegemonic body politic that actually endangers them. Women, sex and bodies are written out of liberal and other masculinist citizenship politics, leaving men and 'reason' in possession of the state.

Citizenship debates, then, are about the nature of the political community, about who belongs and who should have what rights. Still, usually, the boundaries of difference and social rights 'are determined by specific, hegemonic, maybe universalist, but definitely not universal discourses' (Yuval-Davis in Ward et al., 1993: 14). This universalist language disguises both difference and exclusion.

'Equal access is not enough' (Dietz, 1989: 2). Strategies for actualising citizenship call for a challenge to the false universalism of liberal democracy, and for the inclusion of those whose current citizenship status is ambiguous or denied. They urge action to address the drastic under-representation of women and minorities in politics and power, including through positive action or provision for group representation. These strategies focus on the system as it now is, but also often entail a redefinition of politics to take account of women's experiences and interests (Jones, 1993). Some focus, too, on women's own negotiation of identities, and processes through which women become bearers of rights, 'becoming subjects', self-consciously occupying a citizen identity (Braidotti, 1992: 184; Leech, 1994: 86).

Women, citizenship and difference

In most states women are still a very long way from equality, and are caught in the dilemma of claiming both that their sex should not be held against them, and that they have certain kinds of experiences, or rights claims, as women.

What then would a woman-friendly, feminist citizenship look like?

Feminists who address gender-blind citizenship theorists argue the need to make gender visible and develop feminist analyses of state and citizenship. The difference they privilege, or seek to render obsolete, is gender difference. They ask how women experience citizenship, and what strategies and struggles are effective in rene- gotiating women's relations with citizenship. But feminists theorising difference and its implications for citizenship need to attend to differences between women, too. Not all women occupy the same gender territory (Jones, 1990). It is necessary to ask Which women? Women are usually a good half of identity groups, including those especially vulnerable to discrimination or exclusion, like racialised minorities and recent migrants. Differences among women must be part of theorising women's experiences of states and citizenship, and of power more generally. 'To say that women experience oppression as women does not mean that each woman experiences the same thing' (Jones, 1993: 223). This approach enables us to recognise the 'distinction between "being" a woman and "being" a particular woman' (Jones, 1993: 223).

Differences between women seriously test the possibilities of inclusive feminist theorising and of transnational femininst politics. More feminist analyses now bring together race, class and gender, and other dimensions of difference, such as sexuality, age and dis/ability. An international perspective asserts that nationality and citizenship status are essential makers and markers of difference too. These differences come together in particular and unstable combi- nations for any one person, each negotiating the shape of multiple identities over time and place. A simple listing or additive model is not enough, for identities are not singular or static. Nor can we stop at 'identity politics', as people mobilise as women or as black or as Muslim, for example, in particular political spaces and moments. We need to look closely at the politics of identity, and at how identities are constituted and come to mean what they mean.

This is a fluid, contested and at times dangerous politics. It cannot be understood apart from the international, as political identities and citizenship statuses are closely linked to historical and contemporary international processes of colonisation, migration, and state and nation building, which are the focus of the next three chapters. These processes have spread state-making and the practices of sovereignty, including citizenship, globally. They have also generated forms of political identity and boundary politics that reinforce some people's claims to citizenship and jeopardise others' claims.

It is no coincidence, then, that the revival of interest in citizenship among left and feminist scholars and activists follows an upsurge of racism and aggressive closure in very different states against migrants and minorities, and simultaneously the rise of fundamentalist and other movements that declare war on women's rights and the secular state. For this reason, some of those feminists most concerned to theorise and support women's difference also urge holding fast to claims for women's equal citizenship rights, rather than 'lose' women into community or family boundaries and control (Connolly, 1993; Curthoys, 1993a).

Citizenship debates, then, take us within the state, and de-link the easy nation-state association of old IR. They provide us with ways into debates about the nature of women and gender relations, and of politics and community. They point us, too, to some grounds on which denial of rights and belonging might generate conflicts and political violence, and become causes of internationalised wars.

Changing states

While most debates focus on what citizenship does or should mean, and feminist debates focus on what citizenship means, or might become, for women, it is increasingly urgent to ask what the citizen is a citizen of (Hall and Held, 1989: 21).

Even as feminists seek to understand the gender politics of states and the possibilities and dangers of engaging the state for feminist goals, those states are changing (Leech, 1994; Peterson, 1995). Some feminists now argue that, however problematic women's relations with states and liberal citizenship, they are preferable to an inter-nationalised market citizenship and the further erosion of state sovereignty by powerful transnational capitalist interests (Harrington, 1992).

'Globalisation' is a short-hand term which draws our attention to the increasing permeability of state borders and the growing power of non-state actors such as transnational corporations in determining much that goes on within it (Featherstone, 1990; Robertson, 1992; Kofman and Youngs, 1996). It reflects the uni-versalising of the market since 1989. Ideologies of economic rationalism and the impact of financial institutions such as the World Bank and the IMF determine much of the shape of state economic and social policies. These include restructuring and 'rolling back the state', with profound and gendered consequences (Afshar and Dennis, 1992). Many women now face a lethal combination of state neglect and/or withdrawal of services, a 'free' market dominated by transnational or state capitalism, and increasing militarisation and use of state violence to ensure both the conditions for market capitalism and for the survival of the state regime (Sen and Grown, 1987; Enloe, 1993).

Even the seemingly more benign western states are moving unevenly from social to market democracies, with hard-won labour and women's rights under attack. This is a further reminder that there is no linear or inevitable 'progess' in state or women's politics, or any stable or inevitable form of state power. States now bargain sovereignty for foreign investment and international debt, and state boundaries are routinely overridden by flows of technology, communications, ideas, tourists, workers, arms, toxic waste, disease, finance and corporate decisions (Appadurai, 1990, Youngs, 1996). At the same time, many states are tightening their immigration controls and police their territory, determining who can enter, and stay, who can claim citizenship rights, and who cannot. They do so in the face of more people than ever being 'on the move', as refugees and as labour migrants for example. Making sense of contemporary movements of people, and states' responses to them, means pursuing a gendered analysis of the international politics of colonisation, nationalism and migration, which are the focus of the next three chapters, and of the global political economy, which I take up in detail in part 3.

2

Women, colonisation and racism

European colonisation was a global process, involving the extraordinary imposition of European power over the rest of the world. The history of colonisation dominates the last 500 years, from the time of Columbus and the 'discoveries' literally making 'the world'. Colonisation was marked by formal political control, economic exploitation and cultural domination, and resistance.

Colonial power made use of certain ideas of women and sexuality to construct and police both women's bodies and racialised boundaries. It also set a racialised hierarchy in world politics, through structural relations of domination, subordination and exploitation. 'Whiteness' and 'non-white' are still significant political identities in the world today.

This chapter explores the sexual politics of colonisation, and the 'race' politics of gender. It suggests that white women are ambiguously placed within contemporary constructions of global power, in ways different from white men, and from 'other' women. These differences draw attention to the gendered, and racialised, dimensions of international relations and of political identities (Doty, 1993). They continue to inform and complicate relations between women, and feminist theorising.

Colonising worlds

European colonisation fuelled and was fuelled by the industrial revolution and the development and internationalisation of capitalism.

It rested on the exploitation of people's bodies, labour and land. While people had always moved from place to place, and there were other empires, European colonisation generated a vast human movement, including administrators and settlers to the colonies, slaves from Africa to the Americas, indentured labour from South Asia to East Africa, Fiji and the Caribbean (Miles, 1987; Potts, 1990). There was much traffic within the formal political and racialised hierarchies of empire. Colonial borderlines became the boundaries of states through formal decolonisation and the internationalisation of the modern state system in recent decades. Colonisation spread alongside capitalist relations of production and a market economy that incorporated the rest of the world, unevenly and unequally, into a now globalised political economy or single world system. This 'continuous expansion of a modernist, secular and materialist social system, spanning the globe, [is] perhaps the key motor force of contemporary history' (Gill, 1991: 276).

European colonisation and later the formal dismantling of empires shaped the political–geographic map of our world. Colonisation and anti-colonial movements generated a range of political identities, not least those of the 'West and Its Others' (Sardar, 1992). Settler states emerged through the nineteenth and twentieth century, and since World War 2 so did those states now loosely labelled as the 'third world'.

The current era is often labelled 'postcolonial', recognising that direct territorial colonisation has largely gone, as has the Soviet Empire. It is postcolonial too in the sense that no-one and nowhere is untouched by colonialism, and because almost everyone now lives in formally independent states. But international hierarchies, relations, and boundaries bear traces—or often are still significantly determined by—colonial relations. 'Postcolonial' can also disguise contemporary structures of global power, which in political-economy terms suggest an intensification of domination power and relational dependence and exploitation (Miyoshi, 1993).

Colonising women

Within conventional histories of colonisation, women are largely absent. Empire and anticolonial nationalisms are told as conflicts and competitions between different men. Colonial histories may be romances of empire, of white conquest or of anticolonial resistance.

Women are further elided through a popular and revealing

analogy between 'women' and the colonised. Here, women's oppression is compared with colonisation, and oppression is something women share with the colonised. This particular connection underscores the masculine character of 'control over' relations in general (Peterson, 1992a), and ways in which dominated peoples, including the colonised, are feminised. But the colonised/women analogy leaves colonised women, and the gender politics of colonisation as it is constructed within both colonised and coloniser groups, unexamined. 'Women' become dominant-group women, in the metropole or less often in the colonies, while the feminisation of the colonised is seen as being done to colonised men. It is unclear where colonised women are in these representations.

In other representations, coloniser powers were associated with civilisation and culture, and the colonised with nature, as women were in the metropoles. The close associations between sex and power in the construction of dominant and imperial masculinities is revealed in the profusion of phallic imagery, for example, penetrating the dark continent and the eroticisation of conquest, leading one commentator to suggest that 'homosocial desire acts as a kind of textual unconscious for the entire discussion of empire' (Donaldson, 1992: 8).

Recently there has been a form of colonial nostalgia evident in films such as *Passage to India* and *Out of Africa*, or more cynically and decadently drawn in *White Mischief* (Enloe, 1990a; Chaudhuri and Strobel 1992: 1). They disguise the violence, racism and exploitation that drove colonial relations, 'the evil and utter madness of imperialism' (Said quoted in Donaldson, 1992: 89). Here the colonies and the colonised become backdrop, part of the scenery, local colour. Within these stories, individual white women may be romanticised, or drawn as heroines—unconventional or liberated in/for their times. These stories accord in some ways with new feminist herstories, part of a retrieval project of (white) women in the empire.

Within the boys' own adventure of empire and the colonies, white women were usually absent—invisible—or passive companions or victims of white men's actions. Occasionally they were made visible, especially in settler colonies as breeders of the white race. But there is another colonial story which locates women in rather different ways. Here, white women are given agency, but for bad. This is the story of the memsahib and other local variations, the gross stereotyping of white women as idle, pampered, petty, parasitic upon empire and tended by servants who are mistreated, spending time and energy only on gossip, complaint and concerns with status and display (Knapman, 1986; Strobel, 1991; Jolly, 1993). A variation of this image goes further, to lay the blame for 'loss of empire' at their feet. White women are here judged as more racist than their men, as disrupting formerly close relations between early colonists and the locals, and as drawing and defending raced boundaries through their snobbishness and sexual jealousy. Causal connections are made between deteriorating 'race relations' and increasing numbers of white women in the colonies—somehow these women are to blame for the ultimate 'loss of empire'.

There is now a growing literature on white women in the colonies, and in relation to empire. Much of this literature is of the 'retrieval' kind, 'women's adventures' and/or feminist stories. It tells us that (white) women were there, though in very different roles and relations over time and place, for example in larger numbers and crucial as reproducers of the race in settler colonies (de Lepervanche, 1989), or as unwelcome intruders in tropical colonies whose officials were concerned with administration and extraction of surplus (Callaway, 1987; Strobel, 1991). These writings are interventions, then, against an ungendered colonisation. They tell a different story of gender and race relations, seeking to refute the scapegoating of white-coloniser women and the trivialisation of their lives as decorative assessories of empire.

These retrieval feminist writings document coloniser women's lives to disrupt the stereotypes, to reveal the variety of coloniser women's lives, views and relations. They demonstrate that life in the colonies was often extremely difficult, their work hard, and their isolation and loneliness frequent. Often, too, they argue that coloniser women were not more racist than 'their' men. Indeed, some had close relations with 'the locals', especially with colonised women, through a range of teaching, helping and missionary activities that were seen there, as elsewhere, as peculiarly women's work. Helen Callaway argues that unlike their image as harsher and more racist, coloniser women represented the humane and 'civilising' side of empire and enabled the emergence of a more equal relationship in the transition from empire to commonwealth (1987a: 244).

Documenting the lives of coloniser women is part of a feminist project, to take women's own experiences seriously. It gives them a presence beyond their usual invisibility or stereotypic representation in masculinist tellings. It often reveals differences among women which caution us against homogenising them within a single

28

category. It may or may not recognise class differences and other boundary politics, which privileged some and penalised other coloniser women in the structuring of colonial society. But critics of some retrieval herstories find fault in their valorising of white women's lives in ways that sanitise or release coloniser women from responsibility as part of the colonising force. For while colonisation was gendered, gender was racialised, and white women were ambiguously placed in terms of the colonial project. They were both oppressed in terms of patriarchal relations, and oppressors, or at least advantaged by 'race' relations in colonialism (Strobel, 1991: 41; Pettman, 1992a). In this situation, innocence is not available as a position for coloniser women, and their stories cannot be told in relation to their men alone. Their relations with 'other' women become highly problematic. Questions of responsibility and complicity juggle with those of power and control.

Many coloniser women, especially missionary women, were engaged in helping and service work with colonised women. But even where the former saw the latter as sisters, in a precursor to global sisterhood, they retained notions of difference in race and cultural hierarchy that represented 'other' women as little sisters or surrogate daughters. Barbara Ramusack (1990) characterises these relations as 'maternal imperialism', with coloniser women a part of the civilising and Christianising project. Colonised women appear as victims of their culture and of their men (and at times, of white men)—to be saved by white women's interventions. So Margaret Jolly uses the label 'colonising women' to indicate these women's problematic location within the colonial project (1993: 104). These presumptions and hidden power relations between women have returned to haunt us, replicated in some contemporary western feminist representations of 'third-world women' as always already victims (Mohanty, 1988; Mani, 1990).

The maternalist trope sees women as connected through their similar women's bodies, maternity and family responsibilities, even though structured through big-sisterly or motherly responsibility and difference between women. But maternity is also used to divide women along lines of class, race and nation, to make good and bad mothers. Here there could be collusion between colonial authorities, colonising women and some local male authorities, seeking control of women's sexuality, fertility and marriage (Jolly, 1992). (There are clear parallels between the tasks 'at home' of public health and maternal education aimed at making white working-class mothers better mothers, and the kinds of education, surveillance and intervention directed at colonised women.) There were ambivalences, too: concern about 'over breeders', and very different attitudes towards the treatment of different women in terms of maternal health and reproductive rights.

Jane Haggis points to the role of colonising women as significant agents 'in articulating and conducting a project of domestication aimed at colonised women' (1992: 1). She explores the use of maternal imagery and language by missionary wives and single women missionaries of the London Missionary Society in South India as they constructed their relations with colonised women. They pursued their project of making good wives and mothers of colonised women in accordance with their own cultural and class notions of desirable family relations and sex roles. There was congruence, then, between their objectives in restructuring family life, sex roles and men's and women's work, and the cultural reconstruction and political economy of empire. They were engaged in a project of domestication, which involved a reproduction of the colonial order (Nair 1992: 42).

A different example of the complexities of raced gender relations in colonisation and women's work for and with other women is revealed in a study of African-American missionary women in southern Africa. They identified with African women in some ways not available to white women, but also felt set apart from them by their commitment to Christianity and a civilising mission, which was shaped by western notions of women's roles and family life (Jacobs, 1990).

Colonising women benefited from empire, as 'the inferior sex within the superior race' (Strobel, 1991: xi). Some had opportunities and choices in the colonies that they would not have found had they stayed at home. Yet while they were privileged in terms of race, cultural and often class power in the colonies, they were more or less constrained or exploited within their own family, social or institutional lives. They were culture carriers, and often shared with men of their family or group views of themselves and others. But they negotiated complex relations and contradictory pressures and identities, interpreting their worlds with reference to personal though socially located ideas and values.

Within structures of power and practices that were both racist and sexist, individual colonising women made their ways. They pursued a variety of relations, or refused relations, with colonised women. Recent feminist writings on colonising women tell of the very different choices and politics pursued, for example, by different

British feminists in India (Paxton, 1990). Another compares Charlotte Geddie, a Presbyterian missionary in 'maternalist sympathy' for ni-Vanuatu women, with Beatrice Grimshaw, a traveller and journalist who represented Pacific women as downgraded and beyond redemption, promoting white-settler and planter interests against missionary endeavours (Jolly, 1993).

Colonised women, too, were never a homogenous group, even as contemporaries in any particular colony. There were always some differences among them that predated colonisation, whether of age and marital status in more egalitarian small-scale communities, or of hierarchy and, for example, caste, class or prior occupation status. (Current rewritings of these differences, however, are informed by different political projects that construct certain understandings of women as more equal with men 'before', or of women's difference as emblematic of 'culture' defined against the colonising power—a politics I will pursue in the next chapter.) Colonised women, too, made their own decisions in the face of colonising power, some converting or collaborating, others resisting or subverting, others sidelined in competition or deals between different groups of men. The search for colonised women's stories often displays a familiar tension between recognising their agency as opposed to their relative powerlessness and at times atrocious treatment at the hands of colonisers. We still know little of most colonised women's lives, though feminist recastings of colonial stories are making more women visible.

Domestic politics

Colonising and colonised women's relations were further complicated by their many personal encounters, especially in domestic service. The close proximity of the women in these relations was within households, in forms of family labour usually designated private, away from the public/political sphere attended to in political science, sociology and much history. It is complicated by the gendered and often sexualised nature of domestic labour generally.

The politics of domestic-service work varied enormously, and in places was itself part of the 'education' and domestication project targeted at colonised women. In Australia, for example, many young 'half-caste' Aboriginal girls were seized by the state and trained in domestic arts before being placed in white homes as domestic servants. Subject to supervision but rarely protected by state

Aboriginal Protection Boards, they were a source of cheap labour for white families. They and other Aboriginal women who laboured in white city and country homes relieved white women of domestic labour and childcare responsibilities, even while some faced the removal of their own children on the grounds of being unsuitable mothers. The cruel irony here, as in other colonial situations, was that the very women whose sexuality and maternity, cleanliness and reliability were so often found wanting were responsible for childcare and house duties for 'superior' women.

In these situations, Aboriginal women and girls were especially dependent on particular white adults against whom they had few defences. Stories of mistreatment and humiliation at the hands of white women and of harassment and sexual abuse at the hands of white men abound (Tucker, 1987; G. Ward, 1988). There is a virtual absence of reports of friendship between white and Aboriginal women historically (Tonkinson, 1988: 34). Jackie Huggins, an Aboriginal historian, argues that Aboriginal women suffered more at the hands of white women than of white men (1987). Some older Aboriginal women do recall particular households or white women employers with affection, and resist tellings that cast them as helpless victims in their own lives. But the unequal relations, in terms of race, culture, class and often age, is part of the living memory of many Aboriginal women. It is also part of contemporary living in forms of racialised domestic service in western, Middle Eastern and Asian households today (see chapter 9).

Domestic labour is often sexualised, and in colonial situations racialised gender stereotypes frequently represented colonised women as promiscuous or exotic. These representations connect in difficult and dangerous ways with other dimensions of the sexual politics of colonisation.

The sexual politics of colonisation

Retrieval herstories challenge

the extraordinary presumption that sexuality between white men and colonised women was indicative of racial harmony. Even when such sexual relations did not constitute rape, and when indigenous women embraced a sexual or love relation with colonising men, there was still an element of conquest: sexual access to local women legitimised the colonial relation. Sexual relations between white women and 'men of colour' on the contrary betrayed the imperial accumulations of the power of race, class and sex (Jolly, 1993: 108).

Particular constructions of women and sexuality were used to police women's bodies, and the boundaries of race. Colonising women were distinguished from colonised women through racialised gender stereotypes which replicated the good mother/bad mother in the good woman/bad woman dichotomy (though colonising women could become bad women by unruly, unrespectable or sexually licentious behaviour; and lower-class or independent single colonising women might likewise be perceived as beyond the bounds of protection). Colonising women were generally represented as pure, non-sexual, mothers, civilising influences on 'their' men. They were the property or possessions of their men and their community. Their fidelity and the restriction of their sexual relations to same-race men were essentially part of keeping the race pure. Any suggestion of a sexual relationship between a white woman and a colonised man was quickly read as rape, though in some cases white women were also blamed for 'encouraging' attention (Strobel, 1991; Bynum, 1992).

Colonised/black men's sexuality was constructed as savage, violent, voracious (though with specific characteristics attributed to different groups of men). This complicates the previous notion of colonised men as feminised. A contradictory bundle of images could be activated simultaneously or in different situations. Colonised/black men were seen to have too little of some masculine characteristics, such as responsibility and stability, and too much of others, especially in terms of a sexualised hypermasculinity, which was a threat to white women, and to black/colonised women too. So restrictions were placed on the movements and relations of black men—in the name of protecting white women (though they were more likely generated by white men's sexual anxieties and fears around appropriating the bodies of colonised women and the land and labour of colonised men. Indeed, it seems that the spectre of the black/colonised rapist against whom white womanhood must be protected arises especially at times when colonial authority is questioned, and black/colonised men must be 'put down' (Sharpe, 1993). Such panics over supposedly vulnerable white women allowed the far more common rape of colonised/black women by white men to go largely unnoted.

Colonised women's sexuality was variously represented, in racialised gender stereotypes that distinguished, for example, between African and Asian women, or between Melanesian and

Polynesian women. Often they were seen as sexual creatures (using the word advisedly), more of nature and less controlled and chaste than good white women. As temptresses or as amoral, they could be held responsible for the seduction of white men. This image was complicated, though, by some missionary, humanitarian and early feminist representations of them as victims of their men's brutish natures, or savable through Christianising and domesticity. But this could have a related effect, in detaching women from 'their' men, and putting them under the 'protection' of white men and, sometimes, of white women.

In a complex sexual politics of colonisation, excluding and controlling boundaries were drawn around white women and black men, leaving white men free to transgress the boundaries, and use, abuse or even care for colonised women (Pettman, 1992a). Even where concubinage was preferred to the importation of white women, as in early stages in some tropical colonies, the women involved remained dependent and vulnerable, and were policed in ways that maintained racialised boundaries and carefully determined who counted as white (Stoler, 1991; Baustad, 1994). The children of colonising men and colonised women usually stayed with the mother, thus keeping the white race pure. White men who lived with and loved colonised women were often persecuted or at least socially stigmatised—more so than those who were more secret and often more abusive in their relations across the line.

Tessie Lui argues that 'race is a *gendered* social category that rests on regulating sexuality and particularly on controlling the behaviour of women' (1991: 163). Distinctions between legitimate and illegitimate children are bolstered by norms and in many places legislation and sanctions condoning or prohibiting certain kinds of marriages and sexual relations, as in South Africa until very recently. These in turn relate to social entitlements, which in colonial and race power societies go far beyond rights to individual inheritance and social status. Sex is seen as the vulnerable link in maintaining group boundaries, so it is especially important for colonising—and, if they can, colonised—men to control same-group women's sexual behaviour and domestic lives. Sex, gender and women's bodies become part of the material for the construction of group boundaries. 'Women's bodies were the contested terrain on which men built their political regimes' (Lui, 1991: 163).

The 'race' politics of gender

White women's bodies were subjected territory in colonised and racialised societies where dominant-group men strove to guarantee the reproduction, physically and socially, of the boundaries of colonial race power. Here marriage functioned to appropriate colonising women's reproductive labour rather than to protect those women. This was clear, too, in the slave societies in the southern United States, where 'sexual liaisons between white women and black men threatened the institution of racial slavery in a way that sex between white men and black women did not' (Hodes, 1993: 402), for a child's legal status followed the mother. Martha Hodes suggests, though, that individual southerners showed a certain amount of tolerance towards relations between white women and black men during slavery, because of dominant views of white women outside the planter class, and especially of poor white women as depraved; perhaps, too, because serious threat to the slaveocracy was unthinkable. Even during the Civil War, there was no evidence of fears of the black rapist, when the threat to privilege was seen as external, from the north. After emancipation, as ex-slave men gained the vote and some other legal rights, defending dominant-race power entailed the elaboration of a racist discourse which constructed black and white masculinities and femininities through 'marking the body' (Wiegman, 1993: 446). Naming black male sexuality as dangerous to white womanhood initiated a horrific period of lynching and terrorism against black men, and generated representations of black men's sexuality that are still with us today. White women were dangerously located within discourses that 'justified' lynching on their behalf, and were used symbolically to guard the racialised borders (Carby, 1986; Pettman, 1992a; Ware, 1992). At the same time, the construction of black women's sexuality as loose placed those women beyond the bounds of chivalry or (controlling) protection—subjected to harassment and abuse, and then blamed for it.

This story of shifting discourses of race and of newly systematic attacks on black men after emancipation echoes the emergence of discourses of the native rapist and of white women as needing protection in colonial India in the wake of the 1857 revolt. Anticolonial struggles or local attempts to claim political rights could be deflected into representations of native or black men's 'pathological lust' for white women. This demonstrates 'the fear of a native assault on English women to be a screen for imperialist strategies of counterinsurgency' (Sharpe, 1993: 41–2). A discourse of rape was used to put down anticolonial rebellion and to 'justify' the often horrific violence of colonial power. At the same time, the combined threat to European power, and a newly dominant medical discourse about degeneracy and 'scientific' racism consolidated racialised boundaries. This in turn led to the suppression of concubinage and the encouragement of European women coming to colonies as wives, even while the latter were blamed for the former and for worsening race relations through their supposed sexual jealousies.

Janaki Nair also tracks the increasing separation of coloniser and colonised, and the rhetoric of racist superiority in India after 1857. Increasing numbers of colonising women in India became part of a 'complex grid of power' (1992: 27), where knowledge of Indian women and their subordination was used to deflect criticism of empire and to undermine then-current English women's movement rhetoric against their own 'colonisation' by English men. Blaming white women distracted attention from the elaborate process of institutionalising domination practices and, in settler colonies, of reproducing the new nation.

The sexual economy (Wiegman, 1993: 446) that underlay ex-slave and colonised constructions of black men points to powerful material interests behind racialised discourses, and body and boundary policing. Collective sexual hysteria swept white South Africans in the form of 'black peril' in 1893, 1906–8, and 1911–13—coinciding with economic depression (Strobel, 1991: 5). Similar moral panic in the Australian Territory of Papua saw the passage of the *White Women's Protection Ordinance* in 1927 (Inglis, 1974), at a time when consolidation of colonial control generated new contacts and conflicts.

Retrieval herstories reject white women's responsibility for deteriorating race relations (hopefully without denying that some individual colonising women were dreadfully racist). They explain the apparent coincidence of growing numbers of white women in different colonies and the stricter policing of racialised social boundaries as part of an intensification of the colonial project, involving denser white settlement and accompanying conflicts over land and labour (Knapman, 1986). They remind us that there was a political economy to colonisation. Racial ideologies underpinned hierarchical relations and rationalised the colonial project, facilitating the material interests at stake. These varied over time, between different colonial powers and within their relations with different colonised peoples.

While there is a political economy of sex operating in these circumstances, there is also a psychosexuality, where difference itself is a danger and the boundaries which are drawn are multiple and unstably related to each other. The powerful associations of women with difference and of the female body with sexuality suggest other uses of the women/colonised analogy. 'As figures of difference, women are connected with sexual insatiability, class instability, natives, the colonised, and the potentially threatening, unassimilable other' (Brown 1993: 19).

So while white women—as individuals—may have been boundary police, they were also policed and contained within particular locations in the colonial adventure. Colonising men's ideological use of racialised gender identities, and their fear of the loss of 'their' women and of 'pure' bloodlines, meant that white women were used symbolically as markers of the boundaries, in defence against colonised men. The 'whiteness' of womanhood was used in colonising discourse, and women's whiteness continues to inform both racist discourse and some feminist discourse today (Carby, 1986; Ware, 1992).

Imperial feminisms

Traces of empires and of colonial relations are still with us—as are the structures of race power they built. British women who did not go to the colonies still grew up and lived within an empire. Richard Handler and Daniel Segal reject 'the master narrative of "Western Civ" in which a self-made Europe (having spent its toddler days in Greece or wherever) went forth and remade the world in its own image. In our view, Europe, and its national diplomats, did not go forth; they returned' (1993: 4).

Colonial images in popular literature and the arts played a part in defining metropolitan and other European cultures and identities. 'Englishness' was defined against other nations/states such as the French, and against other peoples who were both colonised and racialised, including the Irish. Women's writings as early as Aphra Behn's *Oroonoko* (1688) contributed to these images, and slave trade Abolitionist literature also spread representations of ambivalent difference (Ware, 1992; Ferguson, 1992). Many of these writers did not themselves have first-hand experience of others' lands or people. Those who did included Victorian women travellers, whose tales of adventure and of other women's lives, in harem literature for example, brought difference home (Melman, 1992; Pratt, 1992).

White women in settler colonies such as Australia also mobilised in suffrage movements, claiming inclusion for colonising women in an imperial citizenship (though the aim was as often to civilise Australian men as to civilise colonised women; Lake, 1993). They sought status as partners in building the new nation/race, using 'other' women as mirrors of their own progress. Some early feminists did include Aboriginal women in their search for women's autonomy and rights. But often they still saw them as little sisters to be saved, replicating maternalist moves in other colonies. These representations played dangerously into wider race-making processes, which constructed the colonised as children, appearing to legitimise dependence and domination relations.

British first-wave feminism arose alongside an especially virulent phase of imperialism, and feminists laid claim to the vote and inclusion within an imperial state. Antoinette Burton explores the appropriation of the helpless Indian woman 'as a specifically feminist-colonial possession' (1991: 69) as a way of contributing to Britain's civilising mission. 'The Indian woman' was usually cast as passive victim, despite prominent Indian women working with British suffrage organisations and organising their own women's organisations in Britain and in India. A few British women, like Annie Besant, aligned themselves with colonised women's struggles against British colonisation. Other British women engaged in campaigns against aspects of imperialism, as Josephine Butler did in opposing the harassment of Indian women under the *Contagious Diseases Act* in India, which simultaneously presented colonised women as victims and part of white feminists' civilising mission—the white women's burden.

A number of British feminists were also engaged in anti-slavery campaigns, in which black American women also participated, though again the predominant images of them were as abject victims (Midgley, 1992: 6). Recent feminist writing has traced the roles of white women in the anti-slavery movements in the UK and the US. Vron Ware suggests a connection between the first women's movement born out of the campaign to end slavery, and the second in the US out of the 1960s civil-rights movement. *The Vindication of the Rights of Women* in 1792 and subsequent arguments for women's rights relied on popular sentiment against slavery and associated women's oppression with it. The women's movement was at first linked with rights for black people. 'As the movement for women's rights progressed, women were able to exploit the power of the slavery analogy in interpreting their own servitude but without needing any longer to refer to the slaves whose bondage had at once outraged and inspired them' (Ware, 1992: 109).

Slavery's abolition in the United States did not bring about black freedom. In the face of the rapid increases in the numbers of lynchings from the early 1880s, Ida B. Wells, an African-American, led the anti-lynching campaign. She developed a critique of lynching and its strategic use of the supposed vulnerablity of white woman-hood to the black rapist as a guise for racial terror, designed to protect white male supremacy. She worked closely in Britain with Catherine Impey, the editor of *Anti-Caste*, which was both anti-slavery and anti-imperial, but fell out with other white feminists in Britain and the United States over the explosive mix of racism and sexism, and the dangerous positioning of white women in the politics of lynching.

The ongoing impact of historical memory and its implication of white women in race power is demonstrated in Alice Walker's story 'Advancing Luna—and Ida B. Wells' (1982). Here a white woman civil-rights activist is raped by a black activist in Georgia. Knowing the demonisation of black men as an excuse for white violence, Luna remains silent, and only later tells the narrator what happened to her. The black narrator asks 'Who knows what the black woman thinks of rape? Who has asked her? Who *cares?* Who has even properly acknowledged that *she* and not the white woman of this story is the most likely victim of rape?' (1982: 93). Her anger is fuelled by recognition of ongoing race power: '[T]he power *her word on rape* had over the lives of black men, over *all* black men, whether they were guilty or not, and therefore over my whole people' (1982: 95). The issue then is: 'whether, in a black community surrounded by whites with a history of lynching blacks, [a white woman] had a right to scream as [a black man] was raping her' (1982: 101).

This is a dramatic illustration of 'the difficulty of excavating a genuinely postcolonial space for feminism' (Donaldson 1992: 7).

Colonial presences

'Colonising women are a contemporary presence, not an ancient absence' (Jolly 1993: 104). This complicates relations between different women, and feminist politics and theorising about difference. So indigenous and ex-colonised women require that white women take responsibility for their own racialised and ethnic positioning, and interrogate the continuing social significance of race, including whiteness, before alliances and political friendships are possible.

In settler states, the term 'postcolonial' is not accepted by indigenous peoples who remain trapped within white-dominated immigration states. Here colonial relations have been modernised, and aboriginality or its equivalent may be reconstituted as a social-needs and administrative category by the state in its attempt to manage difference. In Australia, for example, relations between the colonisers and those who now constitute themselves as the first nation are bitterly unresolved, though the recent Mabo high court judgement recognising some forms of native title did give Aboriginal people status as indigenous owners (Rowse, 1993). However, the profound 'trauma injury' (Atkinson, 1990) of colonisation and dispossession continues to shape the lives of the survivors. It is found in ongoing poverty, structural violence and institutional racism, and family and community violence that particularly affect women and children. Naming this damage can feed into colonially generated racist images of Aboriginal men as violent, families as deviant and women as irresponsible mothers. This in turn can invite state intervention, replicating the history of disruption to families, the seizing and institutionalisation of children, and the imprisonment of men and women in horrifically high numbers.

In this context, Aboriginal women are torn between reluctance to speak, lest racist hearings see their words used against their communities, and the need to resist setting community concerns against women's concerns in accusations of undermining or betraying 'the race'. Feminist writings that do not attend to these painful conflicts can compound the problem. Uninvited or apparently insensitive interventions meet a critical reception. A white feminist academic published an article on rape in Aboriginal Australia, positioning herself as 'breaking the silence' on intraracial rape, and authorising her writing in collaboration with her long-time informant and friend, an older Aboriginal woman (Bell and Nelson, 1989). A number of Aboriginal women academics objected strongly. They challenged the deployment of a categorical distinction between traditional and 'angry urban activists', a division long used to divide Aboriginal people and to deny radical spokespersons legitimacy. They reiterated the primacy of colonisation in the lives of all Aboriginal women, and called attention to white women's complicity in colonisation. 'Just because you are women doesn't mean you are necessarily innocent. You were, and still are, part of that colonising force' (Huggins et al., 1991: 506).

There is a politics of representation here, about how Aboriginal women and gender relations are represented, who speaks for them, and who is allowed to speak about what (Larbalestier, 1990; Pettman 1992c). Given the usual absence, or at best marginal presence, of Aboriginal women in the production of authorised knowledge about themselves, claiming a voice is a political act. It is also an expression of anger that the many Aboriginal women already working for—and sometimes writing about—Aboriginal women's safety, and addressing rape within Aboriginal communities, were silenced in the article; and that those women often are not recognised to speak, when a white feminist academic is.

The politics of voice involve a contest about who speaks and who is silenced (though Aboriginal women may choose to remain silent rather than be incorporated into or appear to legitimise others' talk about them). Debates continue about how to 'write' other women, in the academy and in society, where racist discourses infuse popular representations of difference (Yeatman, 1993). Aboriginal women writing about family and community violence go to careful lengths to locate these dangers within the context of colonisation, and attend to the possibility of appropriation for racist ends. They caution white feminists to attend to the dangers of activating racist stereotypes or facilitating state harassment of black men or communities, for example, in campaigns to make the streets safe for women, in situations where black male sexuality is criminalised and 'race' is coded with crime and disorder. Similar 'representation debates' are ongoing elsewhere, including in newly liberated South Africa (Hassim and Walker, 1993; Lewis, 1993).

The colour of feminism?

A study of colonisation reveals relations of domination and subordination structured through global political economy and constructed along different axes that continue to position different women differently. This makes pertinent black feminist challenges to white feminists, in bell hooks' reminder that it is white men that they want to be equal to (1984), and in Hazel Carby's demand, What exactly do you mean when you say 'We'? (1982: 233).

These questions reflect the challenges to white feminism made by black and third-world feminists through the 1980s, as their own experiences were not included in some feminist representations of women in general. They identified silences and presumptions which have universalised white feminists' experiences, in accusations that mirrored accusations those feminists made of masculinist universalising strategies in maintaining sex power.

In settler states and the old metropoles, colonised/black women pointed to their very different experiences of family, sexuality, work, patriarchy and the state (Amos and Parmar, 1984; hooks, 1984). Many black families have long been headed by women, and are often the only available security against poverty and racism. Many black women work outside their own homes, significant numbers of them in domestic labour for white households. Their sexuality is still constructed against that constructed for white women, as exotic or easy, in ways that place them beyond the bounds of 'protection', and that routinely subject them to approaches, innuendos or outright sexual attack. Black families are often seen as deviant, and black masculinity as dangerous. Black mothers are also seen as deviant, as too strong, as castrating matriarchs, as bad women for doing what good men are supposed to do. These racialised gender readings are saturated with meanings and underwritten in power relations that flow directly from experiences of slavery and colonisation.

The domination practices of colonisation and racism act to naturalise and normalise dominant-group characteristics and interests, including 'whiteness' and particular ethnicities. So in Australia only Aboriginal people and racialised minorities are seen to have race or ethnicity. White feminists become imperial through their association with these domination practices, to the extent that they do not 'own' their own whiteness and ethnic location, and the social significance of these (Frankenberg, 1993). When taking their own experiences as those of women in general, they effectively exclude other women, and reproduce the power relations and boundaries of colonised difference.

Indigenous, black and third-world feminists demand that white feminism recognise the variety of women's experiences, and learn to listen to women with very different understandings of social relations from their own. They also demand that white women understand white as a privileged political colour. Individual white women without personal knowledge of black women and without conscious racism are still implicated in colonisation and racism, through their identification and treatment as white in a world where

42

race makes a difference. Here recognising difference is not enough, for raced difference is power difference.

Colonising women in settler societies and first-world dominant-group women still relate to other women through unequal power relations. Today, many black and indigenous women meet the state in the person of a white woman, as teacher, health worker or social-security officer, for example. While class and the particular site of state vary, historical experiences and current institutional racism mean that even the welfare aspects of the state are problematic and threatening for many minority women. That these experiences, including state surveillance and intervention, are shared with poor immigrant and white women, is a reminder that we are talking about power—although power constructed and defended along different, and at times compounding, axes.

Relations between white women and colonised, ex-colonial and racialised women speak to historically constructed power relations. They immensely complicate attempts at feminist theorising. Alternatively, they offer the opportunity to analyse difference beyond gender, to give an account of differences among and between women. All men are privileged as men in patriarchal relations, but minority men occupy ambiguous status in other terms, and may themselves be oppressed and exploited in the wider social formation. Some women are privileged in terms of race, culture and/or class power, even while being constrained by their gender. They are, thus, in a stronger position to mediate the effect of gender in their everyday lives.

Recognising the multiple axes of oppression (King, 1988) and the contingent identities that each of us occupy or subvert destabilises any simple identity or category politics (Meekosha and Pettman, 1991). Women's identities as colonised, indigenous or black may be most salient in particular contexts, though these identities are gendered, too. Many racialised women remain suspicious of 'white' feminism. Other third-world and minority women name themselves as feminist, and reject any presumption of white ownership of feminism (hooks, 1984; Mohanty et al., 1991). They raise crucial questions about what to make of the category 'women' in the face of these differences, and how to work towards a feminist political project for the liberation of all women.

This doesn't mean giving up on gender, for gender relations structure social power and determine what it means to be male as against female in any particular society or moment. It does mean recognising contests around difference, including sexual difference, as power plays. It means dealing with racism as a primary structuring relation between black and white women, and decolonising feminisms (Donaldson, 1992: 3), before black women are prepared to talk with white women about sexism—especially in their own community (Huggins, 1992: 20).

3

Women, gender and nationalism

*All nationalisms are gendered, all are invented, and all are
dangerous . . . in the sense of representing relations to political
power and to the technologies of violence.*

(McClintock, 1993: 61)

International Relations as a discipline paid remarkably little attention
to nationalism until very recently. This partly reflects its construction
as a discipline focusing on relations between states, which has
reinforced disciplinary boundaries and the dichotomy of inside/out-
side (Lapid, 1993). The dramatic changes and conflicts of recent
years caught the discipline by surprise. In turn, academic writings
about nationalism frequently ignore women and gender relations.
Yet even a cursory look at nationalism's construction and politics
reveal women's significance in marking the boundaries of difference.
Both nation and nationalism are constructed on and through gender.

Women are constructed as mothers of the nation, and markers
of its boundaries. 'Women become the subjected territory across
which the boundaries of nationhood are marked' (*Gender and
History*, 1993: 159). Interrogating nationalism means recognising
women's roles and the uses made of them in both constructing and
reproducing nationalism.

Making nationalism

Nationalism is one of the most powerful political forces of the last
200 years. Currently in resurgence, it is literally remapping the very
territory of states and international relations, most dramatically in
the former Yugoslavia and Soviet Union. The break-up of the last
vestiges of the huge polyglot empires of the past is accompanied
by much violence and danger, especially in the wake of the

enormous arms trade and arms races of recent decades (Anderson, 1992). These changes are destroying the formerly easily deployed concept of a coinciding nation–state, central to but rarely analysed in IR. They lead us to ask Whose nation? and Whose state? and to examine the often difficult relationship between nation and state.

Nationalism speaks of a people, of 'us', of belonging. It calls up criteria for belonging that popularly assume shared history, language or religion. It frequently posits a people–time–land connection—we have been here forever—which presents a particular problem for settler-state nationalisms (Stasiulis and Yuval-Davis, 1995).

The nation is an imagined community (Anderson, 1991) calling up far too many people to know each other personally, but assuming recognition and belonging among them. Nationalism is a modern phenomenon, facilitated by the rise of the modern state system, and especially the ideological heritage of the French Revolution, which declared the people as sovereign. The nationalising of the state powered it as representative and protector of 'the people'. Nationalism was generated, too, by cultural and technological developments fuelled by the industrial revolution: the growth of literacy, mass education and the print media, nationalising and standardising 'culture', and citizenship. Thus, despite particular nationalisms' claims to primordial beginnings, it is a modern political form. It eclipsed dialects and a range of local and lesser myths and loyalties. These may have been repressed or obscured, rather than destroyed. They may form the place for alternative constructions of identities, for oppositional politics when the centre weakens, or when the contradictions between the nation's claims to represent and the political economy's marginalisation of or discrimination against others becomes intolerable (Bhabha, 1990).

Nationalism relies on excluding and forgetting. Nationalism constructs 'the people', simultaneously including/excluding us/them. The nation is a form of identity and difference. It creates the outsider, the other, the stranger. The nation produces its boundaries and simultaneously produces the foreigner, minority, immigrant, exile (Lerner, 1991). Nationality is relational, for it derives from difference. '[N]ations are forever haunted by their various definitional others' (Parker et al., 1992: 5). What is significant is not only difference, but the political import of difference as threat or inferiority: difference is hierarchised. So one way to approach nationalism is to ask how, and who, the nation is used to exclude and subordinate (Lerner, 1991).

The drawing of the nation, like other political identities, both obscures difference/s within the boundaries and creates differences between those defined as inside as opposed to outside those boundaries. In this sense it marks the limits of belonging which only too easily can become the boundaries of the moral community. Beyond these boundaries violence becomes thinkable—indeed, do–able. In this sense, and despite IR's presumption of nation subsumed in/by the state, it is the drawing of the nation that creates the outsider, the enemy. Nation is compounded by and in places contradicted by the state. The state's nationalism is frequently an expression of ethnic majority nationalism, but when it becomes too exclusive in the majority's images and interests, it triggers minority ethnic opposition. No state is 'pure' or ethnically homogenous, though Somalia is close. There is no necessary or inevitable logic about which nations claim, or succeed in establishing, a state.

In nationalism and the state, conflicts of loyalty between the particular and the universal are resolved through asserting the higher claim of the particular. Indeed, the nation is an attempt to solve the problem of why loyalty should be given to this particular community, rather than to humankind (Seth, 1993: 5). The nation simultaneously legitimises the particular and certain universal ideas and ideals. There is a tension here regarding nationalism as shaping the international order, which in turn draws a line in terms of who constitutes a people for the purposes of recognising the right of national self-determination. IR and its international order are thus characterised by a 'pragmatic reconciliation between the prescriptive principle of state sovereignty and the popular principle of national self-determination' (Mayall, 1990: 45).

Nationalism is peculiarly contradictory and paradoxical. Nationalism is not reactionary or progressive in itself, though its costs are dreadfully evident today.

> Nationalism has been illiberal as well as liberal, generous and expansive as well as xenophobic, democratic as well as undemocratic, future oriented and backwards looking . . .
>
> [I]t is not that nationalism tends to be either progressive *or* reactionary, depending upon the conditions under which it arises and operates, but rather that nationalism is *simultaneously* universal and particular, appeals to nature and to culture, is atavistic and modern, liberal and illiberal, democratic and undemocratic . . . It *encapsulates* the binary oppositions of modern thought and culture—nature/culture, universal/particular and so on—but it does not permanently reconcile, let alone transcend, the tension between these (Seth 1993: 12–13).

Nationalism has been described as Janus-faced, looking both backwards to a mythologised past, and forward in its constitution of a contemporary political project (Kandiyoti, 1991b: 431). But the nature of the particular political project that any one nationalism pursues varies enormously. Beyond similarities in the construction of the national collectivity, its boundaries and criteria for membership or exclusion, we might recognise different kinds of nationalism, and different nationalist projects within each of these. Nationalism has mobilised many people against colonialism and foreign occupation, and against unrepresentative and repressive regimes. It has also mobilised against other people simply on the grounds that they are 'different', even while functioning to construct that difference, or at least to give it political significance. Nationalists pursue political projects that range from racist and exclusivist to inclusive and multicultural. Particular nationalisms may be charged with association or articulation through other agendas, conventionally labelled as left or right wing, and they usually incorporate a range of tendencies and contradictions within their ranks as well. Nationalism and the nation are always in process, despite the naturalising and normalising discourses that disguise their politics.

There is no 'nationalism in general' (Parker et al., 1992: 3).There are different ways of classifying categories of nationalisms, with names such as dominant, hegemonic, imperial, often referring to first-world state projects; settler-state nationalisms, indicating another contradiction in their construction against both mother country and indigenous peoples, and also their immigrant make-up; anticolonial nationalisms, constructed historically; postcolonial nationalisms, as third-world states build their nations; and ethno-nationalisms, as minorities or incorporated territories seek independence or autonomy. Currently, new or revived nationalisms reflect a new global politics, which I will explore further in the next chapter. It is necessary to attend to the specificities of different nationalisms. But first it is important to note the extraordinary similarities in the ways that very different nationalisms construct 'women', and their construction of the nation as female.

Gender and nation

Nationalism constitutes the nation as above politics, and so disguises the politics of its making. This is the extraordinary power of the nation as that thing which people will kill and die for. Indeed, the nation is closely associated with sacrifice, with death and rebirth (Lerner, 1991; Elshtain, 1992a; Poole, 1985).

The nation is often called up in familial language—motherland, kin, blood, home—language that is strangely different from the Realist representations of power politics and rational self-national interest. In a complex play, the state is often gendered male, and the nation gendered female—the mother country—and the citizens/children become kin (Elshtain, 1992c; Pettman, 1993). Catherine Hall suggests that the common theme of the nation as female 'implies the gendering of the citizen as male', and relatedly that we often think of the state as masculine (Hall, 1993: 100). In this construction of the nation, 'women are the *symbol* of the nation, men its *agents*, regardless of the role women actually play in the nation' (*Feminist Review*, Editorial, 1993b: 1).

The nation is frequently represented as a woman under threat of violation or domination, so her sons must sacrifice for her safety, and for her—or their fathers'?—honour. Thus the defence of Egyptian honour against colonial power was represented as the defence of female purity, and early twentieth-century Iranian nationalists represented the nation as a beautiful woman raped by foreigners (Brown, 1993; de Groot, 1993). There is a common historical association of the indigenous and colonised with the female body, where cultural expression is feminised. This leads to construing imperial power as 'male heterosexual rape' (Parker et al., 1992: 9). Foreign occupation is likewise depicted, for example, by the French against German occupation in World War 1, and the Greek Cypriots after the Turkish invasion, and recently in the 'rape of Kuwait'. The metaphor of rape to represent national or state humiliation reveals 'how deeply ingrained has been the depiction of the homeland as a female body whose violation by foreigners requires its citizens and allies to rush to her defence' (Parker et al., 1992: 6). It also confuses the rapes of actual women with the outrage of political attack or defeat, and in the process women's pain and rights are appropriated into a masculinist power politics. Eroticising the nation/country as a loved woman's body leads to associating sexual danger with boundary transgressions and boundary defence. It can materialise in competition between different men for control of women. Indeed, a triangle, a love story, a fairytale is often constructed, necessitating a villain, a victim and a hero. The sexual subtext and gendered politics of nationalism are further complicated through the feminising—and hypermasculinising—of 'other' men.

The language of nationalism and war call up affective relations, bonding, familial loyalty, and love—quite different from the free, competitive individual of the rational market/polis. Ross Poole argues, in a problematic formulation, that the language of war is not, as we might expect, of violence and death, but of caring, courage and self-sacrifice—in Australian parlance, as mateship. 'War is not so much the construction of a new and virulent form of masculinity, as the recovery, for masculine identity, of that relational form of identity constituted within the family. It is, in this sense, the return of the feminine' (1985: 78; see also Jean Elshtain (1987) drawing parallels between the good soldier and the good mother).

In a further move, men appropriate giving birth, women's power, to themselves. Nationalism, war, sacrifice and death are closely associated. The birth of the nation comes through the killing and maiming of young men, on territory where women aren't supposed to be. Indeed, 'proving' manhood seems to be part of becoming a nation; thus, the birth of the Australian nation on the killing fields of Gallipoli, a masculinist birth, a 'mission impossible' (Lake, 1992: 305), achieved without women.

Nationalism fashions a distinctly homosocial form of male bonding; deep, horizontal comradeship (Anderson, 1991: 7); and a willingness to kill or die for one's mates. This is a passionate brotherhood, a 'virile fraternity' (Parker et al., 1992: 6). It is also a particular form of masculinity, which is a heterosexual masculinity. 'The nation finds itself compelled to distinguish its 'proper' homosociability from more explicitly sexualized male to male relations, a compulsion that requires the identification, isolation and containment of male homosexuality' (Parker et al., 1992: 6); hence moral panics about homosexuals, and women (usually seen as alternatives), in state militaries.

The nation is represented as a body, the body politic. This body can be threatened from without, but also by pollution, contamination, by the enemy within. Defence against such threats can take the form of violence against scapegoated minorities, such as Jews in Nazi Germany, and the obscene notion of 'ethnic cleansing', named in the bitter break-up of Yugoslavia, but familiar in its intent and atrocities in numerous other national and communal conflicts.

'Nationalism typically has sprung from masculinized memory, masculinized humiliation, and masculinized hope' (Enloe, 1990a: 44). Men have particular roles and relations with nationalism through their identity as protectors of nation and women (and children), as citizen warriors. But women are called up by the nation too. Women can share in the national identity as soldiers' wives, mothers and daughters, not by transforming but by generalising their domestic identity (Poole, 1985). Women are frequently represented, especially in mobilised or besieged nationalism, as mothers of the nation. This representation locates and constrains women in particular ways.

'[T]his trope of the nation-as-woman of course depends for its representational efficacy on a particular image of woman as chaste, dutiful, daughterly or maternal' (Parker et al., 1992: 6). Jean Elshtain (1987) pursues these images in terms of war's production of gendered as well as national civic identities. Here the nation's men are 'Just Warriors', the defenders and protectors; and its women are the virtuous ones, the 'Beautiful Souls' the protected ones. Their status as passive, non-political, domestic, underlines women's dependent status and men's roles as political actors.

But only the women of the nation are the beautiful ones. Other men's/nation's/state's women, especially those who have been racialised or made exotic, licentious, tempting, dangerous, inferior, are not 'beautiful' like the home/national woman is. (Though home/national women may place themselves outside the bounds of protection by unruly, ungrateful behaviour, or by dishonouring themselves/their men/their nation by sexual or other associations with 'other men'.) Here we are not talking only about discourse, about ideology, but also about the material effects of category and collectivity politics. Who you are seen to be may cost you your life.

This is a reminder of the difficult relationship of protector and protected, witnessed often as a slide from protected to possession to controlled. Women become vulnerable to attack by own-group men if the burden of protection is too heavy, or if those women are seen as ungrateful or disloyal. It further demonstrates women's difficult relationship with the nation, as women are terribly vulnerable to rape in nationalist conflicts and wars, both as spoils of war and as a way of men getting at other men, by demonstrating their inability to defend their women. Violence against women thus becomes an assault on men's and national honour. There is a complex move here, from actual women's bodies and the dangers they face, to nationalist discourse using images of women's bodies to mark national or communal boundaries. Here policing the boundaries too easily becomes the policing of women's bodies and movements (see pp. 99–104).

The significance of women in the construction of national collectivities and political identities goes beyond the symbolic use of their bodies as a metaphor for the body politic and place. While no complete overview is possible here, I trace aspects of these relations, drawing on examples from very different kinds of nationalisms in different places and times.

Women and/in dominant/state nationalisms

Dominant nationalism is state nationalism, or empire nationalism. It mobilises public and institutional power to dominate, exclude, even destroy others. It functions to make the state its own, to conquer and rule 'others'. It takes different forms, and may seek to assimilate or to separate out minority or other people. Consolidating the 'homeland' in its more virulent form includes, for example, the sterilisation and forced abortion policies of Nazi Germany (Bock, 1992).

This is an extreme example of nationalist reproductive politics and of violence against women's bodies. But women's construction as mothers of the nation in a wide range of nationalist projects has long had the effect of placing 'their reproductive capacities at the centre of their service to the nation' (Hall, 1993: 100). Dominant and hegemonic nationalisms are often concerned with the purity of the race, and so subject dominant-group women to systematic control in terms of marriages, sexuality and children. I noted these restrictions under colonialism and in settler-state nationalisms in chapter 2. These were pursued through reproductive-politics and women's-rights debates which sought to boost the maternal health and family support of the 'right' women. In Western European and settler states currently, they show in institutional racism, which denies minority and racialised women equal health and reproductive rights.

Dominant nationalism is also excluding in its casting of the boundaries of belonging, for example, through the association of whiteness and Englishness with British nationalism. Dominant nationalism's control of the state means that immigration and citizenship policies can be formulated according to criteria determined with reference to the national interest, which may mean, for example, allowing immigration when there is a labour shortage, while still withholding social rights and, in many cases, citizenship (see chapter 4).

Women and/in settler-state nationalisms

Dominant nationalisms in settler states illustrate the combined impact of colonisation, immigration and nationalism on the current state system. Historically, settler states as diverse as the United States, Argentina, Australia, Israel, and South Africa (until 1994) pursued nation-building and securing the state on racialised and culturalised exclusivity (Stasiulis and Yuval-Davis, 1995). Settler-state nationalisms are drawn against both mother country and indigenous people. They are 'nations of immigrants', who then face particular problems constructing the nation and claiming state/sovereignty in the face of first nations, whose time–place–people connection contest imposed moral and political bases. In Australia, for example, the myth of *terra nullius*, unoccupied land, and racist ideologies including scientific racism, 'justified' the dispossession and exclusion of Aboriginal people. Australian nationalism of those decades distinguished itself from 'old-world' and especially British nationalism, though often still in an empire frame. It sought to build 'Australia for the White man', setting up strict barriers against 'non-white' immigration, which lasted into the early 1970s.

Australian nationalism, then, was white, British or Irish, and, apparently, male. The 'ideal type' was a lone male—bushman, soldier, later urban-worker or surfer. Women were usually invisible, or, as we saw in chapter 2, visible only as breeders of the white race. Their relations with others, especially sex and marriage, were policed, and they were chided by nationalist politicians when birthrates fell for endangering Australia's security in a hostile and overpopulated region. Some women, including feminists, sought their place as equal partners in the new nationalist project, new women for a new land. Some sought to compensate for and to civilise the manliness of the nation, constructing themselves as citizen mothers alongside male citizen workers or soldiers. They won the right to vote very early on in the story of women's suffrage. One state, South Australia, was the second where women won the vote in 1894 (after New Zealand in 1893), and the first to allow women to stand for parliament as well as to vote. But when these rights were generalised in the new federation of states in 1901, they were accorded only to white women (Pettman, 1995c).

White–settler nationalisms' exclusionary project generates counter-nationalisms. So Aboriginal people in Australia mobilised both for equal rights in the state and for recognition of their particular claims as indigenous people (Coe, 1994; Rowse, 1993).

53

Aboriginal protest and politics constructed Aboriginality in a conflation of 'race' and culture against the dominant white Europeans.
There is much contest now over retellings of Aboriginal and colonial
history, with familiar tensions between casting Aboriginal people as
victims especially when forced displacement has jeopardised current
claims to land or compensation, and as agents, demonstrating
strength and survival. These retellings often recast the racialised
colonial boundaries of 'Aborigines' and 'whites' in ways that point
to the primary faultline of raced power and the ongoing consequences of colonisation. In the process, the gender politics of first
nation-building can be obscured, though there are now many
Aboriginal women who are telling their own stories—stories that
include both coercion and choices in relations with white men.

Anticolonial nationalisms

Anticolonial nationalisms mobilised against European empires and
western domination, defining the nation against the nonrepresenta-
tive colonial power, trying to build a nation to claim a state. Most
of these nationalist movements took as their physical boundaries
the territory and borders constructed in empire, which usually did
not coincide with precolonial collectivities. This frequently involved
a double move—to recover 'tradition' against the west, and to
modernise to be able to compete with and displace the west. Many
anticolonial nationalist movements were reformist, opposing or
seeking to modernise feudal and older political and cultural forms.
They pursued a nationalising project to build a new nation/successor
state. In so doing, they defined national difference in cultural terms,
against the west (Chatterjee 1991: 521). This difference they located
in the private, in family and sex roles—the very domains to which
both modernising and traditional politics usually relegated women.

Anticolonial and many postcolonial nationalisms deploy a dichotomy of inside/outside, defining an arena of relative autonomy
against an intrusive west. They locate their own subjectivity in
culture, family and home, supposedly superior to and some distance
from the materialist and predatory west (Chatterjee, 1990: 249).
Mobilising the inside/outside distinction, nationalist rhetoric makes
woman 'the pure and ahistorical signifier of "interiority"'
(Radhakrishnan, 1992: 84). This renders women themselves mute,
as 'Woman takes on the name of a vast inner silence' (1992: 85).

In the process of developing a new nationalist consciousness, 'tradition' is reinvented. 'In the new script for the past the women's question held a key place' (Chakravati, 1990: 27). Women are constructed as the bearers of the authentic/authenticated culture.

So it should not surprise us to learn that 'the woman question' often appeared on the public agenda in association with the rise of anticolonial nationalism, and in response to political, economic and cultural encroachments by the west. Early supporters of women's rights were nationalist elite men. Women themselves were mobilised within nationalist movements, but their scope for action and especially for pursuing their own gender interests depended in part on the terms in which the particular nationalist project was visualised. In Muslim colonies and states, for example, 'the woman question emerged as a hotly contested ideological terrain where women were used to symbolise the progressive aspirations of a secularist elite or the hankering for cultural authenticity expressed in Islamic terms' (Kandiyoti, 1991a: 3).

There are now significant collections and texts on women's relations with anticolonial and postcolonial nationalism, many by third-world feminists.

Kumari Jayawardena (1986) traces the complex relations of nationalist and feminist movements in Asia and the Middle East in the late nineteenth and early twentieth century, a retrieval project that rejects certain constructions of feminism as only western, only recent. Women's and feminist movements were part of wider social reform and anticolonialist agendas, aspiring to modern political rights and relations. Women's emancipation was often seen as part of national liberation, supported by middle-class nationalist men who opposed particular abuses and the oppression of women such as footbinding in China or *sati* (widow burning) in India. There were bitter conflicts over women's roles and rights, as nationalist men sought a new woman, but not a western one and conservative men mobilised against the changes.

Women were agents and actors in these politics; but they were also often supported by and spoken for by men. Women also organised for their own liberation, in wider nationalist struggles or in women-only organisations. In the 1920s and 1930s especially, there were remarkable outpourings of women's journals, writings, and conferences in Asia and the Middle East. There were links between some colonising women and local women, and significant international networks of socialist and feminist women. Colonised activist women travelled internationally. There were Asian women leaders at the Second Congress of the Communist International in

Moscow in 1920, and many women in British colonies, for example, were familiar with the struggles of British suffragettes (Jayawardena, 1986).

There was also a political economy pushing towards changed roles and more public participation for women. Both the developing capitalist economy and the nationalist anticolonial struggle needed women's labour and support, calling into question 'traditional' women's roles. This in turn led to a reaction against the changes, and to a highly dynamic conflict about women's roles in the past, and for the future. In this politics, women's bodies, relations and roles became the battleground for different idealised versions of the past, and constructions of nationalist projects for the future.

Nationalising women

In comparing nationalist and women's struggles internationally, we discover specificity, but also remarkably similar constructions of women in relation to nation—a reminder that nationalism is always gendered. In recent and contemporary nationalisms in wartime North America and Europe, and in anti-imperial and liberation struggles, women's labour and support were needed. Women were mobilised into the nationalist project in ways that unsettled old roles, and made places for women as actors. Yet women were still trapped in the symbolic use made of them as mothers of the nation, and notions of honour that constrained their movements and associations. Deniz Kandiyoti points to women as both actors in and hostage to nationalist projects. She notes representations of women in these projects, as 'victims of social backwardness, icons of modernity, or privileged bearers of cultural authenticity' (1991b: 431) and as objects of male discourse. Lata Mani confirms this analysis when she argues that '[t]radition was thus not the ground on which the status was being contested. Rather the reverse was true: women in fact became the site on which tradition was debated and reformulated' (1990: 118).

The symbolic uses of women are now well documented in feminist analyses. For example, in colonial and anticolonial India, there was competition between the imperial patriarchy of British colonial authorities and the Indian nationalist middle-class men who sought to challenge them. Colonial authorities sought to eliminate some traditional practices, while encouraging or freezing others into law (Sangari and Vaid, 1990: 7). When British colonial authorities appeared concerned for women's rights, and moved against particular oppressive practices, they also disregarded women, including those women resisting the practices. They needed a colonised people who required saving, constructing passive native women victimised by native males, from whom the colonising males would protect them. British rule was justified in part in terms of a civilising mission that cast British colonisers as rescuing or protecting oppressed colonised women.

Lata Mani (1990) analyses debates in colonial discourse, among Indian nationalists preindependence, and Indian leftist, liberals and traditionalists now, over *sati*. These arguments usually totally ignored women's resistance and agency, using 'women' to pursue other objectives and agendas. It was essentially a masculinist debate, where 'Indian women were not conceived as agents but rather formed the enabling ground or "site" of the discourse' (Mohanty and Mohanty, 1990). In the face of these appropriations, Indian feminists seek to reclaim a politics that places women's struggles within a history and politics of colonial/postcolonial power relations (Mani, 1990; Sander Rajan, 1993; Grewal and Kaplan, 1994)

There were complex relations of conflict, competition and collusion between colonial authorities, and both nationalist and conservative Indian male leaders. 'The woman question' in India was contested between colonial authorities and Indian men, between Indian nationalist and conservative men, and between Indian men and women, with colonising women also entering the debate at times. Each involved 'recasting women' (Sangari and Vaid, 1990) in accordance with the particular project. The politics of gendered identity construction reveals that '[b]oth tradition and modernity are eminently colonial constructions' (Sangari and Vaid, 1990: 117). This is significant for contemporary debates about whether women's rights as human rights are universal or culturally specific. A position of innocence or noncontamination from processes of colonisation and modernisation is not possible. Thus Rey Chow notes that China and other places subject to western imperialism are already 'westernised'. She challenges representations that turn China into a timeless 'culture garden', typical of the orientalising/third worlding of many western texts. These representations then allow constructions of 'third-world women' as victims, as cultural, not political; as outside social relations and outside history (Mohanty, 1988; Spivak, 1989). They also allow for the punishment and silencing of those feminist and other 'third-world women' who are judged as inauthentic, as 'not traditional enough' (Ram, 1993).

The politics of tradition/the sexual politics of culture

The language of culture and tradition disguised the politics of colonisation, nationalism and gender relations. Further, it relegated women to the domestic sphere, the home and family. In Indian nationalist discourses, for example, the construction of middle-class womanhood proceeded against both the west and other classes and castes. This saw the introduction of a new division between public and private, a form of housewifisation which was to develop further after independence. This division is not simple or set. 'A sphere marked out as "private" at one stage of nation-building may reappear with the full trappings of the "public" at another, their boundaries being fluid and subject to redefinition' (Kandiyoti, 1991a: 430). In this reading, the emergence of 'the woman question' and its subsequent subsuming within the nationalist project is a modernisation of patriarchy, rather than its displacement (Chatterjee, 1990: 250).

Women's relegation to the domestic, figuratively at least (many, especially poorer, women continued to work outside the home) meant that 'the woman question' was called up when it suited wider nationalist aims, and banished when women's actions threatened male political or nationalist priorities. So 'women' were largely subsumed and incorporated within the nationalist movement. Despite the heavy work that women did for the nation, symbolically and on the ground, their particular rights and claims were contained and domesticated. In most anticolonial movements they remained a category or occasionally a political constituency. Gender relations and the gender power of dominating practices were kept beyond political scrutiny. In this way, the role of gender difference as both structuring and structured by wider social relations is obscured (Sangari and Vaid, 1990).

There is a political economy of gender beyond its cultural, family or 'women' associations. Some changes in productive relations, for example, colonial land settlement or postcolonial development policies pushing women out of rights to land use or into outwork, are facilitated by the construction of women as supposed to be 'at home' (Chowdry, 1990). Elsewhere, as family and kin businesses or work networks disintegrate in the face of western competition or new production, and women are forced into 'unprotected' factory work, a high value placed on family honour through women's seclusion and surveillance reinforces class, caste and community differences, in favour of wealthier families. In this context, Santi

Rozario names 'purity' as a form of 'symbolic capital' (1992: 11). The honour of a caste or kin is mobilised to control women. She argues that intercommunal politics between Muslims, Hindus and Christians in the Bangladeshi village in which she worked have little to do with values or traditions per se, and cites the shift from bridewealth to dowry since 1971 as an example. Rather they have everything to do with access to scarce resources and political power. A political economy of space and gender difference is thus more revealing than a cultural essentialism or relativism, as the latter entraps women and denies a voice to those who wish to challenge local or transnational patriarchies.

The historical specificity and political economy of the construction of gender relations and of particular women is obscured by the construction of women within the traditional and domestic in colonial and much nationalist discourse. In this construction, women are homogenised, their voices silenced and their differences frozen. Women are 'always/already victim', passively waiting to be saved (Mani, 1990). In a dangerous replicating move, some 'white' feminist texts represent the third-world woman in a similar mode: object of men's oppression, victim of their own tradition. Here, they become peculiarly creatures of culture, in a way that by implication or contrast, white women are seen to have overcome. Such a representation robs those women of a history and a politics, and again denies the differences, including power differences, between women. These differences are now attended in many feminist works, including by first-world white feminists and increasingly now by third-world feminists; though this binary is itself also now under attack (Lazreg, 1988; Grewal and Kaplan, 1994).

Women's bodies/boundary wars

'Nationalism is gendered—women's bodies are the boundary of the nation, and the bearers of its future' (*Feminist Review*, 1993b: 1). The use of women as boundary markers suggests why the control of women and especially their sexuality is strategic in the maintenance and reproduction of identity and of the community (Peterson, 1994). In this context, the ideological weight some men give to women's outward attire and the sexual purity of women in the community can be noted. They see women, in Cynthia Enloe's formulation, as the community's, or the nation's, most valuable possessions; as those responsible for transmitting the whole nation's values and through this its political identity; as the bearers of the community's future generations, or 'nationalist wombs'; and as the members of the community most vulnerable to abuse, violation or seduction by 'other men' (1990a: 54).

This raises questions about the continuities and breaks at the moment when anticolonial nationalism wins its state, and turns its attention to consolidating the nation in the state. Here again women may be trapped within the new project. Ritu Menon and Kamla Bhasin (1993) have documented one of the most sustained operations to salvage women and through them, community and nationalist honour. Partition and the creation of Pakistan was accompanied by horrific violence and massive dispossession, displacement and migration. In the process, an officially estimated 50 000 Muslim women in India and 33 000 non-Muslim women in Pakistan were variously abducted, abandoned, or separated from their families. This led to the extraordinary 'Central Recovery Project' of the government of India, and an equivalent but less vigorously pursued project of Pakistan, over the years 1948–56. During this time some 30 000 Muslim and non-Muslim women were 'recovered' by their respective government agencies.

These recoveries were often forced, as many women were married and absorbed within the 'abducting' community. Referring to the evidence of much resistance on the part of Hindu women, Menon and Bhasin note:

> Abducted as Hindus, converted and married as Muslims, recovered as Hindus but required to relinquish their children because they were born of Muslim fathers, and disowned as 'impure' and ineligible for marriage within their erstwhile family and community, their identities were in a continuous state of construction and reconstruction, making . . . them . . . 'permanent refugees' (1993: 13).

Menon and Bhasin ask 'Why should the matter of national honour have been so closely bound up with the bodies of women and with the children born of 'wrong' unions?' (1993: 14). They conclude that India had been unable to stem the establishment of a separate Muslim homeland, so against the official proclamation of India as a secular nationalist project the Indian government pursued a communal identity, which located women as boundary markers and reproducers of true community members.

These struggles, of women and over women's bodies and rights, are not in the past. Women's roles and rights are central to the politics of national and political reconstruction involved in contemporary Islamification projects in Afganistan, Pakistan and Algeria, and in the rise of fundamentalisms including the Christian right in the United States. I will take up this discussion again in the context of postmigration and postcolonial identity politics, and of re-ethnicisations in first-world states in chapter 4.

Feminist nationalisms?

Nationalist movements and communal identities pose particular problems for feminists. The powerful appeal of nationalism and communal values extend to women, too (Connolly, 1993). There is, often, a difficult relationship between nationalism, women's rights and feminist struggles, though these are negotiated in different ways over time and place. We are left observing that in these relations too, nationalism is often contradictory. Nationalist movements mobilise women's support and labour, while simultaneously seeking to reinforce women's female roles and femininity. In their turn, many women support nationalist movements as women, and particularly as mothers. Their involvement may unsettle older roles and relations, and may politicise and radicalise women. Some women support nationalist movements as individuals or patriots, while others claim a particular role or investment as women or as mothers. We can further distinguish those women who make feminist claims for restructuring gender relations within nationalist politics (Molyneux, 1985; Jayawardena, 1986).

I noted previously that women in nationalist movements who work for women's rights and women's liberation may be supported by nationalist men, especially those whose politics are progressive or radical. More often, women are asked to set aside 'sectional interests' until the national cause is secured—the classic 'Later, not now' (Enloe, 1990a: 62). This has some appeal, and in particular circumstances urgency, as colonised or minority status, discrimination or persecution—even death—may follow from particular national, racialised or ethnic collectivity membership. But these dangers are experienced in gendered forms. And there is now considerable evidence that those causes that are marginalised in the struggle are likely to be marginalised in its victories, and especially in the consolidation and institutionalisation of victory in the state (see chapter 7).

Thus in wars and in nationalist and other liberation movements, women are mobilised in struggles, and used symbolically in them (Kandiyoti, 1991b). There may be a sequence here, as women are used early on in 'women's' and auxillary roles, as nurses or cooks, and later, when manpower is short, as substitutes for men's labour. They may be used, too, in ways that exploit their femininity, and other men's understanding of them as less political and as less violent. Usually, they have been pushed back into the home—or at least excluded from formal power—at the conclusion of the struggle; hence the importance of feminist recovery projects, in first, transitional and third worlds, which reinsert women in past nationalist and liberation struggles. These reveal that women were there, and some were there as feminists. There are also rewritings that seek to assess what gains, if any, women have made through their involvement, as individuals or as part of women's rights struggles, afterwards.

Women in struggles/women's struggles have been made visible through women's conferences, writings, and the build-up of international networks especially through the UN Decade for Women. There are now extensive writings on and by women in first, third, and now disintegrating second worlds. These reveal the full gamut in politics and interpretations of women's experiences. Some of these will be pursued in later chapters on women's political action and liberation movements.

Concluding then—the nation never just is, anymore than the state just is. Nationality and citizenship, like race and ethnicity, are unstable categories, and contested identities. They are all gendered identities, and the constructions of 'women', inside and outside their borders, are part of the processes of identity formation.

Contests and conflicts continue over the borders and boundaries of belonging, over the body politic and over women's bodies as the markers, reproducers and transmitters of the nation. Thus while some see nationalism as a political ideology, along with liberalism or socialism, for example, others see it more closely aligned with religion or kinship relations (Anderson, 1991: 5; Parker et al., 1992: 4). The language of kinship, family and home in nationalist discourses link blood and soil (Lui, 1991). Controlling the sexual behaviour, marriages and children of women thus becomes central to community reproduction and defence. These elements of sex and control locate women centrally in the symbolic and material construction and reproduction of the nation.

The very power of the nation and its articulation of gender rules and gender power make feminist theorising about and politics towards nationalism extremely difficult. We can ask, then, how have different feminisms engaged with or sought to distance themselves from different nationalist projects? We can also ask whether, in the light of these understandings, the notion of a feminist nation is imaginable—or is it a contradiction in terms? (Parker et al., 1992: 8).

4

Women in postcolonial and postmigration political identities

The discipline of International Relations has not taken migration as part of its research agenda, except occasionally as a particular state's foreign policy issue or when 'refugees' become an international crisis. Nor have questions of political identity and the construction of 'us' and 'them' been much explored (*Millennium*, 1993). These gaps stem from the obscuring effects of the nation–state couplet, and IR's assumption of a fixed relationship between people, territory and identity, which is simply not so on the ground.

In recent decades, women have made up increasing numbers of migrants, including labour migrants. Eighty per cent of refugees are women and children. Women's experiences of displacement are rather different from men's. Women are caught up in postmigratory identity politics, especially when they are used to mark the boundaries between different communities or cultures in their new place.

Women are crucial, too, to postcolonial identity projects, including to neotraditionalist or fundamentalist movements, for whom women's roles and status are central issues. These new identity politics challenge the secular state, which IR presumes. They are also often transnational, involving diasporic communities and deterritorialised identities. They further disrupt the IR hyphen in the nation–state.

People on the move

International migration is by definition a form of international relation, involving the crossing of state borders, legally or illegally, and, often, changes in citizenship as well. International events and conflicts generate flows of people across borders, as the fall of the Berlin wall and the conflict in the former Yugoslavia demonstrate. An international political economy of labour migration propels movement from poorer states and regions to richer ones; while most refugees move to neighbouring states. Immigration and refugee issues become foreign policy problems, and in turn rebound in politics within states (Mitchell, 1989), not least around issues of national identity, citizenship politics and racism. State responses and state-making processes aggravate or defuse these politics, in the former situation, often with international reverberations.

Huge movements of people over the last 500 years and especially since the late 1940s enormously complicate and unsettle associations between people, place and identity. An estimated 200 million people moved 'voluntarily' between 1500 and 1980 and many moved in various forms of forced migration. The slave trade from 1500 to 1800 forcibly transplanted millions of people. International indentured labour taking South Asians to East Africa and Fiji constructed 'race' hierarchies within and between states, in terms of power and difference that still matter in the world today (Doty, 1993; Pettman, 1995a).

International migration in the last 500 years has gone through several different phases. From 1500 to 1800 comparatively small numbers of Europeans set off for the colonies, and slaves were imported into the Americas. From 1815 to World War 1 there was a dramatic upsurge in the numbers leaving Europe, calculated at between 48 and 60 million people, going mainly to North America, Argentina, Australia and New Zealand. In that time some 10 million Russians moved to Siberia and Central Asia, and some 12 million Chinese and 6 million Japanese moved to East and South-East Asia (Hune, 1991).

There was very little migration in the Depression between the World Wars, though World War 2 displaced many millions across state borders in Europe especially and contributed to postwar migration. Migration since then has been enormous. To continuing flows from Europe to settler states was added a reverse flow, from south to north. European labour shortages and postwar reconstruction and industrial development drew in migrants, often from colonies and then ex-colonies to old metropoles. Labour migration, both temporary and permanent (though this distinction is not always clear or useful), widened to include new 'receiving' states including Gulf states and Japan, in a fracturing of the third world.

There was also extensive intraregional migration. Immediately after World War 2 large numbers of people moved from Eastern Europe to 'the West', a traffic that revived with the disintegration of Soviet power. People moved, too, from Egypt and other Arab states into the Gulf states, from North Africa across the Mediterranean, from Central and South America into the United States, and lately from poorer South and South-East Asian states to comparatively richer neighbours. Smaller in numbers but proportionately of greater significance are trans-Pacific migrations and remittance networks enclosing Pacific ministates and larger, richer Pacific-rim cities such as Sydney (Australia), Auckland (New Zealand) and Honolulu (USA) (Connell, 1991).

Over time, as states shift position within the international political economy, their migration statuses change. Italy, for example, was a country of emigration in the postwar decades, but is now an immigration destination, with growing numbers of migrants from north and sub-Saharan Africa and from the Philippines. States also experienced shifts in sources and kinds of immigrants, with demographic and political consequences. Some countries still deny the migrant presence, for they forbid or discourage migration for settlement, and so identify the 'strangers' as temporary labour migrants or as 'resident aliens'. This has profound effects on the choices and images of those others, especially where states have significant numbers of illegal immigrants, as in the United States and Japan.

We are now witnessing a new phase of international migration, marked by rapidly increasing numbers and the diversity of states involved, and particularly by the ways in which migration has now become a global phenomenon (Adelman, 1993: 32). This current phase is characterised by transformations in terms of its global reach; accelerating numbers; diversity of types of migration, including permanent and labour migrants as well as refugees; the feminisation of many migrant flows; the politicisation of migration, stimulated by political events such as the Gulf War; and the rise of 'new' nationalisms and racisms in European countries aimed against 'foreigners' (Castles, 1993).

There are now an estimated 17 million refugees outside their home-state borders, 80 per cent of them women and children. In addition, some 45 to 50 million people are 'on the move' internationally each year. Debates about kinds of migration are also complicated by their tendency to merge into one another: 'temporary' labour migrants from Turkey to West Germany, for example, were declared 'here to stay' in the 1980s; single labour migrants in many states later sent for or were joined by their families; refugees who became citizens in new states sponsor relatives under family reunion categories; wealthier or better-educated escapees from their states move as a 'brain drain', as many Hong Kong residents seek to do before the territory's return to China in 1997. Other border crossers become part of a cycle or circle of multiple migration or transnational negotiation of kin and domestic political economies, as, for example, many men and women from Mexico move to and from the United States (Donato, 1993).

Women on the move

Until very recently, these flows were tracked as numbers and not according to gender. The migrant/labour migrant was seen as a male, with or without dependants. Even where this was or is so, the gender politics involved need closer analysis—when men went, for example, to South Africa or to West Germany, why was it men? Which men are later joined by wives, fiancées and children? And which states specifically forbid reunion or make it very difficult? Under apartheid in South Africa, working men's hostels became part of migratory and identity politics. In many large European industrial cities family-less men gather on Sundays in cafes and squares in nostalgic exile.

When women do join their men, their opportunities and post-settlement experiences are often affected by the receiving governments' presumption that they are dependents rather than workers. Migration is very expensive; to repay fares, to pay for agents and accomodation, and if men are laid off or injured, many recently migrated women do 'work'—often without former kin networks and during the time of maximum childcare responsibilities (Martin, 1986). Here the shock of change is evident in high stress, exhaustion, insecurity and ill-health, as they try to negotiate the new terrain. But women may also find some changes liberating, earning their own money, getting a driving licence and making women friends at work. Some women were active in union or feminist politics back home, and pick them up again in the new place.

What happens when men leave women behind? Women must work even harder, taking on men's tasks in rural areas, for example, or finding some form of paid employment if the money doesn't come back. Women seen as without protection might be vulnerable to their husband's male relatives or friends who are supposed to be 'looking after' them, or to bank officials, moneylenders or potential employers. But here, too, the increased responsibilities may be experienced by some women as liberating. Women may be most burdened but some also feel most independent when their men migrate and they alone are responsible for children (Zlotnik, 1990: 379). What then happens when the man comes back, or when the woman goes to a strange place to join him? Or on her return with him after his studies or work? Some women return to stricter state or community gender rules, or to face rising fundamentalisms insisting on seclusion or constraints that were not there before. Other women return alone, if a marriage 'out' fails, to uncertain status and difficult choices in some cases, or to welcome family support and loving friends in others.

Women's stories of their border crossings point us to the gendered processes involved in migration, and the gender relations behind different patterns of movement for men and women. Some tell of a marriage politics of migration, going as wives in chain migration to men they do not know. Some women are exchanged by male kin in men's politics, though we cannot guess from this what individual women make of the move, or the marriage. Women can lose their citizenship when they marry 'out', or be held at ransom when their immigration status or residence depends on their continuing marriage (WING, 1985).

Approximately half of all people officially outside their country of birth over the last two decades are women (Zlotnik, 1990). But women do not only move as dependants of men. Some flee from husbands, families or communities that are besieged or turn violent (Wong, 1994). Many go alone or with other women as migrant workers, making up the majority of legal migrants from Mexico to the United States, and in domestic labour to the Gulf states. Some 95 per cent of Filipinos living in Italy are women. They include those who worked at home as teachers or nurses, but at much lower pay. Some of them have children, left behind in the care of female kin. Women migrating alone to improve their own or their children's futures is not new, though in many states their construction as either dependants or single workers makes for difficulties when sending for children left behind, or for husbands or fiancées.

In South and South-East Asia especially, a young woman going alone across state borders may be moving as part of a family income-generating strategy, prompted in part by the changing international division of labour, which is increasingly exploitative of cheapened feminised labour (see chapter 8). It seems that there is a major difference here, in that many more men migrate for economic and individual reasons, while many women move for family reasons which reflect gender power in those families and in the wider international political economy (Zlotnik, 1990; Pedraza-Bailey, 1990).

It is hard to put together the 'big picture' of migration phases and flows, and personal and family dynamics, often encouraged along kin and social networks already in place in another state. Family politics and gender relations influence who will go where; and individuals choose, sometimes flight, sometimes journeying or adventuring. There is a whole literature, an immigrant genre, which includes many migrant women's writings (George, 1992; Gunew and Mahyjuddin, 1989). There are films and documentaries, supplementing and contradicting mass-media images of different women. Here are migrants and exiles and expatriates, refugees and cosmopolitans and multinationals, and stories of the negotiations required on the ground. These help us to understand why women cross borders, and how they experience the different statuses they might then inhabit. These stories also reveal something of the industries or businesses, the players—from international recruitment agents to border guards and owners of local transport—who are involved. Some border crossings entail considerable cost, and risk, for illegal migrants especially.

IR could gather clues and cues from those whose worlds are made and experienced away from the high places of state and academy that produce its authorised knowledges. It could also converse with others in the academy, in postcolonial literature and cultural studies for example, whose commentaries are fraught with difficulty and danger, as any academic discourse is, but which do attempt to engage with some of the experiences of border traffic that is currently reshaping our world.

Framing those decisions are structural factors and whole sets of international relations, only some aspects of which may be visible to the participants.

An international political economy of migration

International relations directly affect international immigration flows. The Gulf War dislocated some 400 000 Asian workers in Kuwait and 100 000 in Iraq, many of them women from states such as the

Philippines, Sri Lanka and India (Abella, 1991: 92). The Berlin wall 'fell' in part because of the sheer pressure of numbers flowing across the crumbling borders of old Soviet power. The end of the Cold War and the drastic changes in state authority patterns and foreign policy included the Soviet 1991 'free exit' law (Cohen, 1992)— though Western Europe, which had long advocated such a freedom, set about hastily restricting immigration and asylum rules to contain the new 'threat'. The changes also left large numbers of labour migrants on the other side, including those from Vietnam and other socialist states who had come to work or study in Eastern Europe.

The appearance of the first Russian au pairs in London in 1989 and of Polish women traders in West Germany (Morokvasic, 1991) signals both an international relations and an international political economy of migration. Many movements of people are from poorer to richer states, as some become exporters of labour and others importers. States also 'lose' people in a brain drain that amounts, often, to a subsidy for the rich and a further impoverishment of human resources in the poorer states. This is not only an economic choice. Many repressive and discriminatory regimes 'target', often literally, intellectuals, professionals, teachers and artists who might oppose them.

Shifts in the international political economy (IPE) since World War 2 are reflected in migrant flows, though there are lags and other effects, including chain migration after the original motivations have passed. Declining demand in the 1970s 'marooned' many labour migrants in older decaying industrial Europe. They were subject to attack and scapegoating as the cause of it all. Now, more likely, transnational corporations move to cheapened labour, especially in those countries whose repression discourage trade-union and democratic rights activities.

There is also an IPE in the 'push' factors in dislocating and impoverishing effects of modernisation and development. Some people lose access to land or are displaced by new manufacturing industries or cash cropping, with growing un/underemployment and increasing commercialisation requiring money for goods or services. These shifts often hit women especially hard, as do widespread structural adjustment policies. With the growth of a global assembly line of casualised, feminised labour, many young women move from rural to urban or export processing zones, or cross state borders in feminised labour migrant flows as domestic workers, for example. There is an IPE, too, in states, localities and families becoming dependent on remittances sent back in return for the export of labour. Remittances to the Philippines from those 'exported' amounted to some $US5.98 billion from 1986 to 1991 (*Asian Migrant*, 1991). In 1988 remittances were equivalent to 58 per cent of exports for Bangladesh, over 20 per cent for Pakistan, Sri Lanka and India, and 14 per cent for the Philippines (Connell, 1992). There are now very large numbers of men and women who work in states where they do not have citizenship or other social rights, and often not even rights to reside or work (Yuval-Davis, 1991). Why in conditions of globalisation and free movement of finance, production, goods and technology, can we not have free movement of labour, and indeed of people? (Barry and Goodwin, 1992). This points to the privileging of capital and not labour in the contemporary world. It raises ethical questions about immigration and people's rights to leave, enter and remain in states. It is, too, a reminder of how important states are as players in international migration (Zolberg, 1986).

Border patrols and border politics

Every state declares its right to determine who can enter, stay and acquire citizenship rights as part of its practice of sovereignty. Border defences through immigration and citizenship regulations are at least as important and often more important than military defence of physical boundaries against armed attack, though it is the latter that is privileged in mainstream IR. Some states pursue close relations or enter into bilateral agreements with others on migration issues, as Australia has with Italy, and with Vietnam. Some states' refugee intakes reflect foreign-policy links and ideological alliances, as numbers of Vietnamese went to the US and Australia after the 'fall of Saigon'. All states make calculations on numbers, sources and kinds of migrants to be encouraged or prohibited. In these complex politics, different women find themselves included or excluded in terms of what kinds of women they are seen to be.

States make gendered immigration policies including ideal types (Fincher, 1993). They might prohibit some women's migration on the grounds that they are undesirable mothers or 'breeders', while seeking women from particular states as good women, or single women as wives for disproportionately male migrant groups (de Lepervanche, 1989; Pettman, 1992a). Women's nationality, ethnicity and class in the home country affect chances and conditions of migration, and post-settlement options and obstacles.

Women's experiences after migration are filtered through axes of class and ethnicity as well as gender. They depend in part on whether women are legal immigrants or not, entitled to permanent settlement or citizenship, though we know the gaps there can be in women's and minorities' legal and social rights. Immigrant women experience the multiple effects of discrimination and difference. They can also fall between the category cracks—where social movements, identity politics and state provision may construct women *and* migrants as alternative categories (Meekosha and Pettman, 1991). The emergence of 'visible-minority women' in Canada, and non-English speaking background or ethnic minority women in Australia draws attention to the significance of migration and difference in many women's experiences of states. But these big categories also homogenise migrant women, disguising class, cultural, age, sexuality, political and other differences among them.

Migrant and minority women fight against routine invisibility, subsumed within the community, and hypervisibility should their words or actions not accord with the symbolic place accorded to them in the construction of the inner space of difference and of 'tradition'. Despite this dialectic, women are defining their own needs, including as paid workers and as claimants on state services. They are mobilising within their own organisations and emerging as subjects, even where they are discouraged or even forbidden from so doing because it is seen as 'betraying the race', or the community.

Immigration affects domestic politics in other ways, as political pressures force more restrictive immigration policies, as 'the Jewish lobby' (more precisely the pro-Israeli or Zionist lobby) becomes a factor in US politics and 'the ethnic vote' is discovered by settler-state politicians. States in turn try to manage the politics of difference, usually through an awkward and shifting combination of control and restriction of immigration with containment and accomodation of 'ethnic' or migrant claims. The state's control and surveillance processes, and information gathering including for census purposes, can create or freeze identities that were previously much more fluid, multilayered and negotiable on the ground. So the state becomes a player in postmigratory politics, too.

Whose nation? Whose state?

'Immigration' becomes an issue about national identity, or even about national security in panics about influxes, invasions and threats to 'our culture' or to social harmony. Here, difference itself is seen by some to create intolerance or racism, disguising the political uses of difference, and its pathologising as polluting the body politic. Closure against outsiders is argued as 'natural' as we all stick to our own. But a lot of ideological work goes into racialising migrants. 'Immigration' becomes a code word, meaning 'black' in the UK or Asian in Australia, while the often larger number of 'white' immigrants goes largely unremarked upon.

'Ethnic' organisations and anti-racist groups mobilise against institutional and popular racism, and for migrant and minority rights. They confront states as players or arenas with particular cultural understandings and racialised/ethnic interests of their own, though disguised in the usual normalisation of dominant-group interests, which is what the nation–state is about. IR becomes complicit in this process by not asking whose nation? and whose state? (Anthias and Yuval-Davis, 1992).

It is now very difficult to separate out immigration and citizenship debates from issues of 'race' in many states. Indeed, it is difficult to separate out 'race', ethnicity and nationalism in many instances. The rise of the 'new right' in the UK and other Western European states for example focuses on a redefinition of the nation in terms of race and culture, and closure against the strangers at the gates. The new revived, reconstituted nationalisms are defined against racialised immigrants, so marking themselves as white. They are 'ethnicised' through an exclusivist construction of 'Englishness' for example. In this sense 'black Englishness' becomes a disruptive notion, and 'Germanness' cannot incorporate people long resident or locally born of 'foreign' descent.

There is an unstable hierarchy of difference, as, for example, ex-East Germans occupy an ethnicisied category as different from and inferior to their West German co-citizens. So Irish people in the UK also experience racialisation for certain purposes, in stereotypical difference and at times danger through associations with 'terrorism'. But they do not routinely experience the 'at-sight' racism that black and other 'visible' minorities do just walking down the street.

In the midst of erratic and contested moves towards a European community, there are fears of Fortress Europe and questions about its gendered effects (Kofman and Sales, 1992; Bhavani, 1993; True, 1994). European states in Brussels show more concern about immigration than about social rights as a 'European' issue (*New Community*, 1991), and 'immigration' becomes an explosive political issue, exploited by Le Pen in France and neo-Nazis in Germany. Freer movement across state-member borders for the 'real' citizens is coupled with more surveillance and control of racialised outsiders seeking entry, and of those already 'in'. Within the ECU, some 17 million people or 5 per cent are of 'non-European' origin. They are sometimes represented as the thirteenth state, to indicate their conditional or pariah status. Little matter that some 9 million of them are under 30 and often born in Europe (Walker, 1993). A tripartite membership is emerging, of full citizens; then those with legal but not social rights, whose ambiguous citizenship makes them 'denizens'; and finally foreigners, with no secure rights (Brah, 1993). This last group can be further broken down, for the growing numbers of 'illegals' sets them apart as a super-exploitable under-class, outside state or union protection. In this situation, there are many racisms, within and between states, reconstituted in part through recasting dominant or 'old' nationalisms.

Postmigratory identities

Denied in these racisms is Europe's implication in those others' being there. Many can say 'we are here because you were there' (Sivanandan, 1982; see also Centre for Contemporary Cultural Studies, 1982). With so much British history played out in other people's places, some of those people then came back along the colonial routes. So 'postcolonial' and 'postmigratory' are terms applicable in the old metropoles, too. Here, new social categories and political identities formed and shifted meaning. 'New Commonwealth' (a designation used to separate racialised colonials from the whites of settler societies) is remade to include 'Afro-Caribbean', also replacing the place names of islands such as Barbados and Jamaica; while the term 'Black' expanded in the political mobilisations of the 1960s and 1970s to include all those who had experienced colonisation and who now identified with an antiracist political project in Britain.

As Black became a political colour and an oppositional stance, some—especially younger or more radical—Asians became Black too. Their construction as Asian or South Asian was already something of a leap in cultural imagination, enclosing a variety of caste, linguistic, regional, religious and nation–state affiliations, and in some cases warring collectivities at home. The pliability of identities was further reflected in the racist designation 'Paki' to roughly include all South Asian groups, as well as those 'multiple migrants' of the South Asian diaspora, from Idi Amin's Uganda, or Trinidad, for example.

Name changes often signal a new or different political project. So 'Black' signalled a move from assimilation to a more robust and oppositional identity politics. Name changes also signal shifting borders of belonging and exclusion, within and across states. Now, some whose own family and locality identifications were obscured or overlain as South Asian or Black mobilise as Muslim, as religion is also politicised and ethnicised.

We need to resist popular western associations of 'fundamentalism' with Islam (Sahgal and Yuval-Davis, 1992). Many Muslims, including Muslim women, oppose fundamentalism, and many more are not fundamentalist. Many fundamentalists are not Muslim. The extreme Hindu right, including the Bharatiya Janata Party, rejects the secular state and claims 'India' as Hindu. To do so, Muslims are declared outsiders and invaders, or else traitors, or dupes, if seen as descendants of those forcibly converted to Islam. Some conversions are more recent, such as those of untouchables to escape imprisonment in the Hindu caste system. As memory and history are reconstructed to lock populations into rigid designations and boundaries that belie the shifting, fluid and multiple identities of actual people, 'recovery' includes acts such as the destruction of the mosque at Ayodhya (Chattopadhyay, 1993). In this project, women are bearers of 'authentic' culture and subject to communal disciplining in the turn away from the modern secular state and its citizenship promises. But women are not only objects in these politics. Some organise and pursue exclusivist projects with a passion, too (Mazumdar, 1995).

Christian fundamentalists, too, mobilise around 'traditional' notions of family and women's place, and against abortion rights, for example, some directing violence against abortion and women's health centres in the United States. Here the connections between racialised and religionised projects show in their concern especially about white women's autonomy, disregarding black women's reproductive choices. Catholic fundamentalism is contested by liberationist priests and many laypeople who support women's rights, but the Pope's temporary alliance with Islamic conservatives in the 1994 Cairo population conference should not surprise us.

As Punjabis, for example, became Muslim, crises like the Gulf War contributed to hostile associations of Muslims and other South Asians with Iraqis, or Arabs; these, in turn, encouraged new kinds of international affiliation. The inside and outside are unclear, and are fought over.

So in the context of 'the Rushdie affair', 'Bradford Muslims' becomes a recognisable, postmigratory and modern political identity (Madood, 1992). It is also profoundly gendered. Here, identity politics homogenise ethnicities, as ethnic brokers or oppositional spokesmen call up 'the community' as their constituency and moral backing. Women are apparently subsumed within the community, and are spoken for. This process may be exacerbated in some forms of state sponsored multiculturalism privileging 'culture', so often located in family practices and domestic forms. Religious and other more 'traditional' leaders, almost always men, become custodians of now authorised difference. Identity-making processes in the 'new' world are as thoroughly gendered as they were in the 'old' ones.

Women as territory

In postmigratory politics, some groups seeking to present themselves as 'model minorities' and those seeking to maintain or reestablish control over their postmigratory community resist feminist organising and public naming of 'family troubles' such as violence against women (Bhattacharjee, 1992). This is especially so in more conservative and fundamentalist communities, which condemn women's organising autonomously and feminist work as 'foreign' or western subversions.

As usual, women take up different positions in support of, against or away from these identities. Some women find a political cause—a justification for acting or a comfort in a strange or hostile place in the new ethnicities. Others fight bitterly against what they see as reversals in women's rights and attacks on their claims as citizens. All women are entangled through the symbolic uses of them to mark both the borders and the nature of difference. So members of the UK-based group Women against Fundamentalism (WAF) organise and protest, despite the fury of fundamentalist men about their 'acting up' (Sahgal and Yuval-Davis, 1992).

Rachel Bloul's study (1993) of 'The Affair of the Veil' in France in 1989 clearly demonstrates the gender politics of both host/dominant and migratory/minority political identities. Here it is not only the symbolic uses of women but also the politics of masculinity that lie at the heart of the 'ethnicisation' project, and affect both 'home' and migrant identities.

'The Affair of the Veil' began when three Maghrebi girls refused to take off their headscarves in class; they were subsequently expelled. It blew into a huge media event, in which the girls', and most other women's, voices were silent/silenced, and Maghrebi and French men made use of images of 'the veiled woman' in contests over the rights of women and over possession and power in the public sphere.

French men who were not noted for their support of feminist causes championed the individual rights of Muslim women against their 'community', and expressed concern that cultural practices such as wearing the veil (or in this case headscarf) were incompatible with being French. But some French religious leaders, both Christian and Jewish, did support the veil. Muslim/Maghrebi opinion was divided. Women (49 per cent) and older people (66.7 per cent) were more opposed to the veil in school than men (42 per cent) and younger people (43.6 per cent), reminding us that such 'traditional' practices are not remnants so much as contemporary and emerging remakings. But whatever their position, most Muslims argued in favour of freedom and individual rights, mobilising French dominant public discourse on morality and politics. In yet another twist, the girls involved removed their scarves some months later after their father was ordered to so instruct them by the king of Morocco.

This much publicised contest is a warning against presuming a united position on the part of either the dominant group or of an immigrant or ethnic minority. Indeed, this study reveals the very different configuration of identity politics in two 'migrant' neighbourhoods in the same town in north-east France. The more 'traditional' factions in support of the veil were often younger, better-educated male students, members of transnational associations such as the Muslim Brotherhood, rather than older state- or region-based community or welfare associations.

In the mobilisation of postmigratory identities, outside the 'home' territory and in circumstances where 'the state' lies beyond control, 'women themselves become the territory' (Bloul, 1993: 4).

> Muslim women have become the privileged site for the affirmation and display of such identity, whatever these women's individual decision regarding the 'veil' is. French men's reactions demonstrate their under-standing of this collective use of women. [T]he existence of 'veiled women' in the French public space is perceived by French men as a Muslim, male challenge to their own control of the republican, French, fraternal space (Bloul, 1993: 17).

In turn, the apparent existence of an 'Islamic threat' inside France further ethnicises French identity.

Ethnicity, then, is a form of politics taken up in pursuit of a particular project, which might be inclusionary, for example against discrimination or for positive state action for rights of minorities; or exclusionary, in defence of conservative interests within, and competition without, for state or other resources. There is the possibility of using 'new ethnicities' for oppositional or alliance politics (Hall, 1988; Vasta, 1993a). But there is also the danger of ethnic absolutism (Gilroy, 1993) if identities are essentialised or if 'culture' is used to claim virtue or naturalised goods. This is not to deny ways of organising everyday life, of making meaning and associating with others in a communicative community. But this community too is in process, and shot through with power relations in which women's difference becomes both a structuring device and a signal to that structure.

There is a complex politics of identity and representation, as dominant groups mobilise against visible difference, remaking themselves as they mobilise. Their targets then react to mobilise in new ethnicities and alliances of their own. There is a politics around who is represented in the state, in the media, in access to resources; and around how 'they' are represented, including whether their own representations are attended to (Hall, 1988; Mercer, 1988). In this politics, the fewer you are the more representative you are expected to be, whether as a black filmmaker, an ethnic member of a mainstream organisation, or a third-world woman academic.

Making 'the people' and 'the community'

In these politics, the state is player, agent, and site of struggle. As we observed in Chapter 1, states are in the business of making 'the people'. This task is difficult enough given the diversity and difference enclosed by almost every state's territory. (The 'nationalities problem' is an old one, though resurfacing in violent form in the wake of disintegrating state empires (P. Hill 1993).) It is made much more complicated by reactions to the 'visible differences' brought into the state through recent migrations.

Homi Bhabha writes about the process by which the nation is told, or narrated, in the cultural production of political identities. This is an elaborate process, 'turning Territory into Tradition, turning the People into One' (1990: 300). This involves 'forgetting to remember', in order to reach the 'naturalized, nationalized space of the imagined community' (1990: 311). In this story is a clue to why nation–states break up, for much power and elaborate work goes in to 'making' them, and there is no inevitable success or stability in the process.

Bhabha refers to 'the people as a form of address' (1990: 304). How different states go about that address requires close scrutiny, including for example the moment when, officially, immigrant-receiving states like Australia or Canada declare the national project 'multicultural' and make a place, albeit often a contained and marginal one, for ethnic minorities (Kobayashi, 1993; Pettman, 1995a). Here multiculturalism becomes a state strategy for managing difference, especially when faced with mobilised immigrant or ethnic claims for fair or special treatment. While criticised by left and antiracist activists as coopting ethnic leaders and domesticating difference, multiculturalism makes a space that some can seize (Tsolidis 1993), to extend entitlements by turning the state's rhetoric back on itself in the way liberal feminists urge for citizenship. But in the problematic and contradictory politics around multiculturalism people must tread warily.

Multiculturalism is also made suspect through its association with long-term labour migration, leading one critic to label it as an 'import strategy' for transnational capital, in the global management of its labour needs and requirements for so many to move in search of jobs (Miyoshi, 1993). Global capitalism's frontier or border cities, such as Los Angeles, have little resemblence to 'warm' multiculturalism, and more to severely divided and militarised camps. In these situations, it is not only majority against minority or old nationalisms against newcomers (and of course there are always divisions and crossovers in each of these). But minorities and migrants may be set up against each other, replicating old colonial divide-and-rule strategies. So African–Americans will soon be outnumbered by Hispanics as the largest racialised minority in the US. Some Latinos with US citizenship also say there are too many illegals, too many immigrants, and fear the newer Hispanics, from Guatemala and El Salvador, for example, as inviting a backlash which may catch up with them, too (Chavez, 1993).

Multiculturalism does, however, allow—at least in theory—for a state–nation. This entails a notion of civil nationalism, where citizenship or membership of the state is the presumed basis of association, very different from an exclusivist nation based on a story of kin or blood, for example. If the state becomes too exclusivist, if the dominant ethnic group or mix appears closed or turns violently against others, reactive ethno-nationalism may well tear the state apart; as has happened in Rwanda and Sri Lanka (Hennayake, 1992).

Postcolonial nationalisms

The idea of states, and of nations, is now globalised. Successor states were created by colonisation and by anticolonial struggle for control of the colonial state and territory. Some poorer third-world states depend for their existence on the fiction of sovereignty, on international recognition within a state system and on international aid including military aid. The end of the Cold War removed a strategic motive for great-power propping up of otherwise fictional states. But much of IR still thinks in terms of a world of states, when this is only part of the story.

Nationalism has bequeathed the notion of national self-determination to peoples who find themselves in and against states, or against whom the state directs its techniques of violence. Where states fail to nationalise their populations, and cannot or will not deliver them security and services, other forms of identity mobilise against the state (Peterson, 1995). These are variously labelled ethno-nationalist, communalist, neotraditionalist or fundamentalist. Very different movements share a rejection of the secular modernist project that includes the IR state. They construct a 'return' to what are represented as more indigenous or authentic roots.

So the Iranian government forced veiling on women, some of whom had taken up the veil as a political protest against western consumerism, the commercialisation of sex and the commercialisation of women's bodies associated with it. The notion of 'westoxified' women (Tohidi, 1994) replayed earlier nationalist constructions of women as vulnerable to seduction by western and modern forces, as potential bearers of moral decay. So, too, the first act of the new mujahidin government in Afghanistan was to make veiling compulsory (Moghadam, 1994a: 8).

The veil has emerged as a symbol of contest over power and the public sphere in other Muslim majority states, including Pakistan, Algeria and Egypt. Some women take up the veil voluntarily, in support of Islamicist politics. Others do so to smooth their negotiation of public space or workplace in situations where western dress for women (but not for men) signals sexual availability, or cultural or religious betrayal. A recent study of the new veiling in Egypt confirms that it is often urban, educated, middle-class and young women who decide to wear the veil (Odeh, 1993), as it is often younger, urban and middle- or upper-class women who are more Islamicist in Malaysia. But where family and community honour are read through women's clothing and public behaviour, the cost of resistance may be considerable. In Algeria there are reports of schoolgirls attacked or killed for appearing in the streets in western dress.

Some outside readings of the new veiling reproduce racist or culturalised representations in terms of Muslim women as victims, more oppressed and backward than liberated western women. Here some western feminists inadvertently imperialise their writings and reproduce 'the third-world woman' with these associations, as do sometimes, third-world academic feminists (Lazreg, 1988; Mohanty, 1988).

One way is to learn to listen to what different women are saying about their own actions and the meanings they give to the veil. Another is not to abandon women to 'culture' or to male-dominated conservative political projects which appropriate 'women' in competition with other men, and to recognise that Muslim women, too, organise in defence of women's rights, often at enormous personal risk, including in some states imprisonment, rape and torture (Cherifati-Merabtine, 1994a; Poya, 1992).

The international network Women Living Under Muslim Laws (WLUML) was formed in response to several events in 1984 (Shaheed, 1994), including in Algeria, the arrest and jailing of three feminists for the 'crime' of discussing the government's plans to introduce new family laws that severely reduced women's rights; in India, the Shah Bano case highlighting Muslim women's exclusion from secular state codes and their containment within religious law; in Abu Dhabi, the condemning of a pregnant woman to be stoned to death for adultery two months after giving birth; and in Europe, the formation of the Mothers of Algiers, women formerly married to Algerian men and seeking custody of their children. Transnational feminist networks cross state borders and link women who have themselves crossed borders, as refugees, exiles, dissidents, migrants, students and workers.

WLUML and WAF remind us that culture, ethnicity and other forms of identity politics, like nationalism, are not fixed or uncontested, and not necessarily progressive. While we could do worse than take up the call of earlier feminists to judge the condition of states by the way they treat 'their' women, we need to ask, too, how they treat others. It is possible to assert difference without using it against others. Too often, though, in mobilised political identities, those outside the borders of belonging are beyond the moral community. In exclusivist identity projects, violence against those outsiders becomes permissible.

Postnation? Poststate?

State- and nation-making processes, and international political identities are still largely conceived in the spatial and territorial terms of 'old' IR and statist development models (Inayatullah, 1992). Dramatic shifts in global relations and power are noted in some IPE texts, where countries of origin (Miyoshi, 1993: 745) for a single product reflects transnational and increasingly globalised processes of production, trade and consumption. We also need talk of diasporas, of transnational and global infusions in the making of many contemporary political identities.

Arjun Appadurai (1990, 1993) writes of the new world of deterritorialisation and of transnational movements.

As populations become deterritorialized and incompletely nationalized, as nations splinter and recombine, as states face intractable difficulties in the task of producing 'the people', transnations are the most important social sites in which the crises of identity are played out. (1993: 428)

Diasporic networks and transnational movements mean that 'patriotism itself could become plural, serial, contextual, mobile' (1993: 428).

Appadurai is concerned to interrogate 'the hyphen that links nation to state' (1993:412).

[T]he nationalist genie, never perfectly contained in the bottle of the territorial state, is now itself diasporic. Carried in the repertoires of increasingly mobile populations of refugees, tourists, guest workers, transnational intellectuals, scientists, and illegal aliens, it is increasingly unrestrained by ideas of spatial boundaries. (1993: 413)

He urges us to consider 'the difference between [the US] being a land of immigrants and being one node in a postnational network of diasporas' (1993: 423), a distinction which can usefully be pursued with reference to other states, too.

Nowadays, many kinds of mobilised ethno-nationalist identities depend upon forms of communication, support and funding that are transnational. There is a complex politics of displacement here, where overseas news becomes home news for many. The inside and the outside of states cannot be separated in the old IR way, and the domestic and the international are scrambled.

But the links of the 'wandering people' are not only between new state and 'home', or between new migrant ethnicity and a different majority state. There are Greek, Macedonian, Indian, Chinese, African, Jewish and Muslim diasporas. There are multiple migrations, as, for example, descendants of South Asian indentured railway workers fled Idi Amin's Uganda for Canada or for the UK, some of whom are now returning. Afro-Caribbeans discover African connections in the inner cities and youth cultures of the UK (Gilroy, 1993). Some South Americans move 'back' to Spain. Relatives' letters, phone calls, visits and remittances build webs of meaning. So, too, do political pamphlets and speakers, funds and grievances, and new languages for making claims.

New worlds?

Here we return to a paradox of world politics, the simultaneous trends towards integration and towards fragmentation. New transnational and diasporic identities and associations display a polyvocality that is picked up in the notion of a postmodern world. The grand narratives, of the liberal enlightenment of progress towards a (western, male, middle-class) rational universe, or alternatively of world transformation through proletarian struggle and Communism, have been found wanting.

Now we see different worlds, but these are all located within global structures, and relations of power and penalty. While there are many tracks across state and other boundaries, and much of the world is 'hooked in' to global circuits of power and communication, there are places and people who are increasingly bypassed, and sometimes literally left to rot. We see some wars and human tragedies daily on our television screens, but others are hardly mentioned. The current conflict in the Sudan, where over a million people have died, suggests that some people are expendable. Both cities and continents have new configurations of their heartlands, the armed camps and border territory, and the no-go zones. In this world, refugee camps become a permanent feature, and violence and the effects of militarisation are daily events for many women and men (Appadurai, 1993, Miyoshi, 1993).

Location becomes significant in untangling political identities and power relations. Location is spatial, linked back into political geography. But it is also social and performative, in terms of the identities and roles that people take up in making themselves. So to structure we add agency, to gender, we add other axes of difference that mutually constitute ourselves and others.

The gendered politics of boundary-making are central to an understanding of international political identities. They are also central to the core foundation questions of IR, about the causes of war and the conditions for peace, which are the focus of part 2.

THE GENDERED POLITICS OF PEACE AND WAR

5

Men, masculinities and war

War was—and for some still is—the heartland of the discipline of International Relations. IR was founded as a separate discipline in 1919 in the wake of World War 1, charged with investigating the causes of war and conditions for peace. IR began in a time of intense feminist and women's anti-war activity, but it did not admit their understandings to the discipline, nor attend to the gendered politics of peace and war.

War and 'security' were central issues for early IR, and in the debates that heralded Realism's victory over the field after World War 2. War can be regarded as 'a defining assumption' of the discipline, which focuses on the 'high politics' of the state and war. Of particular significance is the 'special place that security, with its set of archetypes of male experience, occupies in the foundation of the discipline of IR' (Grant, 1992: 84).

'Security' means very different things for most women than the meanings given to it by IR. War and peace are feminist issues. Women are located in particular and dangerous ways, both in discourses about war and in war politics on the ground. Violence, including state violence, is often sexualised. Feminist understandings and re-visions of security are by no means monolithic, but they do reveal war and peace as gendered processes, and suggest strategies for a more secure world.

War and political violence

War is not so much a 'thing' or an event as a set of social practices that exist, usually, along a continuum of political violence, within and between states (Nordstrom, 1994a). War is a form of politics, involving both the organised capacity to use large-scale violence, and the predisposition to resort to violence to resolve conflict or pursue interests. What is so significant about war in the international system, and in the IR discipline that seeks to make sense of it, is that war is understood as an inevitable and indeed legitimate part of that system.

It is necessary to distinguish, then, between the causes of war, as part of the system, and the causes of particular wars (Suganami, 1990). The latter are often 'trigger' causes, backed and facilitated by international links and processes transferring information, strategy, supplies, weapons and personnel.

> Foreign strategists and 'advisers', arms and supplies, soldiers, merce-
> naries, power-brokers, and development and interests groups move
> among countries; guerrillas and soldiers travel to other countries for
> training and strategic planning; refugees and displaced persons flow
> across borders time and again; and blackmarketeers negotiate networks
> of profit on everything from land, ivory and drugs to computer
> technology and nuclear weapons. This imbroglio of alliances, antipa-
> thies, and mercenaries on both sides of a conflict enables fundamental
> ideological assumptions, strategic orientations, and specific tactical
> practices to be transferred from group to group across international
> boundaries and political affiliations (Nordstrom, 1994a: 19–20).

So US covert military operations in Central America included training in counterinsurgency tactics for Salvadorian and Contra troops; and South African intelligence forces were heavily engaged in Renamo's survival and the bloody war in Mozambique. Bilateral state military aid, training, and the use of US, French, British, Israeli and until recently East German advisers in different third-world states spread military and anti-guerrilla tactics and strategy (Enloe, 1993). There is a heavily international component to even the most apparently local or 'internal' war or state terror.

War-making is closely linked with state-making and state-break-ing. Wars and their 'endings' set state borders and international hierarchies of power. The particular construction of the IR state as sovereign gives it a monopoly of legitimate violence and appropri-ates 'security' to a militarised defence of the state and its interests. In this construction, war can appear as not so much the breakdown of international relations as its continuation by other means (Bull, 1977).

This naturalisation and normalisation of war is all the more extraordinary in the face of the increasing destructiveness of war over the last 200 years, and especially in this century. Before the French Revolution wars were—for most people—more like natural catastrophes that 'hit' when advancing or retreating soldiers marauded or forced conscripts, or when the fighting came close. Popularising sovereignty and rising nationalism meant total war in terms of the mobilisation of ideological commitment and labour of most people. Technological advances have vastly increased the destructiveness of war, and blurred distinctions between civilian and combatant. In World War 1, 80 per cent of casualties were soldiers; in World War 2, only 50 per cent. In the Vietnam War some 80 per cent of casualties were civilian, and in current conflicts the estimate is 90 per cent—mainly women and children. The 1994 Save the Children Fund report notes that some one-and-a-half million children have been killed and four million children seriously injured in wars in the ten years prior to 1994, with many of the survivors severely traumatised by their own or others' torture and abuse in conflict situations. In light of these figures, talking of war as if it is something mainly to do with men is a nonsense.

Many soldiers are actually still children or very young men, often forcibly conscripted by despotic or human-rights abusing governments or guerillas. This further complicates issues of complicity and responsibility in violence, and aggravates the already difficult problems of demilitarising individuals and learning peace. Besides the dead, many seriously injured and permanently disabled survive, and others are killed or maimed long after the fighting officially stops through use of landmines for example. Environmental disaster, famine and disease often accompany and follow war, and between them generate huge movements of people, as refugees and as displaced persons, putting even more pressure on states' and people's capacity to provide and survive.

Behind any particular war or political violence is a war system that permits war to happen. Standing militaries, training and defence funding take up large proportions of almost every state budget; arms trades, military aid, scientific research and development constitute a huge process of militarisation, mobilising resources for war. There is also a culture of war, marked by willingness to resort to violence for political ends. While IR and other theorists of war debate the circumstances under which the use of force is justified (and there is a whole tradition of 'just war' theory in theology, for example, as well as politics (Waltzer, 1977; Elshtain, 1992a), the underlying question relates to the ethics of war and whether any form of killing can be justified. These deeper ethical issues are often disguised in IR, which asks not when is it legitimate to kill another person, or even 'enemy soldiers', but when is it legitimate for a state to declare war on or defend itself against another state (Zohar, 1993).

War involves sustained, large-scale and politically directed violence, often between states, though frequently involving anti-state forces from within the borders. Political violence is broader; it includes state terror enacted by state agents or by vigilante gangs with state complicity, for example, directed against all or parts of the state's own population. This terror is designed to disable opposition or resistance, to so intimidate a population as to forcibly 'depoliticise' it, and to break down the very fabric of everyday life and social relationships. This terror is usually gender specific, and international. It is still largely ignored in IR war literature—yet another legacy of the inside/outside dichotomy and the privileging of relations, especially war relations, between states.

Also ignored in mainstream IR are other and wider definitions of violence with rather different implications for thinking about war and peace. Johan Galtung's notion of structural violence (1975) brought to peace research attention the causes of death and suffering that do not result directly from war, though they are often defended by force and militarisation, directly or indirectly. A contemporary estimate suggests that while on average one million people die from war killings a year, some nineteen million die from immediately preventable causes associated with poverty and the grossly unequal distribution of goods and services, which the current international system props up (Nordstrom, 1994a). In these circumstances, the opposite of war may not be peace, but justice. Third-world women especially argue the interconnections of poverty, environmental degradation, gross social inequality, exploitation, militarisation and violence (Sen and Grown, 1987; Mies and Shiva, 1993). Widening definitions of violence also deepen our definitions of peace, so peace becomes more than negative peace, more than simply not-war (though that itself is important enough, often); it becomes positive peace, where people's own security is built collectively in their everyday lives (Brock-Utne, 1989).

Man, the state and war

Kenneth Waltz, in the classic IR text *Man, the State and War* (1959), organised a vast literature on the causes of war into three clusters or levels of explanation or analysis: man, the state and the international system.

[T]he nature and behaviour of man, signal the causes of war: Wars result from selfishness, from misdirected aggressive impulses, from stupidity (1959: 16).

The prescriptions vary, but common to them all is the thought that in order to achieve a more peaceful world men must be changed, whether in their moral–intellectual outlook or in their psychic–social behaviour (1959: 18).

Waltz then analyses theological writings, from St Augustine on, and philosophical writings, including classical and modern political theorists concerned with the nature of man. They often tell of dramas: Hobbes' state of nature, for example, or Spinoza's men caught between their reason and their passions. Such pessimistic and turbulent readings of man were incorporated early into Realist IR, into such key texts as Hans Morgenthau's men's lust for power (1978).

Other explanations of war align more with the 'great men of history' school in images of mad or bad men, of a Hitler or a Saddam Hussein for example. Popular representations of 'human nature' also often include notions of 'natural' aggression. Yet 'human nature' cannot explain both war and not war, nor how it is that so many men, and states, can go for generations without war. It also excludes the possibility of a political peace project.

For Waltz, 'the state' refers to the internal structure of states, and he debates whether some kinds of state are more peaceful or warlike than others. There is a popular association (in democracies) of democratic states with peace, though the extensive involvement of the US in many wars internationally might unsettle this assumption. Marxist analysis classically focused on capitalism—and later imperialism—as causes of war, as states dominated by capitalist interests were pushed into wars to defend or extend trade or financial interests or colonies.

Waltz mentions too that wars may issue from governments charged with the protection of their people. This could suggest there is something in the make-up of the state itself that both legitimises and materialises war as a routine form of international politics. This connects directly to Waltz's third level of explanation, the international system, which for his purposes includes the nature and behaviour of the state in that system.

The third level, then, is one of international anarchy, of the security dilemma located at the very centre of IR. With no overriding world authority or system of enforceable international law, each state must rely on its own power and defence. Here the logic of sovereignty allows Waltz to treat each state as a unit, and to conclude that '[i]ndividuals participate in war because they are members of states' (1959: 179). 'Even good men and good states resort to force' (1959: 187) because of the operations of the balance of power. The alternative to the balance of power is suicide. So while the causes of war are multidimensional, the underlying and permissive cause is the international system. Ultimately, 'wars occur because there is nothing to prevent them' (1959: 232).

This is a classic Realist text; it presumes states are entities and unitary actors and concentrates on wars between states, which are seen as striving for power as dominance and security through military preponderance in a world of conflict and danger. War and the world are either totally ungendered, written in a language of 'man' where women are invisible, or they are profoundly gendered, assuming only men are political actors and states are masculinist constructs.

Men and war

To reapproach these levels or dimensions of explanation from a feminist frame, we can ask, as Waltz did, Is 'man' naturally aggressive? And we can rewrite the question to ask Are *men* naturally aggressive? Ancient and modern political theorists construct man/men who are competitive, whose 'nature' may be domesticated in a social contract within the state in an exchange of state protection for citizen obedience and soldiering. Popular understandings of men's natures often associate masculinity with violence and/or militarism in ways that naturalise or even heroise male violence. Other explanations of men's apparent aggression include hormonal testosterone levels, sociobiological readings from animal studies, versions of history in which 'man the hunter' is primed to kill, or the idea that men have to learn to be aggressive if the species is to survive, as women with small children cannot fight or hunt.

These images reflect popular and widespread associations of men with violence and war, and women with peace and nurture. Analyses of the gender of violence that draw on psychoanalytic theories point to the socialisation of boy and girl children, or learnings from and written onto the sexed body which create difference. Object theory posits a fundamental difference in gender identity formation, as sons must break entirely with their mothers to establish their adult sexual identity. So boys are 'sent off' in a trauma of separation from their mothers as 'Not-I', which many experience as profound rejection and alienation, and they cope by suppressing/repressing emotional connectedness. On the other hand, daughters are expected to maintain connectedness and are brought up as emotion-keepers and carers. From 'boys don't cry' to the expectation that daughters but not sons can show affection and vulnerability, the die is cast (Sylvester, 1992).

This story tells of the rational and autonomous male who is a far cry from the passionate and socially committed patriot–soldier expected to submerge his individuality and risk his life for others. It recalls Poole's assertion that the emotions and behaviour expected of soldiers are more those associated with the feminine and the family than the rational public world (1985; see also Elshtain, 1987: 225). What, then, is involved in the move from self-interested competitor to being willing to die for one's mates? The masculinity-militarism couplet is here revealed as complex and contradictory.

There is a further tension between the autonomous, independent and force-wielding citizen–warrior, and the military hierarchy and discipline that requires the submission of young men. While western political theory asserts men as reasonable, independent and autonomous, military training involves institutionalisation, coercion and humiliation—apparently directed towards breaking down these characteristics. These processes regularly include the vilification of women and consciously play on young men's sexual insecurities and identities (Spretnak, 1984; Stiehm, 1989).

Pursuing sexual difference in its association of men with violence and women with nurture, some feminist commentators assert that military training is socialisation into an extreme kind of masculinity (Roberts, 1984; Reardon, 1985). The young soldier must prove he is neither a girl nor gay to be a real man, and a good soldier. Cynthia Enloe (1987) makes the point that so much ideological work and power would not need to be brought to bear on soldiering if all men were 'naturally' aggressive. Much brutality and violence in wars is directed at same-side men and boys, including forcing reluctant men to fight. At the same time, the gendered imagery of war and statecraft, the supposed demasculinisation of the US through its Vietnam defeat and humiliation and the 'wimp factor' seen as pushing both Bush and Clinton into foreign military adventures, point to a gender script in war-making.

Masculinities and war

Not all men are violent, and some men are peacemakers and nurturers. What, then, makes some men violent, and other men not violent? And what makes not-violent men agree to fight other states' men? Bob Connell (1985) suggests a move from asking about men's violence to asking about masculine violence. Masculinity, like war, is a cultural construction, a set of social practices, so Connell asks What kinds of masculinity are more likely to be violent? He finds hegemonic masculinity implicated in violence in the ways it splits not only men from women but separates 'feminine' characteristics and values and assigns these to women and inferior men. Subjugated or subordinated masculinities may not necessarily be peaceable; indeed, much violence is against own-group men and women. But hegemonic masculinities command the state, including the military and the police, who are themselves heavily implicated in institutional violence, mainly within their own state. And Connell argues that certain hegemonic masculinities have now been globalised (1993).

Feminists draw attention to the relationship between public state-regulated violence and the private world of the household and male violence (Mies, 1986; Tickner, 1992), until recently—and often still—of little concern to states. This may be part of the trade-off: consolidating state power in return for men's control of their own households and women. Feminists ask questions about possible connections between different levels of violence. Many men experience power over and learn or practice violence against women and children at home or in relationships, and against other men in the street, bar or club (Roberts, 1984; Hanmer, 1989). What do these more private or localised violences have to do with men's willingness to use violence in the name of the community, nation or state? And what are the possibilities for reforming masculinities to encourage men's taking more responsibility for parenting, caring and combating male violence? The 'new men's movement' includes both pro-feminist political analyses (Hearn, 1987; Seidler, 1989; Connell, 1995), and dangerous tendencies to romanticise and recover the heroic male of older stories (McEachern, 1994).

Mike Donaldson asks 'Why, in specific social formations, do certain ways of being male predominate, and particular sorts of males rule?' (1993: 646). Hegemony entails establishing and maintaining power, which crucially includes naturalising or normalising power relations. For Donaldson, the subordination of women, heterosexuality and homophobia are bedrocks of hegemonic masculinity. He suggests it is a system from which all men benefit, though not all men support it. While at one level being a member of the privileged or normalised gender is a benefit, maleness and masculinity are infused with class, race, age and sexuality. An easy association between masculinism and any individual man's social experience or sexual identity is problematic.

It is useful to recognise the existence of different, shifting and contested masculinities, as with other kinds of political identities, while continuing to insist on the gendered politics of categorising practices and power relations, which are signalled by and through difference (Peterson, 1992a). Might the state need different kinds of masculinity for different functions in maintaining its war machine, for example, the brute force of the foot soldier, the rational planning of the military strategists and commanders, the intellectual and scientific masculinism of defence researchers (Enloe, 1987)? Is a singularised 'masculinity' or even hegemonic masculinity a disguise of cultural difference in exemplary men-and-war scripts? Are there appeals to different notions of a good man or a good soldier in, for example, Japan or Chile? (Enloe, 1993: 74). The particular understandings of what it is to be a man, and the skills and practices that are called on in the name of states and patriotism, may vary.

Civic identities, gender and war

As we saw in chapter 1, modern constructions of the citizen and the soldier universalise (some) men's experiences and exclude women, especially from the prerogative state and war. Explorations of the connections between men, masculinities and violence need to attend to forms of political and state culture that build a political community on the understanding that its male members are prepared to lay down their lives for its survival and interests. Much feminist analysis of the citizen–warrior explores the politics related to state authority and power (Elshtain, 1981; Stiehm, 1984; Hartsock, 1984; Grant, 1991; Peterson, 1992a; Tickner, 1992). State practices of legitimation and domination are reinforced through mobilisation of nationalism and patriotism. Here it appears that men's membership in certain kinds of political collectivities, especially as citizens, soldiers and patriots, holds a key to understanding the normalisation of political violence.

Jean Elshtain suggests that

> [t]he young man goes to war not so much to kill as to die, to forfeit his particular body for that of the larger body, the body politic, a body

most often presented and re-presented as feminine: a mother country bound by citizens speaking the mother tongue' (1992: 141–2).

War is the means to attain recognition, to pass, in a sense, the definitive test of political manhood . . . The freedom of individuals and states is not given as such but must be achieved through conflict. It is in war that the strength of the state is tested, and only through that test can it be shown whether individuals can overcome selfishness and are prepared to work for the whole and to sacrifice in service to the more inclusive good. The man becomes what he in some sense is meant to be by being absorbed in the larger stream of life: war and the state. To preserve the larger civic body, which must be 'as one', particular bodies must be sacrificed (Elshtain, 1992c: 143).

So greater love has no man, than he lay down his life for his country. But while the association here with citizenship, soldiering and sacrifice is gendered male, the civic mother must bear and bring up sons for the state. There is a complex and painful family drama here. The ethos of sacrifice speaks to gender and generational power relations. 'Young men have been designated a sacrificial class, sent by their fathers to fight other fathers' sons' (Ruddick, 1983: 477). She adds in a footnote that the state or nationalist fathers often send other fathers' sons—poorer, or minority sons—to fight for them. bell hooks and other black and minority feminists remind us of contradictions here, when dominant group women urge their men on to wars, or acquiesce to states' sending minority men to be used as cannon fodder while those men's citizenship rights at home are denied or compromised (hooks, 1989). In other states where wars come closer, women, children and non-combatant men are sacrificed. Those responsible for choosing war are rarely those who pay the price.

States/wars

Janna Thompson (1991) asks why so many young men, poorer men and women are so cooperative in terms of sacrifices and support for state wars. Much feminist analysis focuses on psycho-social and identity-making processes. The state is itself implicated in these processes, producing and managing political identities, and (attempting to) nationalise loyalties. In so doing, it draws boundaries around them and us, creating the other, the outsider, the enemy.

Feminist analysis suggests that the state is male, or alternatively that it is masculinist and male dominated (see chapter 1). States are structured around centralising authority and legitimising practices that rest ultimately on the threat of force. Some states are more militarist and activate violence more routinely and systematically than others. State regimes such as Nazi Germany and more recent military dictatorships in Argentina and Chile generated ideologies of hypermasculinity, which proved especially dangerous to women and inferiorised or dissident men.

But feminist IR argues that there is something in the nature of states and their defining characteristic of sovereignty that rests on violence and militarism. Spike Peterson argues that the state's 'historical and ongoing role in the construction and reproduction of the *legitimation* of violence and domination—specifically its 'depoliticization'—warrants our closest attention' (1992a: 58; see also Rosen, 1990). The state's monopoly of the legitimate use of force, and of the power to say what is legitimate, is centred in the prerogative state, not much attended to by non-IR feminists (Hancock, 1993). States are organised on the basis of a capacity for violence. This is the warfare state, claiming a huge proportion of state budgets for 'defence', and often acting to undermine interstate security (Peterson and Runyan, 1993: 84). Here states function as protection rackets, and often themselves directly endanger those they claim to protect. All too easily security becomes military security, security of the state or its current government.

The culture of war

Feminist IR draws attention to the cultural construction of political identities both masculinised and militarised, and to the language and images of IR, in its theory and practice, which infuse political understandings of power as dominance and militarise security threats and solutions. Feminists, postmodernists and critical theorists (overlapping categories) problematise 'the world' as IR makes it (Peterson, 1992a; Sylvester, 1993, 1994a; George, 1994). They deconstruct war as a cultural system, whose concepts, language, images and understandings represent particular, especially very powerful, views and interests. Thus Realist IR and strategic studies (tellingly located down the 'hard end' of IR) dominate definitions of security understood as 'power over'. In naming the world, they make it (Klein, 1989).

In response, then, to claims of security, we ask Whose security? What questions are being asked and what can't be asked? 'My country right or wrong' eliminates the possibility of asking Why patriotism? or of pursuing a rigorous critique of the politics and interests leading to particular wars. Who is heard and who is silent/silenced in national security and foreign policy debates? Whose experiences of danger and violence are being written out of the account? As usual with such exclusions, silences and partial accounts, women's and minority or dissident men's experiences of war and peace cannot be written in without disrupting the current categories, concepts and understandings of the discipline, and of 'the world'.

Pursuing these questions enables us to track a culture of war, which predisposes people to expect and support the use of force in international relations. This culture and its everyday practices are being constantly reproduced, rewritten, resisted. War, and the militarisation that enfolds and supports it, are cultural processes, complete with their own gender scripts.

Carol Cohn (1987) reflected on her time with defence researchers and planners to analyse the elaborate use of abstraction and euphemism, talk of 'clean bombs', 'collateral damage', 'surgical strikes', which domesticates and disguises the lethal pain and damage that is actually being prepared for. During a tour of the dockyard where a new Trident submarine was being constructed, the group was invited 'to pat the missile' (1987: 695). Deadly weapons are nicknamed Pal and Bambi, allowing a dissociation from what is happening. She points too to the sexual subtext, using terms such as 'a better bang for your buck', or describing nuclear explosions as 'orgasmic thumps', in a familiar eroticisation of power and destruction.

The Gulf War became a kind of 'open learning' in strategic studies through CNN and US military analysis, where 'clever bombs' and 'friendly fire and technique' almost invisibilised the human cost, fear and death (Campbell, 1993). A cartoon at the time carried the caption 'A "smart bomb" trying to work out the difference between a frightened 18 year old Iraqi conscript and a frightened 80 year old Iraqi grandmother' (Squier, 1993: 3). Once again the Gulf War demonstrated profoundly gendered discourses, a sexual subtext and the association of 'wimp' with weakness, silencing many critics. The discourses revealed processes of personalisation—where 'Saddam' stood as a substitute for Iraq as a state and for its people—and abstraction—de-peopling Iraq, obscuring its 150 000 dead and the devastation endured by many more (Cohn, 1993).

Jean Elshtain (1987) tells of hundreds of stories across time and place, associating men with war and women with peace. War is productive of gendered as well as national civic identities. Dominant among them are the 'Just Warriors', the soldier–protectors, and the

'Beautiful Souls'—the women who are the protected ones, who wait and weep. Here war is male, and peace female; men are naturally aggressive, or alternatively, sacrifice for kin and country; women are peaceable, the nurturers and comforters. Men and women, protectors and protected, are constructed in relation to each other, just as, or as part of, the related construction of masculinity and femininity (Runyan, 1990).

These war stories justify and romanticise war, and reproduce gendered representations of men as citizen–soldiers and women as dependants, regardless of what actual men and women are doing in war and peace politics. These stories and representations are used to shame men into fighting, and to 'silence doubting or peaceful men and women' (Stiehm, 1989: 229). 'Womenandchildren' (Enloe, 1993: 166) are symbols, victims and reasons for violence. The existence of those designated as needing protection becomes a rationale for violence. Much ideological work goes into constructing women as good women, and persuading women to behave as good, faithful, defenceless—worth dying for—to make men feel responsible for them and willing to fight for them.

This brings us to the difficult protector/protected relationship, which constructs women as dependent on men and states to defend them against other men and other states. The protector/protected dichotomy represents war as masculine, and combat as a contest between men, disguising the systematic targeting of women and children in war zones. It can also make women more rather than less vulnerable, to their own men, as well, when the burden of protection becomes too heavy or is resented (Roberts, 1984). Family violence against women is more prevalent in military situations, homeland wars, and when the men come back from fighting. It is a small step, too, from protected to possession to control, where women's movements and relations are policed, demonstrated, for example, in the jailing of adulterous wives of POWs by the Vichy government in France (Fishman, 1992), and the public shaming of women who 'fraternise' with enemy men (but not of men who 'fraternise' with enemy women).

The protector/protected relationship is by definition unequal, and unequal relations rest ultimately on the threat or act of violence. There are also profound and dangerous political consequences of portraying women as in need of protection. They have no control over the conditions or costs of protection, which often entail them behaving as victims, weak, passive and grateful. Being seen as victims undermines women's-rights claims. It depoliticises their actions, and makes their agency or politics appear unruly, rebellious, ungrateful or asking for trouble. If women 'act up' or are seen as out of place, they can be considered beyond the bounds of protection. The costs of protection include women's giving up autonomy (Runyan, 1990). Once again, they appear to lack the prerequisites for full citizenship and claims as political agents and subjects.

War rape

The protector/protected relationship also makes women especially vulnerable to other men's/states' violence as a way of getting at 'their' men, demonstrating their failure as protectors, 'emasculating' and humiliating the enemy. Violence against women becomes an assault on men's and national honour (Pettman, 1995b).

Rape has long been a weapon of war and nationalist conflict (though usually of 'theirs' and not 'ours', apparently). War rape appears to be a usual part of interstate and civil wars, though recent media attention has focused on institutionalised military rape of the so-called 'comfort women' by Japanese soldiers in World War 2 and on rape camps in ex–Yugoslavia, to the exclusion of the more than 50 armed conflicts currently being waged. Rape is not a war crime, though now there is pressure to make it so (Tetreault, 1995).

In France in the months following German occupation during World War 1, the actual rape of French women was rapidly translated into representations of a feminised France whose national honour had been violated. Consternation over the 'child of the barbarian' generated fierce arguments over whether French women forcibly made pregnant with 'enemy babies' should be allowed or encouraged to have abortions. An official commission of inquiry was conducted into the rapes, but soon after the war the rapes were subject to 'virtual amnesia', publicly at least (Harris, 1993).

In the 1930s and during World War 2 the Japanese military were involved in the forcible recruitment, transportation and rape of hundreds of thousands of women, especially Korean women, provided for troops for 'morale' and servicing purposes, and to reduce dangers of political and community reaction to ongoing rapes (Dolgopol, 1994; Seidel, 1993). The victorious Allies had information and documentation of these atrocities, but did not pursue them in postwar war-crimes prosecutions; hence, they maintained a public silence on war rape, and condemned the women who survived it to containment within that silence, only recently broken.

Many German women were raped by occupying Russian troops in the closing moments of World War 2. Greek Cypriot women were raped by Turkish soldiers, and were again cruelly dealt with when rape was used as grounds for husbands to divorce and fiancés to be released from obligations towards them. Many thousands of Bangladeshi women were raped by Pakistani soldiers in the separatist war; some are still not permitted entry into their own homes (Tetreault, 1995). Attention to women's experiences in wars and political violence repeats stories of rape, shame, distress, and silencing.

Reports from Bosnia and Herzegovina estimate the numbers of women subjected to rape and other forms of sexual violence is between 20 000 and 35 000. The Report of the Commission of Experts appointed by the United Nations Security Council to investigate reported war crimes in the former Yugoslavia found systematic and widespread use of rape and other forms of sexual assault. While there were victims and perpetrators on all sides, the overwhelming experience was of assaults on Bosnian Muslims by supporters of a Greater Serbia project. Rape was closely associated with a policy of 'ethnic cleansing', designed 'to instil terror . . . in order to cause them to flee and never return' (United Nations, 1994: 34). Here, as elsewhere, war rapes function as a strategy to deliver 'a blow against the collective enemy by striking at a group of high symbolic value' (Bernard, 1994: 39). The strategy included forced pregnancies, and not releasing women until it was too late for an abortion, 'to make Bosnia a Serbian state by implanting Serbian babies in Muslim mothers' (Robson, 1993: 4). This theme was taken up by the Pope in his plea to the raped women to have and love their 'enemy babies'.

While most of the rapes were done to women and girl children, some men and boys were also raped or sexually mutilated, or forced to perpetrate sexual violence on others, including on members of their own families. Such violence, and the feminisation and castration of enemy men, pushes us back to the connections between proving manhood and nationhood, between masculinity, militarism and violence. It is further evidence that all politics is gendered, and that much dangerous politics is sexualised. Bodies, boundaries, violence and power come together in devastating combinations.

State/sexual terror

Rape is not confined to interstate or civil wars, but is also systematic and widespread in so-called dirty wars and in state terrorism. Women and girl children in particular, but also some men and boy children, experience rape and sexual torture, both for presumed political or identity offence (belonging to the other side may be enough), and to 'get at' their male relatives. In some cases rape and sexual torture are aimed at forcing soldiering men to surrender. Politically active women are especially vulnerable (Amnesty International, 1991 a, b).

The politics of sexual terror are demonstrated by the rape scenario, often performed in public, in front of family and community members. Both there and in detention, sexual torture includes the use of domestic and familiar objects and situations, with the objective of prolonging the terror long after the actual torture ends. Torture is gender specific, with women experiencing mutilation of breasts as well as genitals, and humiliation through the denial of clothes and of sanitary pads during menstruation or post-rape bleedings. Sexual violence is aimed at them as women, in deliberate attacks on their images of themselves, and their relations as women and as mothers. Local and national cultures of honour and shame, social valuing of women's virginity and notions of sexually 'experienced' women as soiled goods link into the intentions and effects of the torturers. Particular constructions of masculinity and femininity are mobilised to maximise war damage to others.

Elaine Scarry (1985) writes of bodies and pain in torture, of the political nature and impact of such terror. Those killed and/or mutilated are often left in public places, as warnings and witnesses to the danger of resistance, or of category membership or family association with 'the other side'. The terror is aimed not only at those whose bodies are attacked, but through them at the body politic, so that both person and society are so disintegrated they are paralysed and negated. Survival becomes as dangerous as resistance is. Rape and sexual torture become part of the political process, as strategies of power and domination. Yet most academic writings about war and politics maintain the silence on these strategies, and continue to obscure the body at war.

There is an ominous repetition in the stories of war rape and sexual torture internationally. The same techniques and scenarios recur, from Mozambique to El Salvador to the Philippines (Aron et al., 1991; Hilsdon, 1993; McIntyre, 1993). Carolyn Nordstrom argues that there are extensive international linkages along which cultures of militarisation and strategic tactics of warfare (including terror tactics) are transmitted from country to country and conflict to conflict. As soldiers, advisers, and mercenaries forge alliances across political regions, as military training manuals circle the globe to inform one war after another, and as media link countries worldwide to carry everything from news to popular war films to pornography—ideas and values about what constitutes 'acceptable' processes of war are internationally forged . . . [D]irty war tactics—those that use terror against both civilian and military populations to try to control political acquiescence through fear—are a major form of warfare today. Sexual violence is a mainstay of dirty war practice (1994b: 9).

War rapes are part of war culture and, similar to other forms of rape, are exercises in political power, not the results of any inevitable male nature. This brings us back to connections between certain kinds of masculinity and sexual violence. Why is rape so often associated with domination practices? When systematic war rape is revealed, are we 'witnessing men out of control or men under control?' (Enloe, 1993: 121). And what are the links between war rape and the widespread reality of rape in 'domestic' relations in supposed peacetime? Both appear as part of a culture that normalises and naturalises rape and privatises violence against women.

There are questions here, too, about the eroticisation of power and notions of the male body or penis as a weapon. Many post-Vietnam films present the white US soldier as the war's victim, and disguise the gender, class and race dimensions of the conflict (Selig, 1993). Those men's recovery is often suggested through violence, a 'remasculinisation' to overcome the humiliation of defeat (Jeffords, 1989). Where women are made visible, it is as prostitutes or gang-rape victims. The forgetting or denial of 'other' victims by many whose only experience of war is through the media is well summed up in the response 'it never happened; and besides, they deserved it' (quoted in Nordstrom, 1994a: 8).

Looking closely at representations of men and war complicates some feminist claims that western political theory evacuates the body, and displaces sex onto women, and that men in politics are disconnected and disembodied; for the body looms large in war stories, in ways both dangerous and sexualised. There may be another split here, between 'enlightenment' man in the polis or market, and military—and especially—patriot man, in war and readiness for war.

Writing/speaking rape

The eroticisation of bodies, torture and power relations weigh heavily on the already painful and risky business of talking and writing about war rape. Breaking the silences around women's pain are a necessary first step towards strategies both to support survivors and to organise for change. But it is only recently that feminists have made rape visible as a crime against women's bodies and rights. Feminists argue that rape is about power, and by extension war rape is about collectivity power and domination strategies.

As I have noted, women's experiences have not been incorporated into IR understandings of the world, and women face particular difficulties in becoming subjects in nationalist and interstate politics. Given the long history associating actual women's rape with national, communal and male dishonour, Suzanne Gibson argues 'to respond to war rape with outrage and anger is not enough. We must make absolutely clear the terms in which we object to these atrocities. Our objections must be unambiguously founded upon women's right to physical autonomy' (1993: 258).

Attempts to document war rape come up against some women's denial or silence, used as a survival strategy, and also as an attempt to keep the 'shame' secret to protect self and family. This may involve researchers in 'collaborative silences' (McIntyre, 1993). So IR feminists seeking to help break the silence, while avoiding speaking for or exposing other women, struggle to find ways that do not appropriate their pain, or write them in ways those women themselves might not recognise or agree with.

There are more dangers in writing the unspeakable (Nordstrom, 1994b: 7), for fear that the endless repetition of horror is ultimately numbing, and will 'turn off' some people. Worse, it may turn some people on, given the eroticisation of both violence and women's bodies. So women's pain can become 'warnography' (Gibson, 1993: 254). This is an issue in drama and film reenactments of terror, when representations of terror can become complicit with what they seek to critique and the audience become voyeurs (Taylor, 1993). There are difficulties, too, in finding ways to write and talk that do not feed into and consequently reproduce 'the woman as victim' as the primary image of women in circulation. But while feminists and activists politicise war rape and speak of torture not shame, of survivors not victims, many of those so terrorised do not survive.

Feminist re-visions of security

Taking women's own experiences of violence and security seriously means focusing on everyday life, on bodily and psychic pain, on anger and silences within regrouping or surviving families and relationships, on coping with and loving 'enemy' children. As private terrors become political issues, women who did not personally experience them may be presumed to be a victim because so many others in their group were.

Taking women's own experiences of war and political violence seriously demonstrates the gendered and sexual politics of violence. Security and danger take on new meanings, as most immediate threats to women and children often turn out to be local and sexualised violences. In much state terror and civil war, as in family violence, perpetrators are known, and may stay around. A more comprehensive view of security, which begins by asking what, or who, most threatens particular groups of people, will disrupt any notion of 'national security', for the greatest threats to people's security in many cases are local state agents or military personnel, or 'home' men who are constructed as soldier–protectors of the very people they endanger.

Taking women's own experiences seriously also means making visible and supporting the strategies and actions of the many brave women, men and children who struggle to maintain or repair everyday life, to build peace and unlearn violence even while war or state terror continues. So Save the Children Fund reports document the horrors witnessed and visited upon children, in Mozambique and Rwanda, for example, but also counsel against the 'disaster pornography' (Burman, 1994: 238), which even sympathetic western aid agencies and journalists may unwittingly propagate. Children often display an extraordinary resilience and innovation to survive and negotiate the day (Boyden, 1994). Women's and communities' own work reveals them as more than victims, and provides clues to living beyond the violence, even in horrific circumstances—though rarely without scars. Traditional healers and women community carers work to 'take out' the violence and practice peace and social health (Gibbs, 1994; Nordstrom, 1994a).

Feminist perspectives on security begin with women's own experiences of everyday life, and bodily danger and safety. They reveal very different understandings of the individual, the state and war from those deployed in the discipline of IR (Tickner, 1992: 55). They seek to unravel the connections between different levels and kinds of violence, and to understand cultures of violence and rape, whether practised institutionally by the state or anti-state forces, or 'privately' against women in their homes or their neighbourhoods. In the process of challenging the public/private dichotomy that has for so long positioned women and violence against women away from state or public concern or responsibility, they also reveal the sham dichotomy, presumed by IR, between an international space where violence is legitimate, and a domestic or private space where individual morality is opposed to violence. In all this, feminist perspectives can draw on extensive cross-cultural and transnational understandings of women organising against war and violence, and for peace and justice, which are taken up in the next chapter.

6

Women making peace

The last chapter explored associations of men with war, and representations of women and peace, used, often, to rationalise and justify war. It looked, too, at women as victims of men's wars. This chapter reviews associations of women with peace as they are mobilised by women peacemakers, and explores debates about women's difference and the possibilities of a feminist ethic of care and non-violence. Some feminists remain profoundly suspicious of the stereotype of 'the moral mother' (di Leonardo, 1985), but maternalist imagery is widespread among women organising for peace and social justice.

Associations of women with peace obscure the deep divisions and differences among women and within feminism concerning the politics of peace and war, and the gender of violence. Mary Burguieres (1990) identifies three clusters or tendencies in feminism, each with very different understandings of peace and war, and of gender and sexual difference. The first are pacifist or maternalist feminists who see women as peaceable, in a gender difference that makes possible a women's peace politics. They valorise characteristics commonly associated with women, and seek to utilise them in the cause of peace. The second are liberal feminists who argue for women's equality with men, rejecting 'women's nature' as part of the ideology that oppresses women. Given the close associations of citizenship with fighting for one's country, they argue for women's equal rights in the military, including combat. The third are anti-militarist feminists who reject sex stereotypes of peaceful women, but who also oppose processes of militarisation and militarised definitions of security and the citizen—processes and definitions they see as profoundly gendered.

Women as peacemakers

Are women more peaceful than men? and if so, why? nature? nurture, through sex role socialisation? social experience, including practices of mothering and caregiving? or through social positioning, as disarmed subordinates in militarised and hierarchised societies?

There is a huge literature, over time, place and culture, of women writing against war, or against particular wars (Cambridge Women's Peace Collective, 1984). They often write as women, and many write as mothers, assuming a different perspective, value system or investment in war from men. Other women write as socialists or nationalists, not necessarily privileging gender in their analyses. Between them, they suggest very different explanations, connections or clues for understanding peace and war than those presented in IR.

Peace movements in North America, Western Europe and white-settler states have been made up mainly of women, and women's difference and maternalist understandings have underpinned many of their actions (Strange, 1990). The original impetus for Mother's Day came from Julia Ward Howe in 1870 reacting against the carnage of the Franco-Prussian War and the American Civil War, with the familiar moral claim that mothers did not raise their sons to kill other mothers' sons. In western European states, rising imperialism and militarisation in the 1880s led to a growing peace movement, often paralleling and at times connected with first-wave feminism. Austrian Bertha von Suttner's widely read pacifist novel *Lay Down Your Arms* was published in 1889.

Women are usually more active and visible in social protest movements than in electoral or party politics. In the late nineteenth and early twentieth centuries mainly women organised and campaigned for child welfare, public health and education reforms, which Linda Gordon argues saved more lives and relieved more suffering than high-tech medical developments (1990: 625). And while the early women's peace movement drew heavily on arguments that women were naturally gentler and more peace loving, it introduced more aggressive and daring tactics (inspired in part by the militant suffragists) than male-dominated protest movements had used until then (1990: 627).

Many women in these peace movements accepted women's different nature, and argued either the necessity of including women in politics for a comprehensive and representative polity, or else saw women's nature as superior, or at least more appropriate for avoiding the horrors of war and social violence. Their assumptions were brutally tested in World War 1, when the peace movement, and suffrage movement, split. Many former peace women rallied in support of kin and country, while others maintained their anti-war stance and an international politics of sisterhood. Patriotic women in the UK handed white feathers to men not in uniform, to designate cowardice. Over 1000 women met in the 1915 Hague peace conference, and specifically rejected the assumption 'that women can be protected under the conditions of modern warfare' (quoted in Strange, 1990: 213). They sent delegates to speak with leaders of fourteen governments involved in the fighting to appeal for peace. They urged a thoroughgoing peace settlement whose humanity and attention to the many dimensions of militarism and insecurity might have helped avoid World War 2, had it been taken seriously by those who instead forced a vengeful settlement on the losers. In 1919 a women's international congress held in Zurich declared that the terms of the Treaty of Versailles would 'create all over Europe discords and animosities which can only lead to future wars . . . a hundred million people of this generation in the heart of Europe are condemned to poverty, disease and despair, which must result in the spread of hatred and anarchy within each nation' (quoted in Wiltshire, 1985: 200). From these understandings grew the Women's International League for Peace and Freedom (WILPF), whose members' theorising about war took nationalism and exaggerated forms of masculinity seriously. They opposed all forms of violence, including parental violence against children (Gordon, 1990).

Similar analyses were developed by feminist peace women in other states. In Australia, for example, the Women's Peace Army represented women as peaceful, with special moral virtues, and responsibility for preserving the lives of their own and other mothers' sons. They also focused on social inequality and campaigned for social and labour rights. They faced the usual hostility against women organising as women for peace in times of war or nationalist mobilisation (Damousi, 1992).

The strong anti-war feminist movement before and during World War 1 drew on many women's writings against war, including critiques of the relationship between patriarchy, masculinity, imperialism and militarism (in Britain, for example, Wiltshire, 1985;

Florence et al., 1987; Vellacott, 1987). Many of those who most opposed World War 1 were already engaged in campaigns for women's rights, suffrage, reproductive choices, labour or socialist politics before war was declared. Labour and left women who worked against war and militarism did not necessarily privilege gender in their analyses and politics. In the US, anarchist socialist Emma Goldman strongly resisted patriotism and the ways in which capitalism and the state undermined workers' solidarity, forcing young working-class men to sacrifice for capitalist/state interests. She campaigned for an education and politics that would reveal workers' transnational interests. In 1917 she was imprisoned for her work organising No Conscription Leagues, and later she was deported. In 1914 the transnational socialist Second International split as many European socialists rallied behind their particular states' war effort. Polish marxist and key player in the German Social Democratic Party, Rosa Luxemburg, remained steadfastly anti-war and anti-nationalist. She spent much of the war in prison, for her founding role in the anti-war socialist Spartacist League (Ettinger, 1988). Opposing nationalist wars and colonisation, she privileged class over gender, though her focus was on young working-class men as victims of wars, along with women of different classes.

Unlike pacifist women, some socialist women who opposed capitalist and imperialist wars supported or at least recognised the necessity for revolutionary violence. Others, such as Quaker women, opposed all wars and violence for any cause, on religious and humanitarian grounds. Similar to socialist and other left women, they often worked within an internationalist perspective in theorising about and organising against war. However, the differences between anti-war women remind us to distinguish between pacifist and non-pacifist views; between opposing all wars and opposing par-ticular wars; between women's and feminist peace or anti-war work; and in turn between different feminists' positions on war/s. These differences, in theory and in politics, warn us against any easy association between women and peace.

Women for peace

Peace movements in different countries have waxed and waned, depending both on local politics and on international tensions. Rising fascism and militarism in Europe in the 1930s and disturbing media reports of fighting in the Spanish Civil War regenerated peace energies. Within this context, Virginia Woolf wrote her feminist anti-war polemic *Three Guineas*, first published in 1938. Exploring links between fascism, war and patriarchy, she argued that 'the public and the private worlds are inseparably connected, that the tyrannies and servilities of the one are the tyrannies and servilities of the other' (1993: 270). She suggested that women locate themselves as 'outsiders' to state and war, and refrain from all support of war, including working in munitions manufacture or ambulance driving, or in urging brothers to fight. She concluded that an educated woman 'has very little to thank England for in the past; not much to thank England for in the present; while the security of her person in the future is highly dubious' (1993: 233) Speaking for a woman of her class, she continues

> 'Our country' . . . throughout the greater part of its history has treated me as a slave; it has denied me education or any share in its possessions. 'Our' country still ceases to be mine if I marry a foreigner. 'Our' country denies me the means of protecting myself, forces me to pay others a very large sum annually to protect me . . . Therefore if you insist upon fighting to protect me, or 'our' country, let it be understood, soberly and rationally between us, that you are fighting to gratify a sex instinct which I cannot share; to procure benefits which I have not shared and probably will not share; but not to gratify my instincts, or to protect either myself or my country. For . . . in fact, as a woman, I have no country. As a woman I want no country. As a woman my country is the whole world (1993: 234).

After World War 2, the European peace movement revived not in the knowledge of or in protest against Auschwitz, Dresden or Hiroshima (though many individuals internationally protested against those and other war atrocities), but in the 1950s with the Cold War and the possibility of nuclear war at home (Strange, 1990). The war in Vietnam generated a huge international protest movement in the late 1960s, bringing together long-time pacifists and war resisters with those who opposed this particular war. Many of the protesters were women, and some organised as mothers, sometimes under banners such as 'Save Our Sons'. Less publicity was given to the local Buddhist peace movement, or to ongoing third-world peace political traditions such as the Gandhian movement in India, though Gandhi himself was often called upon as a model of non-violent action, with some debate about the effectiveness of his politics and about his attitudes to women (Forcey, 1994).

The western international peace movement revived again in the 1980s, with Reagan's Cold-War posturing, with intensified nuclear technology and the stationing of nuclear missiles in different European states, and with the awful warning of Chernobyl. A highly visible development was the setting up of women's peace camps in many places, for example, at Greenham Common in the UK, at Seneca in the US and at Pine Gap in Australia, unleashing media hysteria about 'unnatural' mothers and lesbian tales and revelations that suggested the power and fury behind assumptions about good women and proper mothers. There are questions here: Why *women's* peace camps? Why the enormous hostility to women's acting for peace? Why are 'bad' women labelled 'lesbians'? (di Leonardo, 1985).

In this revival, a number of women-and-peace anthologies were published (for example, McAllister,1982; Thompson, 1983). They often assumed rather than critiqued the notion that women had something very particular to do with, and for, peace (Gordon, 1990). These anthologies brought together writings of different kinds—letters, poems, songs, essays, speeches and art work—in styles academic, polemical, or personal. They presented evidence from wider sources and on connections not usually admitted to IR, recognising women as knowers, and treating objectivity and intellectual distance as part of the problem. They took women's own experiences of war and peace seriously, though they did not necessarily interrogate the choices that rendered some women exemplary or representative, and some women invisible.

Though rather differently constructed, collections from academic conferences on women and peace often also included activists as well as academics, or women who were both, and also attempted to envision different worlds as well as to critique existing ones. These collections are more likely to include contributions from, or on, women warriors, active in national liberation or revolutionary struggles; hence, they have more international/ist content (for example, Forcey, 1989; MacDonald, 1987; Harris and King, 1989).

The anthologies, like peace women themselves, reflected a range of views on women and peace, and on masculinity, militarism and war. They contributed to unsettling common or dominant understandings by directly challenging military values and militarised culture. They presented women as political and moral actors, seeking empowerment, building networks and mobilising for change. In many there were images of spinning, weaving and healing, drawing on women's spirituality as a political resource. Some recover the goddess–mother of presumed earlier, matriarchal lines (long fought over in feminist anthropology). They drew, too, on the words and ways of radical feminists such as Mary Daly (1984), to celebrate womanly ways of knowing and being.

These challenges represented a crucial strategic move, a form of oppositional politics, contesting representations and under- standings of gender along with peace and war. They took images and values often associated with women and reclaimed them, inverting and valorising characteristics devalued or privatised—and exploited—in patriarchal and militarist interests. They also took the feminist slogan 'the personal is political' and applied it in pursuit of keys to violence at different levels, from individual to international and back again, arguing connections which made possible a more complete analysis of processes and practices of militarism.

These writings, and the images and associations they draw on, do speak to and validate many women's experiences and self- images. They call up skills and kinds of care that many women do value and are good at, and that others—including many men—ben- efit from. They have proved very effective in rallying women to peace causes, in terms of the identities and the responsibilities they take seriously, especially as mothers.

Women peace researching

Some feminist peace researchers also draw on and argue for strong asssociations between women and peace. Betty Reardon claims that 'feminism as a value system is the antithesis of militarism' (Reardon, quoted in Roberts, 1984: 196). Birgit Brock-Utne asserts that women's peace work is based on three premises: non-violence; seeking to preserve all life, especially children's; and transpolitical action, somehow beyond particular or party politics (1990: 32). She has focused on sex socialisation and argued that boys are educated for war, a theme pursued by other feminist peace researchers (Roberts, 1984).

We need be wary, though, of a slide from women to peace, or to feminism. Elise Boulding's review of women peace researchers revealed a wide spread of views and research topics, but few called themselves feminist, and some half of her sample did not answer the question about whether women academics approach disar- mament issues differently from men academics (Boulding, 1982:34). Her review offered alternative images for envisioning peace, drawing on sources from outside feminist peace research, including the feminist science fiction of Marge Piercy and Ursula le Guin (see also Hall, 1994).

Feminist analysis might have found a home within comprehensive approaches to peace; however, peace research took a strategic turn in the late 1980s, focusing mainly on arms control and conflict management—often within a statist frame—or on a 'win–win' approach that individualised and psychologised conflict. These approaches were disinterested in power relations, including gender relations (Northrup, 1994), but many women academics, and activists, do work under a peace research label. In 1989 the International Peace Research Association (IPRA)'s Women, Militarism and Disarmament study group was renamed Women and Peace, to include research on the effects of democratisation on women, and to reconceptualise security, to 'transform the reductionist militarist paradigm of security and incorporate concerns for equity, sustainability and justice within a holistic ecological framework' (Valenzuela, 1989: 17). This more inclusive agenda enables attention to structural violence and the possibilities of positive peace. Not coincidentally, this group includes significant numbers of third-world women, from the Philippines and India, for example, which have strong protest and grassroots movements and feminist political campaigns against particular manifestations of militarism and violence.

This is a reminder of the contests around 'peace', and the tendency for some to associate peace with pacifist, anti-nuclear and anti-war movements that recall definitions of negative peace, though stopping the fighting is itself the immediate priority for many women. Feminist and peace understandings often also attend to personal dimensions and especially to violence against women. Many third-world women pursue a wider agenda again, organising against militarism, opposing the presence of foreign military bases or the use of state violence against dissidents and minorities, and linking their analyses of militarism to campaigns for social justice and against poverty (Sen and Grown, 1987; Shiva, 1989). Prioritising social equality or national liberation or democratisation as essential prerequisites for peace and security, many support and in significant numbers join armed struggles against repressive and violent states. Here it becomes even more difficult to maintain a clear dichotomy between maternalist peace women and women warriors; indeed, many women become warriors because they are mothers and peaceseekers (Sylvester, 1987; Cock, 1992) .

The peaceful sex?

Women's organising for peace, women's writings for peace and against war/s, and feminist peace research have all been used to bolster claims that women are more peaceful than men. Other kinds of evidence are called up in the debate, including the consequences of sex socialisation, signs of a gender gap in public-opinion polling about the use of military force, and feminist writings about women's moral reasoning and ethics of care and non-violence.

Much early second-wave western feminism scrutinised sex-role stereotyping and the socialisation of boy and girl children, including social expectations that girls are caring, nurturing and other-related, with images of dutiful daughters and self-sacrificing mothers. Such sex stereotypes were regarded as part of the ideological construction of women's oppression and domestication. The psycho-social processes and gender characteristics involved became ways of explaining women's supposed peacefulness, just as socialisation into masculinity became part of explanations of war. In peace politics, sex stereotyping and socialisation decried by many—especially liberal and socialist—feminists were reclaimed and valorised as peace attributes, or as women's nature rather than learning. (There are questions implied here, about whether as women become more 'liberated' or emancipated from gender stereotyping, they will be less peaceful; and relatedly, if the new men's movement, or some men's growing involvement in parenting or other care-giving responsibilities, will 'soften' men's propensity for violence. Once again, it is not possible to separate ideas about gender relations from explanations of war, peace, violence and security.)

The 'gender gap' in public-opinion polls on foreign policy and defence issues is also taken by some as evidence of women's more peaceful natures, or learnings. This gap is especially clear in questions concerning the use of military force. Public opinion polls in the US between 1946 and 1984 found 10 per cent fewer women supporting military preparedness and military response options (Bacchi, 1985). The gender gap on military force apparently increased slightly in the US during the 1980s. It was at its most obvious during the Gulf War, where shortly before the fighting, men were equally divided for and against the use of force, while 73 per cent of women opposed it. Once Desert Storm was launched, numbers of men and women rallied behind the use of force, but women still outnumbered men in supporting a peaceful settlement 46 per cent to 28 per cent (Gallagher, 1993: 29).

These polls raise many questions. Why do women support peaceful tactics more than men? Why aren't more women peaceful, and why are some men peaceful? The usual gender gap is 10 per cent to 15 per cent, so that means far more men and women agree than disagree on these issues. At the same time, the Gulf opinion-poll results suggest that second-wave feminism is not reducing the gap on defence questions. Indeed, 1980s US research suggests that this gap is especially identified with feminist women, while non-feminist women's responses were very similar to men's. Likewise, pro-feminist men were more likely to oppose the military force option, though not with such a close correlation as found with feminist women (Gallagher, 1993: 35). In 1984 New Zealand banned visits of nuclear-capable warships, resulting in the suspension of US–NZ defence cooperation, a move strongly supported by younger women especially, who predominated in the peace movement, and opposed by most older men (Lamare, 1989). Research into the gender gap foreign-policy attitudes in Denmark in the late 1980s found it part of 'a general left-wing mobilisation of women' and an apparent remobilisation of 'women's values' (Togeby, 1994: 375). These findings undermine arguments for women's nature or essence as intrinsically more peaceful or compassionate, but also question explanations of women's socialisation into passive or nurturing roles as accounting for the gender gap.

A further investigation of women's responses in public-opinion polls on foreign policy in the US since 1945 found that over time women were consistently less aware of and less informed on particular issues, but also women showed greater anxiety, especially about nuclear and security issues. Suggested explanations include that women are more fearful and more women respond negatively to risks then men; or that they are more imaginative and think more about the consequences than men do; or that they are more empathetic and caring than men (though whether we can justify understanding 'concern' as 'care' is not clear). A further and possibly relevant gender aspect of polling is also noted: that more women are willing to admit not knowing, or downplay their knowledge about such issues, while men have a higher 'opinion' response to trick fictitious issues, apparently having an ego or sexual-identity investment in appearing knowledgeable, especially about high politics (Brandes, 1993).

Another suggested explanation for more women's supporting peace alternatives or opposing the use of military force is gendered social location. Might women's disarmed and subordinate status make them more wary of force? Are there clues in the performance of women heads of government or state, often also therefore heads of military command, to see if once 'in', women behave as men do? Some, such as Margaret Thatcher, Golda Meir and Indira Gandhi, were strong leaders who did take their states into wars. In some other states, such as Nicaragua and the Philippines, women became leaders at times of national exhaustion or reaction, symbolising healing and reconciliation, though they were not in full control of their militaries (Richardson, 1993; Howes, 1993). It may be that the larger numbers of women leaders and politicians in the Scandinavian states have different views in terms of the use of force, but their political cultures and states' positioning internationally are also somewhat different. Feminist research on women leaders suggests they do seem to make a difference when they are there in sufficient numbers (15 per cent is popularly asserted as the minimum critical mass) with feminist commitment and backing from strongly organised women's and pro-peace organisations (Bystydzienski, 1993).

A different voice?

The relatively new field of feminist ethics draws on research and debates about women's difference and care work, which have direct relevance to debates about the gender of war and peace. Carol Gilligan suggests that girls and women reason morally in 'a different voice' (1982), which is more concrete and contextual, and less abstract and rational, which focuses more on relationships and responsibility than on abstract rights and principles, and which pays more heed to the consequences of choices and actions. She describes a different theme, of care rather than justice, typically but not only or entirely associated with women (Gilligan, 1993).

Gilligan's findings have been much used by those associating women with peace (and men with war), and much critiqued as well (Larrabee, 1993). Kathy Davis asks 'what it is about the project of a female morality of care that is so attractive or frightening to feminists at this particular juncture in history' (1992: 228), pointing out the political investments behind such debates, and the essentially contested and contradictory nature of 'care'.

Similar questions and contests appear around the work of Sarah Ruddick, who specifically applies questions of gender difference to debates about peace and war (1983; 1992). She has developed the notion of maternalist peace politics based on what women learn, as actual mothers and/or as daughters growing up in a society that expects them to mother. She accepts that women can be violent, including towards their own children, or refuse to or reluctantly mother and that some men do material work and learn from it. (See Theweleit, 1993 exploring men's caring labour and parenting as the basis of a men's peace politics.) She explores maternalist practices that encourage pacifist skills and values. But these practices and the attentive or preservative love she sees them teaching are closely associated with actual women's work, as women are still overwhelmingly responsible for the day-to-day care of children (not always their own), and of others, husbands, the elderly, and for healthcare. This, and popular associations of women's giving life through birthing with a gender interest in preserving life, can obscure the problematic and socially constructed connections of women to peace.

Some critics reject Ruddick's argument for a pacifist content or intent in the practice of mothering, pointing out that mothers' care and emotional investment in their children can as easily be directed into supporting violence against others (Davion, 1992). White mothers stoned the buses and sometimes the children when blacks were bused to white schools in attempts to overcome decades of segregated living and schooling in the US in the 1960s (though other white women joined the civil rights movement). In the US, too, women's handgun ownership is rapidly rising, though usually for self-defence. Women organise, often as mothers, in nationalist, racist and other exclusionary politics, including against 'other' women. Third-world and racialised minority feminists point to the many white women who have rallied behind governments, soldiers and male relatives in imperialist, racist and militarist goals (hooks, 1989; see chapters 2 and 3 in this book). Especially in international perspective, attention to structural violence and state terrorism reveals complicity of dominant-group women in relations of domination and exploitation that daily damage, threaten and often kill women, children and men. Gender alone does not explain politics or responsibility. We need to ask whose peace is defended, and whose experiences of violence are privileged in any 'peace' politics.

Maternalist peace imagery is problematic in its representations of women as necessarily peaceful. It is also problematic in its representations of women as mothers. Many women are not, cannot be or have chosen not to be mothers, while others mother reluctantly or alongside other social commitments. Peace women may respond by pointing out that they are using a language of social mothering, addressing the gender that mothers; though many do authorise what they have to say about peace and war with reference to their own experiences of mothering. Some critics suggest that maternalist language can be heard as heterosexist and anti-lesbian; though of course many lesbians are mothers, and maternalist feminists can both be, or be respecting of, lesbians. Here again there are distinctions and explorations to be made, rather than presumed, between women and mothers, as well as between women and different feminist political projects.

These questions prompt us to ask, in debates around feminist ethics, or around women's caring work and maternal practices, who do women, or mothers, see themselves as care givers *for*? (Tronto, 1987) What are the limits of the female moral community? Do mothers care fiercely only for their own children? When their gender and maternal identity is generalised, is it extended only to others in their communal or national group? or to all others? How difficult is it to translate care and moral responsibility from family and intimates, to public and especially to international levels?

A recurring problem in these debates is the 'levels of analysis' issue. Recalling discussion of Waltz in chapter 5, women as peaceful is a mirror of men as aggressive; so we 'gender' his 'level one' discussions. Yet we recall that this level alone is clearly inadequate. There are powerful processes at the level of the state and the international system and in the construction of civic/political identities that are profoundly gendered, and part of the construction of a culture of war and of the field of IR.

Another cluster of criticisms of an ethic of care or maternalist peace politics raises issues related to cultural and class differences, arguing that 'women' may again turn out to be white, western, middle class. There is some evidence cross-culturally that women as a group are more committed to an ethics of 'care' than men in their state (Stimpson, 1992). There are also suggestions that the characteristics associated with these kinds of care may not be so much associated with 'women' as with subordinate groups. Many African-American men are community carers, too (Stack, 1993). Representations of African and many indigenous cultures make similar distinctions away from the abstract and individuated moral reasoning of the white western male.

Is 'care' a characteristic of subordination (though some members of subordinate groups demonstrate violent lack of care, especially against kin, peers and neighbours)? Might 'care', where it is given, be another power of the weak (Carroll, 1972), lessons learnt from exclusion from the technology of violence and from its legitimate use, vested in dominant structures and groups? Women's relative peacefulness might reflect their disarmed state, including until very recently and still in many states their exclusion from the right to exercise state-authorised violence.

Sarah Ruddick is aware of the danger when she questions 'the effectiveness of a virtue acquired in conditions of powerlessness' (1983: 232). 'Care' and self-sacrifice may be strategies for negotiating conflicts between women's own desires and the expectations of others, where women lack the power to act independently, or might be punished for attempting to do so (Tronto, 1987). The figures on 'domestic' violence across state and cultural borders indicate the danger here. Bill Puka goes further to suggest 'care' as an example of 'slave morality' and cautions against turning 'victimisation into virtue' (1993: 215). He, too, sees caring work as a set of coping strategies to deal with sexist oppression and gender socialisation. In the face of these warnings, others suggest

> [i]t may be perilous to valorize the very traits and behaviors that have propped up vast inequities in past society. On the other hand, to reject caring for that reason may be only reactive, not liberating, for 'care' does entail much that is good and strong. Caution, not outright rejection, would appear to be in order (Cole and Coultrap-McQuin, 1992: 5).

The moral mother

We return, then, to the difficulties of attending to and respecting women's caring work, while recognising that associating women with care is often used to privatise and exploit women's work, and to construct notions of the good woman, thus threatening women who act politically or step out of line. These difficulties are multiplied when we trace different women's use of maternalist imagery—for peace and for war, for causes liberationist or exclusionary, radical or reactionary. They are compounded, too, by the startling similarity in many of the images of women mobilised by anti–feminist men and by some feminist and pacifist women.

The care/justice or peace/war dichotomies used by many peace women and some feminists are seen by others as reproducing the dichotomous construction of gender difference, which is part of women's oppression. Some critics of an ethic of care see it duplicating the usual sexual division of labour in a division of moral labour so that 'the genders are moralised in different ways' (Friedman, 1993: 259).

The 'moral mother' deployed in women's peace work can seem very like the 'angel in the house' of men's moral fantasies (Cole and Coultrap-McQuin, 1992: 5–6). Frequently, women do escape from the house, or at least leave it for political purposes, in the name of or to protect their maternal roles. Their house is not necessarily a safe place, especially if they are seen to question male dominance or interests within it. A stronger feminist position is that women should organise and claim rights for themselves, and become moral and political actors in their own right—which does not preclude caring or responsibility for others. Putting together care with social justice might politicise and build a more inclusive peace project. Guarding against the exploitative tendencies within 'care' is strengthened by a move from female to feminist politics. So, too, recognising the essentially contested nature of both care and gender difference might support their use as political resources in ways that are enabling, including for the carers (Davis, 1992).

Feminist ethics are contested from within, but do assert women as moral agents and as knowledgeable. Like other feminist endeavours, feminist ethics take women's experiences of care giving seriously, including their care of other women, and their own understandings of themselves. So African-American women in southern US states, like many women in different states, are the primary 'kin-keepers' (Stack, 1993). But women in some states or cultures move to husbands' family homes and situations where relations with his female kin are difficult, or even dangerous.

There is no necessary relation between mothering and pacifism. Some mothers understand their attachments and responsibilities as requiring either the sacrifice of their sons for the state or nation, or the use of violence against other women's sons—and daughters. Many women do organise or participate in political action and resistance, and in support of armed struggles, as mothers. But we can make no presumption about their particular politics. We can ask, though, why maternalist imagery is so widespread and so effective in motivating and mobilising women? And why is it apparently so open to appropriation by such different political projects, including both for and against war? Why are there so few differences in the images associated with maternalism in pacifist and armed causes, in feminist, non-feminist and anti-feminist politics? (di Leonardo, 1985: 602)

Mothers in the wars

Maternalist imagery and politics recur cross-culturally—probably universally—in support of the range of politics from left to right, reactionary to liberationist. Maternalist associations do mean something to many different women, but exactly what they mean to any one of them can never be presumed. So in South Africa both ANC-supporting and apartheid-supporting women articulated their political positions in terms of maternalist imagery and loyalties (Cock, 1992).

Many women are motivated by and claim the right to engage in politics as women, or as mothers. They often do so when their mother roles or family members are threatened, or when hostilities or state action make it impossible for them to fulfil their domestic responsibilities. So Chilean women organised against Pinochet when their homes were no longer safe from military or police attack, and when sons or husbands—and daughters and sisters—were 'disappeared'. Palestinian women in exile in Lebanon after 1948, and later in the occupied West Bank, were looked to as mothers responsible for socialising children into Palestinian nationalism as well as culture. Especially in the time of the resistance from the mid-1960s, when carrying out their daily jobs such as collecting water and fetching supplies became dangerous, women organised and protested.

> Their political actions were rooted in ideas of what they perceived to be their culturally sanctioned rights as women, mothers and sustainers of life—to carry out their domestic tasks and raise their children in peace and material security and to be protected from assaults (Peteet, 1991: 90).

Palestinian women also responded to appeals to them as mothers of soldiers—as the PLO leadership encouraged women-directed politics to mobilise more general support for the struggle, though only ambivalently and belatedly recognising women as participants—and daughters as fighters (Peteet, 1991; Hiltermann, 1991). Women's solidarity in the struggles included taking on a more generalised gender identity as mothers of the nation. In the mobilisations associated with the *intifada*, Palestinian women have developed strategies to counter Israeli militarism and to warn and defend young activists. So when an Israeli soldier went to seize a young man and an elderly woman demanded that he not take her son, his retort that it was not her son met the declaration that 'they are all my children' (Giacaman and Johnson, 1990: 41).

Palestinian politics mobilises images of motherhood, of *Um al-Shaheed* or the mother of the martyr (Abdo, 1991), mother to all the young men. This representation is a source of strength and pride for many women, and perhaps some small comfort for those whose own sons or daughters have been killed, injured or taken away. But once again there are contradictions between the ideological and material uses of women for resistance and nationalist politics still dominated by men, and women's own actions, including in support of those politics. Here, as in other nationalist struggles noted in chapter 3, the construction of women as mothers and daughters of the revolution can be used to demand or enforce a false choice, and primary loyalty to nationalist or revolutionary cause, and so to delegitimise feminism as somehow disloyal or self-indulgent. It can also lead to the policing of younger and middle-aged women's behaviour and relations, as they become (revolutionary) national property.

In the aftermath of the bloody overthrow of Allende in Chile and the systematic terror that followed it, women were the first to mobilise against the new dictatorship (Chuchryk, 1989). The Mujeres Democraticas (Association of Democratic Women) and Agrupacion de los Familiares de Detenidos–Desparecidos (Association of the Relatives of the Detained and Disappeared) were early and very courageous examples of women's action. They demonstrate the appropriation and exploitation of ideologies of motherhood for progressive political purposes, though in the process many of the women came to reassess their own views of motherhood, and of existing gender relations. The ambiguities and contradictions of maternal action become clear again here, in women's construction as 'safe' protestors, and suggestions that the regime used the 'mothers' as a brake on overzealous or out-of-control supporters or vigilantes.

At the same time, the Pinochet regime used conservative ideologies of motherhood to appeal to women for support. While it may be tempting to regard women who rallied behind the regime as dupes, many women's mobilisations on both sides of politics as mothers challenge us to ask what are the implications for feminists' taking seriously other women's experiences, when some of those women are not only anti-feminist but also actively involved with a politics that is so costly to, and violent towards, other women.

Many of the women in a number of other South and Central American states who organised against militarist and violent governments did so as mothers, including the well-known Mothers of Plaza de Mayo in Argentina (Fisher, 1989). As well, the Grandmothers of

the Plaza de Mayo organised from 1977 to recover children kid-
napped or born in custody, many of whose mothers were killed or
disappeared (Arditti and Lykes, 1992). The women often represented
themselves as non-political, acting in defence of family and their
roles within it. They drew on Catholic imagery of maternal suffering
and self-sacrifice and turned it against a repressive and dangerous
state. But by entering public space, usually thought of as male, they
politicised motherhood, and subverted the boundaries and meanings
of the public/private divide, so long used to contain and domesticate
women (Radcliffe and Westwood, 1993).

Similarly, Russian women organised in support of soldiers and
their families during Soviet military involvement in Afghanistan in
the Committee of Soldiers' Mothers, reactivated in response to the
Russian assault on Chechnya. Their actions often place them in
opposition to the state. In the early weeks of 1995, they negotiated
with Chechen soldiers for release of some Russian prisoners-of-war
into their mothers' custody, and then worked to assist the soldiers
and their families in avoiding prosecution of soldiers for deserting.

In these politics, women's peace work is far more risky and
costly than in Anglo-European and settler states, (though there are
costs and hard choices there, too). Women on both sides of the
Northern Ireland divide have mobilised against the violence and in
attempts to build contacts and alliances across the fighting lines.
They, like Israeli women demonstrating as 'Women in Black' against
Israeli militarism and in solidarity with Palestinian women, face hard
times negotiating difference from positions of unequal national and
citizenship power (Sharoni, 1995). They are also particularly exposed
to violence and abuse from their 'own', for perceived treachery and
treason (and we need to ask how loyalty to a socially constructed,
though now also materially interested, 'community' comes to take
such moral precedence over loyalty to 'others'—or to 'peace').

It is easier, then, for women to enter public space and become
political actors for the state or nationalist cause than against it. For
many women, acting in the name of mothers, like acting for the
nation, provides the justification to move into the public space.
Their political action can be seen as patriotic and respectful, where
a daughter's politics might appear as unruly or rebellious, and more
of a threat to masculinity and male political power. A small place
is made for women who act within traditional gender roles and
identities. But if women's politics is confined within a politicised
mother role, activist women who reject this role may be especially
vulnerable to attack, from their own side and other men.

The ambiguities and tensions in women's political action are seen where women self-consciously choose to exploit gender stereotypes for nationalist ends. Women acting against states or militaries covertly might arouse less suspicion by exploiting sexist assumptions that see them as passive and harmless, so smuggling arms, passing information or gaining access where men would be immediately suspect. This presumed innocence does not save them from violence though, nor from especially vicious retaliation if they are caught.

Maternalist politics often claim to be non-political, or at least non-partisan. Women who enter the public domain or the political struggle as mothers can find their experiences liberating, building confidence and encouraging them to take up a more overtly political position. Others find it frustrating. They may be politicised by discrimination against them by men, or engage in conversations and analyses of violence that radicalise them or lead them to scrutinise gender relations, and so to argue for women's rights as part of the struggle. This is seen as a move from female consciousness, which seeks rights or safety within family and gender expectations within the nationalist struggle, to feminist consciousness, where activist women view women's liberation as an intrinsic part of national liberation and seek social transformation (Peteet, 1991: 88).

In many states the border lines between resistance, protest, support for revolutionary struggle and joining the struggle are not clear. While representations of maternalist peace politics and women warriors can suggest they are in opposition to each other, women frequently become active or take up arms in nationalist or revolutionary struggles because they are mothers, and see themselves as working for a more secure and equal life for their, and other people's, children. They join other activist and feminist women, including those who have long resisted women's containment within 'the maternal'.

This is a reminder that we cannot fully explore women's relations with peace unless we also look more closely at women in wars. So the next chapter will ask What do women have to do with war? What might we learn from women's own experiences of war? Chapter 7, and the second part of this book, conclude with some thoughts towards an anti-militarist feminism.

7

Women in the wars

This chapter begins by shifting the perspective from the association of women and peace, to ask What do women have to do with war? It pursues the distinction between front and rear, and looks at women's responses when 'the front', and the war, come to them. It traces women's agency in wars, including those women who become warriors in liberation and revolutionary struggles. But whatever women's participation in wars and armed struggles, even as combatants, they are routinely pushed 'back home' and their contribution erased when the fighting stops.

Women warriors are joining volunteer state militaries in increasing numbers. Why this is happening, and what are the effects on the women themselves, and on the military? Given the close associations of citizenship with bearing arms, what are the implications of women's growing roles in state militaries for women's citizenship? And why is there such resistance to women, and to gay men, as soldiers? There are feminist dilemmas in the face of women's claims to equal opportunity in state militaries. Exploring these dilemmas leads back to the problematic links between masculinity, militarism and violence. The chapter concludes with thoughts towards an anti-militarist feminism.

Women in the wars

'Part of the answer to the question "What do women have to do with war?" is: A great deal more than either militarists or many pacifist women are prepared to admit' (di Leonardo, 1985: 611).

'Peace' and 'war' are not always neatly separate or inevitably opposed. Many women opposing war before the declaration of World War 1 then rallied behind the soldiers, often their lovers, husbands, sons or brothers. Not all were bellicose. Many were extremely fearful, and extended empathy and concern to enemy soldiers and their womenfolk, too, as did some men, including some soldiering men. Yet it can be argued that women's moral and political support and war work are essential parts of war-making. Without women's activities, would wars be possible? Women also save men from taking responsibility for war violence, in their work to repair bodies, souls and communities damaged in the fighting or in militarised relations.

On the ground, issues of choice and responsibility are often very murky. There are questions about women's complicity in wars, even when they are personally opposed to or appalled by them, because it is for women—among other things—that men supposedly fight. This recalls the writings of Jean Elshtain (1987) and others about the symbolic uses made of women, including to force men to fight (see chapter 5). Are women responsible for things done in their name? Are they under an obligation to take a stand in politics that use their supposed vulnerability as part of the ideological resources for war? Might there be a parallel here between women in wars and white women in racism, 'protected' by politics that endanger or penalise others? So Adrienne Rich moves beyond Virginia Woolf's disowning her country to assert that as a (United States of) American woman, she has a responsibility to challenge what is done against others in her name (1986).

In almost all wars, most women have supported their states and governments, or at least acquiesced in their war-making. But can we read lack of organised political opposition as support when women are denied political power, and may be subjected to state repression or terror, or to punishment by family and community men if they speak out? Even if they speak out at home?

Questions of complicity and responsibility also recur in terms of women's work in wars. Taking women's own experiences seriously (without assuming that any experiences are transparent or politically innocent) reveals women in more roles than waiting and weeping. Women are agents in wars, including in support of wars. Women's work in war time is as a labour reserve, called on to replace and so to release men or to compensate for men's going off to fight. Could either civilian life or the war effort be sustained if many, let alone most, women withdrew their labour? Women work to provide goods and services to keep the military going, and in armaments factories to produce the means of destruction. Some women have been part of technical and scientific research, including, for example, in the development of nuclear technology and capacity in the Manhattan Project, which led to the bombing of Hiroshima and Nagasaki (Howes and Herzenberg, 1993).

In times of official peace in the 'white' lands (now broken in some places in the wake of the collapse of the Soviet Union and of state communism in Europe) the capacity to fight, and proxy wars in third-world states, are maintained through ongoing militarisation. Huge defence expenditures in NATO and Soviet-bloc states spread a vast technological and industrial military tail, as well as generating much employment and profit from direct and indirect support of militaries (Enloe, 1988). Are women as workers in militarised industry, or as taxpayers, voters and citizens, necessary ingredients in the everyday war machine?

Home and away

Much western women-and-peace writing reproduces IR's, and militaries', distinction between the front and the rear, or home, and locates women in the latter. States such as the US, Britain and Australia did send their troops 'over there' in two World Wars, and continued to do so in other wars outside the west. Some women from these states were at or near the front, too, as nurses or ambulance drivers, for example, experiencing the blood and horror of war first hand (Tylee, 1990; Marcus, 1989).

Numbers of women served in women's auxiliaries in British, US, German and Russian militaries in World War 1, in units that were temporary and were disbanded after the war. More women served in World War 2, as nurses, drivers, and in technical and support roles. Often they were classed as civilians even where they wore uniform and were subject to military discipline. The US Women's Airforce Service Pilots undertook dangerous war work transporting military aircraft overseas, but only in 1977 were they granted military veteran status (Segal, 1993: 83). In Australia some 67 000 women joined the military forces, though most were soon forgotten as 'our boys' assumed the male–soldier identity. During the Vietnam War, women from the US and Australia went to Vietnam in support roles, as nurses, clerical workers and entertainers (McHugh, 1993). Only in the 1994 Anzac Day march did Australian women veterans march separately as women. In 1995, as part of the 'Australia Remembers' fiftieth anniversary of the conclusion of World War 2, women of the Women's Land Army were given medals and recognition for serving their country, too (*Canberra Times*, 30 March 1995).

Other Anglo–American women stayed at home during the World Wars, and lived the terror of war through official and media reports and letters home, or through not hearing from soldier kin. They often had to assume extra responsibilities without support, and then had to deal with injured or angry menfolk returning, or with early widowhood. Their experiences, were, however very different from those in continental European states. In Vichy France, for example, wives of POWs were under enormous pressure and surveillance, facing the threat of jail for adultery (Fishman, 1992).

In many states, war came to the women, children and non-combatant men. They were frequently direct and indirect casualties of the fighting, targets for torture, maiming and murder, victims of starvation and siege, or forced relocation and forced labour. Women and young people were often agents in occupied or fighting zones, as fighters or supporters, and some as collaborators or unwilling hostages. Their experiences of violence and strategies for resistance or survival are told more often in books and films than in the IR literature. Forgetting these experiences is forced as part of the 'normalisation' process, but also brought about by discomfort in the face of moral dilemmas about complicity and choice, responsibility and blame. After World War 2, for example, the fallout between the Soviet Union and the western powers quickly shifted attention to the communist threat, and subverted attempts to pursue war crimes or reconciliation in peace-making. Recently, the break up of the old Yugoslavia and fighting in several ex-Soviet republics brought war back home there. The violence, the danger and the terror make peace work extremely difficult, far more difficult than where war is something that happens in other people's places.

Belgrade feminists Lepa Mladjenovic and Vera Litricin document the rise of Yugoslav feminist organisations and alliances from the late 1980s, including the Women's Lobby and the SOS Hotline for Women and Children Victims of Violence. With the breaking up of Yugoslavia, the Women's Lobby campaigned against nationalist, chauvinist parties, while SOS reported rapidly increasing violence in families, including the use of guns, once the fighting began. Women in Black against War took up their vigil against Serbian nationalist chauvinism and war. But women's groups were hard hit by the rising tide of nationalism and violence. The Women's Lobby kept going, but 'every time the nationalist question came up there was no way to overcome the fact that a lot of women were being hurt. Women suffered but usually did not change their attitudes. There was a great deal of silence and crisis' (Mladjenovic and Litricin, 1993: 114). The Women's Party, on the other hand, faced such severe conflicts among members that they decided to

> 'freeze' their activities until the war was over and then see . . .
>
> SOS Hotline had many problems as well. Despite the fact that the SOS group had a deliberately non-nationalist policy from the beginning, some volunteers were unable to keep their nationalist feelings out of their SOS work. Several attempts were made to reconcile the opposing viewpoints; after that some of the women left and some of them stayed and remained silent (Mladjenovic and Litricin, 1993: 117).

Feminist choices and anti-nationalist politics may be all the more urgent in these situations, but they are all the more difficult and dangerous, too.

In many states, especially in third-world states, war and political violence are an everyday part of children's growing up and of women's attempts to negotiate their lives. Irene Matthews explores two daughters' rememberings of their mothers in wartime: Nellie Campobello, growing up in the Mexican Revolution 'in the very thick of the fighting' (1993: 149); and Rigoberta Menchu, whose own mother also loved the *guerilleros* 'like her own children' (Menchu, 1984: 218), telling of contemporary terrors of state violence in Guatemala. Her mother leaves her family to work for the resistance after seeing her own son tortured and burned to death. Both mothers display a 'generous infantilization' (Matthews, 1993: 161) towards revolutionary or resistance soldiers, who become their children in terms of both care and responsibility. A collection of Zimbabwean women's experiences of war tells of daily harassment and danger, at the hands of guerrillas as well as white state forces, and of the loss of children, including those who joined the guerrillas (Staunton, 1991). At the same time, most women did support the guerrillas, morally and materially. They, too, often spoke of them as their children, as indeed some of them actually were. Other women became guerrillas, and younger women especially were more likely to refer to male guerrillas as compatriots and brothers than as sons.

Documenting the lives of women in war zones recalls the difficulties of writing women's lives without simply reproducing women as victims, while recognising the terrible victimisation of many women and their families on the ground (Nordstrom, 1994a;

see chapter 5 in this book). Alternatively, (s)heroising women can acknowledge how hard it is just to keep going, especially when militaries specifically target the fabric of daily life, and community and family relations for destruction, but it also risks ignoring the enormous coercive power and fatal violence of war.

In these circumstances, it is difficult to think through questions such as Is violence ever legitimate, or necessary, or the lesser of two evils? Unless one is adopting a pacifist position opposing all wars and the use of force, there are profound moral difficulties concerning a feminist position on war. It is tempting to argue that, like 'domestic' violence, the only effective response to war is 'no; never', for if the possibility of a just war or necessary violence exist, states' leaders and others will always act to 'justify' their actions. From a safe looking position, this is an urgent and reasonable position, but when the war comes to women, this choice may be simply unavailable.

Forgetting and re-membering women

Listening to women's stories, the lines between combatants and civilians blur, and boundaries are contested and malleable. Even uniformed soldiers can be unwilling conscripts (and are often children), or reluctant defenders of their homes or rights. Women providing shelter or food or information to guerillas may do so for different motives, including from fear of retribution or to hasten them on their way. But many who are in sympathy or giving assistance may be drawn into more sustained support roles, and may themselves become fighters in the struggle.

Women's stories and feminist writings tell us some of the ways in which different women in different struggles become political subjects (Molyneux, 1985), and the ways by which some of them become women warriors. Do they do so in ways and for reasons different from men? What are the consequences—for the women themselves, the struggle, and the outcome—in the politics that emerge after the fighting is over?

Often, women's participation in and contribution to liberation and nationalist struggles is officially 'forgotten' soon after the struggle ends (Tetreault, 1994). This makes it especially important both to dis-cover women, and to take their own memories and tellings of their own experiences seriously. 'It is not enough for women to have been there; they have to write [or tell? for not all women warriors are literate or have access to publication] and interpret what it means to have been there. Such an activist discourse may become an agent of change beyond discourse' (Cooke, 1993: 177).

Feminist recovery projects have revealed women's roles in nationalist and revolutionary struggles, demonstrating that women were there, and some were there as feminists (Jayawardena, 1986; chapter 3 in this book). There is uneven documentation of women's experiences in contemporary wars, leading to questions about where the media goes, as well as about the politics of collaboration in particular states or struggles. The ethics and politics of voice and representation recur here, with the attendant dangers of exploitation and appropriation of other women's pain or choices. In some cases there are unwelcome attentions, which may expose or further traumatise women, and weariness on the part of those who are visited and asked to speak often, with no tangible results.

So, during the fighting at Engela in Namibia, women refused to tell their stories again:

> We are women in war
> We are wanting to know where help is coming from
> We are not going to tell you of our problems, because we have told our stories so many times, and still no help comes.
> To ask us again is like pouring petrol on fire.
> We are confused. Every country sends representatives here and we tell our stories, and it only seems to get worse. The troubles seem to get worse every day. We have told enough now.
> We are tired.
> We are tired of telling. Our burden is too heavy to pick up.
> We are angry.
> The women of Namibia are angry because of the war (Cleaver and Wallace, 1990: 1).

Women warriors in nationalist and revolutionary struggles

Women do enter into politics and especially into militaries from rather different gender/social positioning than men, though different women, too, are positioned and move differently: as middle-class urban feminists, working-class barrios organisers, or rural female heads of households, with different regional affiliations and ethnic backgrounds, younger or older, mothers or not. Women activists join as nationalists or democrats or socialists, as communalists or religious activists, as individuals seeking their own escape or liberation, as women, as mothers, and/or as feminists. Their own motives, allegiances and identities often change in the process, including as war comes to them, or in the dynamics of the conflict. A recurring motif in different struggles and revolutionary imagery is the armed mother, a construction both related to and opposed to the moral mother of some peace politics. Speaking of Nicaragua, Maxine Molyneux remarks on the construction of a 'combative motherhood'. 'Many of these [soldier] women experience their transition from relief workers to participants in the struggle as a natural extension, albeit in combative form, of their protective role in the family as providers and crucially as mothers' (Molyneux, 1985: 228).

Women have long played significant parts in liberation struggles, in Algeria and Vietnam, for example, in large numbers. But women's participation is more visible in recent liberation and nationalist struggles, sometimes as a result of learnings from other states and women's experiences, and determination not to be forgotten (Abdo, 1991).

While women have long played crucial roles in support of and relief for fighters, significant numbers of women have been fighters themselves. In Central and South America, it is only since the 1970s that women have fought as regular combatants in liberation armies, including in positions of leadership. The first large-scale mobilisation of women was as Tupamaros guerrillas in Uruguay, where the revolutionary movement developed an explicit position in support of revolutionary women (Jaquette, 1973). Shifting guerrilla tactics demanded mass mobilisation, and generated more attention to women's interests and seeking women as fighters. Growing feminist movements in states such as Mexico, Peru and Brazil reinforced the articulation of women's rights as part of the national struggle (Lobao, 1990).

There is often a political economy of activism, too, when poorer women in rural impoverishment or urban barrios, many themselves heads of households and not under male control, organise in response to survival needs or state violence. They may then take their heightened sense of political competence and commitment into wider politics, including into revolutionary organising and fighting. Those women who had already taken enormous risks and been threatened by death squads and state terror were not inclined to accept traditional divisions of labour or restrictions on their partic- ipation in combat roles, though manpower shortages also gave the male leadership an interest in women's 'liberation' (Mason, 1992).

In Nicaragua by the late 1970s some 30 per cent of Sandinista Front for National Liberation (FSLN) combatants, including field commanders, were women. There were similar or higher proportions of Salvadorian women in different wings of the struggle, and 40 per cent of the revolutionary council were women (Lobao, 1990). The revolutionary leaderships recognised women's interests and the ways in which the militarist regimes targeted women. They made moves towards including women in military and political organisation, and asserted that feminist politics and goals were not incompatible with, or secondary to, other goals.

When the state is won

What happens to women, and to gender relations, when the revolution wins the state? Do the politics of the 'cause' affect both women's roles in the struggle and women's rights and gender relations afterwards?

Jewish women fought for the establishment of Israel, but with the formation of that state they were excluded from combat roles. Even though Jewish Israeli women are liable for conscription, they play support, educative, clerical and nursing roles, which reflect the division of labour outside the military (Yuval-Davis, 1985). Unlike Israeli men, they do not continue to be liable for call-up, as their primary responsibility to state and nation is to mother, and to take responsibility for care of children, home and culture.

Soon after assuming power in Nicaragua in 1979, the FSLN moved to declare women's equality and equal pay, and pursued a political and legislative program that asserted women's rights and attempted a reform of gender relations, including giving men and women equal rights in terms of children and equal domestic labour responsibilities, making prostitution illegal, and opposing sexist advertising and media representations (Molyneux, 1985; Collinson, 1990). However, especially after 1982, the US-backed Contra threat of counter-revolution led to a diversion of resources into defence of the revolution (over one-third of the national budget in 1984). In 1983 the Sandinista government introduced two years' compulsory military service for young men aged 18 to 25. While women were still 'allowed' to join the military as volunteers, the establishment of a gendered division of labour and the reinscribing of men as the compulsory soldiers was seen by many as a betrayal of revolutionary tradition and aims. Attempts to secure the state also meant a toning down of feminist demands, for example, for abortion rights, in deference to Catholic and conservative political power.

Nevertheless, women and feminist goals did not simply disappear. The *Proclama* issued on International Women's Day in 1987—itself a mark of respect for feminist internationalism, or an indication of leadership fears of losing women's support for the revolution—reiterated that 'The struggle to wipe out discrimination against women cannot be separated from the struggle to defend the revolution . . . The solution of the specific problems of women . . . are questions which concern not only women, but all of society' (*Nicaragua Today*, 1989: 10). Its declarations included 'We will continue to struggle against irresponsible paternity and the physical and moral abuse of women and children' (*Nicaragua Today*, 1989: 10).

In weighing up the outcomes for women of the Nicaraguan revolution in its first years, Maxine Molyneux (1985) makes a now-popular distinction in terms of women's interests between practical interests, which arise out of women's everyday lives and needs to fulfil their responsibilities and roles, and strategic interests, which revolve around women's emancipation and the related transformation of gender relations. In Nicaragua there was some attention to strategic interests and gender power, though ambivalences and resistance within the male leadership would have made change difficult. But in a situation of growing scarcity and threat, women's strategic interests were downplayed, or subordinated to the wider revolution. Feminists outside and inside the party and government were undercut, and the women's organisation Luisa Amanda Espinosa Association of Nicaraguan Women (AMNLAE) was increasingly contained within the FSLN struggle to hold the state. So 'it is a question, not just of *what* interests are represented in the state, but ultimately and critically of *how* they are represented' (Molyneux, 1985: 251).

In the contradictions and subversions of Nicaragua, women's gains often depended as much or more on their class position than on their gender. So poor women benefited from social reforms giving them access to land in rural areas and to services and support in, for example, access to health- and childcare. These gains were under increasing pressure in the late 1980s. The 1990 elections brought the conservative Violeta Chamorro to power, not least because of the awful war weariness and ongoing cost of resisting the counter-revolution. This shift demonstrated that, while even radical and pro-women revolutionaries might falter once in control of (or fighting to defend) the state, those with an anti-feminist agenda in control of the state are more devastating to women's interests. The Chamorro government called for a return to traditional family values (in a society with almost half its families headed by women). Its liberalisation of the economy saw the cancellation of many social gains. The spiralling of unemployment, and of costs of health and schooling, meant that women's lives and family maintenance became even harder (Seitz, 1992).

At the same time the elimination of a government-supported overarching women's organisation led to the rapid spread of a range of women's organisations, most of them autonomous and many of them explicitly feminist (Luciak, 1993). It seems that women's roles as agents and participants, and lessons learnt in activism, are not so easily forgotten, and can be recharged in the face of direct attack.

More recently, South Africa saw the end of apartheid and the beginnings of atttempts to build a non-racial democracy and military. Immediately before the change, women constituted some 15 per cent of the permanent South African Defence Force (SADF) and 20 per cent of the African National Congress (ANC) army Unkhonto we Sizwe. In the SADF there was a rigid sexual division of labour and strong support for both male and white supremacy. The ANC was committed to liberation including explicitly to women's emancipation, and trained men and women together, though women remained excluded from formal combat roles; thus, there were more radical changes in women's roles and in expectations for change in the ANC. But with liberation, women have been relegated back into the roles of being protected, and have been made invisible in the debates about how to build a new, representative, legitimate military force—where once again the soldier appears to be male (Cock, 1994). It is early times yet for the new South Africa, though, and the Constitution does assert women's rights.

In Eritrea, by independence, one-third of independence fighters were women, and its new leadership was publicly committed to women's equality in a region long associated with severe restrictions on women's freedom and rights. The widespread mobilisation of women and so public a commitment to women's liberation cannot, hopefully, be entirely submerged or erased today.

Back to normal?

Stories from different revolutionary and nationalist struggles suggest an uneven but very widespread pattern of regression in terms of women's claims and participation, after the state is won. This raises many questions, including the startling possibility that (some?) non-state militaries may be more women friendly than states themselves are. Why should it be so difficult for women to translate their activism in wars and nationalist struggles into citizenship rights and effective participation after the fighting is over? Even where there were very large numbers of women bearing arms in revolutionary movements, 'peace' seems to see enormous pressure on those women to return 'home', to give up both jobs and political representation in favour of men.

A similar pattern appears in war histories in Europe and North America, when women are mobilised for war, and function as a kind of reserve labour force, for military and other work. So in both World Wars, many women in western states took jobs that released men to go and fight, including in 'non-traditional' work, in agriculture and factories, and in the new or expanding armaments and military support industries. These experiences were liberating for many women, giving them a sense of social competence and of contributing to the struggle; and allowed married and single women to leave the surveillance of home. At the same time wars often doubled women's work, and created new and at times burdensome responsibilities. While appearing to blur or break boundaries between men's and women's work, wars can actually heighten awareness of gender scripts and relations marked through their transgression. 'Wars may awaken our awareness of the ways sexual territory is mapped because they disrupt the normal division of labour by gender' (Higonnet, 1989: 80).

Women were usually hastened back home when 'the boys' came back. This has led to debates about whether wars are ever 'good for' women, against some popular impressions that they liberate (some?) women or advance women's rights. Rather, it seems that wars help create a temporary expansion of women's public roles and kinds of work, often then removed after the fighting stops (Kandiyoti, 1991b).

This retraction reflected the privileging of those, seen as male, who had earned their full citizenship rights by risking their lives defending their country. But it also reflected the move to return to 'normalcy', a tacit agreement that gender roles had only been suspended 'for the duration', and that part of demobilising and returning to peacetime meant re-establishing the prewar order (Higonnet et al., 1987). While it was never possible to go back (and many poorer and minority women were already 'out' working before the war), the forgetting of women's experiences and efforts was generalised. Postwar discourses and social policies in Western-European states established welfare states that did provide some support for family, but also facilitated women's return to the home and, often, to invisibility within the private sphere. (This was not so in the Soviet Union for example, where the horrific war losses, pressures to build up an industrial and military base and a formal commitment to gender equality kept women in the workforce.) The domestication of women is revealed as a mulitfaceted political and cultural process; it takes a lot of ideological work to (re)normalise and 'naturalise' women's place.

As revolutionary movements assumed control of states, 'forgetting' women's revolutionary contributions appears to be a frequent effect of reconsolidating centralised control of authority. Failure to address power relations, in this case gender relations, during the struggle means that they are not likely to be addressed, let alone transformed, afterwards. Here forgetting is part of the process of legitimising privilege, including gender privilege. Even progressive causes are not necessarily women friendly; nor are nationalist or anti-state movements necessarily progressive, as their victories in Iran and Afghanistan reminds us. We can ask, then, whether women warriors are fighting in their own gender interests, or whether they are fighting for other, including patriarchal or male-dominated, projects (Sylvester, 1987: 504).

Clearly any particular struggle is more or less conducive to women's interests and rights, and only some struggles have a commitment to transforming gender relations. I have noted, too, the different uses made of women in nationalist politics, including by those movements that mobilised women but kept them symbolically within representations of family and nation that denied them full political rights. But the postrevolution regression seems to occur even where women's rights became emblematic of the revolution, especially in the face of legitimacy crises and economic and development 'difficulties' (Moghadam, 1994b).

Women's mobilisation as women, and the articulation of a feminist agenda, with a political strength and tenacity that insists upon womens' emancipation as an intrinsic part of the wider struggle, appears to be a necessary though not sufficient base for securing women's rights and continuing representation (Tetreault, 1994). If women organising within the movement or state can be submerged or made secondary to nationalist priorities, are their strategic interests better secured through autonomous women's organisations? Popular support and alliances with women-friendly progressive men seem crucial, as does continuing access to or support of key leaders in the state. Building a political culture that remembers women, for their participation in the struggle and their ongoing interests, is essential in keeping women's rights and gender power on the political agenda. All this is made very much more difficult in the face of new elite defensiveness or emerging state despotism.

Why are the forces for reasserting the gender order apparently so strong, even within those states where women were well integrated into anti-state militaries and their interests taken up as part of revolutionary politics?

There are many clues that emerge from the telling of women's stories and from critical re-readings of struggles and state politics. In many states, peace does not follow the seizing of state power. Especially in the Cold War, radical and social-revolutionary movements that 'won' states were rarely in effective control of their territory and population. More often, they were beseiged by foreign-backed counter-revolutionary or anti-state forces, and locked out of international economic relations and resources, which condemned them to ongoing deprivation and exhaustion. In Mozambique and Angola, for example, counter-revolutionary and anti-state forces were powerfully backed by South Africa and generated ongoing war, which tore those states and communities within them to bits. The fighting killed many people, displaced many more and disrupted productive activities. Survival, let alone generosity and courage, is extraordinarily difficult to secure.

States hit with legitimacy crises and social distress prioritise state survival and defence, which usually leads to intensified militarisation and the postponement or disappearance of gender transformation policies. Indeed, women's rights and claims may well be given away in return for more men's support of the state, or for fear of antagonising conservative interests, such as Catholic Church elites opposed to liberation theology in Central and South America, or fundamentalist or communalist forces in South Asia and in some Middle East states.

Maria Mies notes the shift in revolutionary rhetoric and imagery from mother with baby and gun to signify the armed struggle or nation, to the founding fathers of the state (1986). Much energy and envy goes into consolidating the new 'state class' after the revolution. Especially in difficult economic times, the state itself is the main source of rewards, so competition for positions within it intensifies. At a more popular level, if the fighting is over, the new state needs to absorb and 'pacify' the large numbers of now demobilised soldiers. Again 'soldier' comes to mean male, and unemployed soldiers are seen to take precedence over married women (even where they are ex-soldiers themselves, or war widows and heads of households). Governments seek to 'disarm' soldier men as a potential threat to state power, and might reward them with 'returned' power over women, rather than risk further discontent through social policies that undermine men's roles and 'the' (patriarchal) family. In attempts to legitimise the new government and defuse counter-revolutionary support, 'women' become a tradeable political card.

Maria Mies suggests a further pressure pushing women 'back home', in a political economy that uncovers 'women's work' as an ideological construction disguised by labels such as domestic, informal, or subsistence economy. As housewives rather than workers, women's labour can be exploited very cheaply; it becomes in effect a subsidy to the formal economy and the state, so it is appropriated for growth and ongoing 'primitive accumulation of capital' (Mies, 1986: 197). Even in postrevolutionary situations where women are declared legally equal, profound inattention to or defence of unequal gender relations ensures that national liberation will not mean women's liberation.

Political economy, state consolidation and male elite power interests range powerful forces against women's liberation. They seem, too, to be a likely combination for explaining why states that won independence in a secular political project declaring women as equal are now supporting or making concessions to fundamentalist and communalist demands about women, and forsaking women to their communities.

The state against the women?

The near-universal tendency for women to lose out in state consolidation politics is apparently confirmed in women's experiences contemporarily, in transition states moving to multi-party and parliamentary elections (see chapter 1). In old East Europe and the ex-Soviet Union, democratisation and liberalisation appear to mean masculism (Watson, 1993). The re-establishment of electoral, party and parliamentary politics has witnessed a drastic decline in the numbers and proportion of women as representatives and office holders. In some South and Central American states, women's rights are now proclaimed, and women's machinery is set up. Some worry that these experiments in 'state feminism' may not necessarily be good for (most) women, but may rather have a debilitating effect on women's organisations by defusing energy, removing a common enemy, and coopting some leading women into the state (Mies, 1986: 177; Valenzuela, 1990).

The challenges and dangers facing women in times of state consolidation and crises are related to the nature of the state, and of (elite) men's interests, including new elite men, who use the state to defend their gender as well as class and ideological interests. But might there also be clues in debates about 'women's nature' and women's politics, rarely brought together in writings about women warriors? If we return to suggestions that women politic differently, in social and protest movements rather than formal politics, and that women have different understandings of power, so that nonfeminist women such as Hannah Arendt stress relational and enabling aspects, power *to* rather than power *over* (Hartsock, 1984), it follows that women's political skills may be less effective or appropriate in the more hierarchical, competitive structures of state power. Reciprocity is not easily translated into rule-bound and coercion-backed statecraft. As states are currently constructed and understood to appear crucially implicated in war-making, they may be implicated in negating or subverting women's and feminist politicking, too.

Conversely, are women's understandings of power, like their presumed skills in peace and care work, a mirror of their disarmed and relatively powerless social location and experiences, rather than their 'natures'? Except in very few states, women have had little opportunity to learn from formal political power, especially coercive and prerogative power. So they may be 'outsiders' as an effect of social history and political power relations, as well as because they are women (Peterson and Runyan, 1993). They are especially distant from the IR state, with its hypermasculinist construction of power, its formulation of IR as power politics, as power over, zero-sum dominance based ultimately or overtly on military force. Could it be that it is not so much 'women' as 'states' that need attending to here, together with processes of militarisation that underpin and reproduce power relations, including gender relations, based on domination and subordination?

Militarising women

There is no clear or easy transition from war to peace, or from revolution to the state. Political culture and power relations are elaborate and tenacious, even while they are changing and challenged. We know far more about war than about how people, cultures and economies demilitarise and build peace. Winning a state, or a war, often leads to intensifying militarisation, as the huge Cold-War arms races and state-defence budgets demonstrated. Even in so-called peacetime, militarisation shapes states' economies and political cultures. Millions of people gain employment and some make large profits from direct and indirect support of militaries.

Militarisation impacts on women's lives, far beyond any immediate or personal connection with the military. Militaries and wider militarisation processes depend on women's work, as well as on particular constructions of masculinity and feminity to build militaries and to legitimise the diversion of enormous resources into militarism. Cynthia Enloe argues that militaries and processes of militarisation need women, and they need them to act as the gender women (1988: 212). She points to women in different but necessary relations with militarism, as camp followers, including as prostitutes and entertainers, as nurses, as military wives and as soldiers. But militaries tend to deny that they need women, even while putting much thought and effort into how to use them.

Women in state militaries

In view of the suggestion that some non-state militaries may be more women friendly than states themselves, and that even where women have taken up arms and fought, they may be denied representation and recognition after the fighting stops, what do we make of women warriors in states' militaries, and of arguments for women's rights to combat roles as necessary for full and equal citizenship? Do women in state militaries fare any better? or differently?

Since the 1970s, women have been joining western state militaries in increasing numbers, and are more integrated into those militaries, though they may still be restricted in their access to some, especially combat, positions. In states with volunteer militaries, who is allowed or encouraged to join the military, in terms of gender, but also in terms of race, class and so on? Who actually is joining the military? Or if there is conscription, who is liable? If young men are called up, why shouldn't young women be, too?

In 1989, women comprised some 11 per cent of the US military, and in 1990 some 11 per cent of the Australian military (Smith and McAllister, 1991). Proportions of officer women to all women vary. In almost all cases women are more integrated into airforce and navy branches than in the army, where the combat exclusion rule especially restricts women.

Which women are joining state militaries again varies, according to demographic and socio-economic circumstances in each state. So African-American women are over-represented in the US forces some four times their share of the overall population. (Over-representation of African-American men in the Vietnam War appears to be one 'trigger' to the US recruiting more women—regardless of colour.) This pattern partly reflects labour market dynamics and discrimination, and the exorbitant price of housing, health and social security, especially for poorer people and single mothers. The US military is in one sense a vast and often superior welfare state. In Australia, it seems young women are more likely than young men to join the military as a career choice, after weighing up alternative education and employment opportunities, rather than from any particular attachment to 'military values' (Smith and McAllister, 1991). Many young women also respond to the opportunities for travel and adventure, and need a respectable reason to leave home. It is debatable whether, in 'peacetime', they join expecting to fight anyone. (An examination of much military recruitment literature and imagery confirms this.)

Why are many state militaries now more tolerant of or actually seeking to recruit women? Two main kinds of explanation appear relevant. First are 'manpower' concerns, especially where there are falling birthrates and lack of suitable recruits (apparently meaning dominant-group men). Women serve as a kind of military labour reserve, as they do in many liberation or revolutionary militaries— which might suggest less need for women soldiers in current post-Cold War 'downsizing' of state militaries. Second are industrial politics in general, including equal employment legislation and expectations in the wider society. Despite some militaries' exemption from such legislation, legal challenges and institutional pressures have grown. These reflect growing feminist movements and reduced tolerance for 'protection' clauses on traditionally male jobs, including in the military (and the church).

Women and/in combat

Debates about women in the military, and especially about whether women should be treated equally in the military, often revolve around the issue of women and combat. These debates reveal as much about gender expectations and gender relations as they do about the nature and needs of the military.

There are many different questions here.

Is the military another workplace, another job, and so simply another site for struggles over equal employment opportunity? This argument is often put forward by military women themselves, who are not much attended to in these debates and who resent the constraints upon their roles, and the consequences for promotion. It connects with other equality arguments, including for a gender-equitable sharing of political and decision-making power in state institutions, especially one so rich and powerful.

As a presidential candidate, Bill Clinton argued that the US military should be more democratic and representative (D'Amico, 1994). Should militaries be representative of those they claim to defend, and so roughly reflective of their state's population? Should they reflect changes in the wider society, including in gender relations, and notions of appropriate roles for men and women outside the military? Or are they a 'special institution', in terms of masculinity, or male power, or state power? Military masculinism is closely associated with high politics, power politics and 'men's business'. Might its effective functioning depend on (its own) perceptions of exclusivity? Does this have something to do with the oft-quoted 'cohesion' that militaries reportedly need to function? Is it to do with 'the manliness of war'?

There are also questions here to do with the connections between militarism and masculinity and violence, and between militarism and citizenship, touched on earlier, and taken up further later in this chapter.

Resisting women soldiers

Much of the anti-feminist resistance to women as soldiers, and especially as combatants, focuses on the women themselves, and their supposed weaknesses or disrupting influence. So the list runs that women can't fight, they are not 'up to it', they lack upper body strength, they get PMT, they have monthlies, they get pregnant, they are emotional, they break down under fire. Brian Mitchell, author of *Weak Link: the Feminization of the American Military* (1989) claims that the heroism of women is exaggerated, and that the army covers for those women who can't cope. Reporting an incident in Panama involving two women truck drivers caught in the crossfire, Mitchell remarks 'None of the [Army] spokesmen denied the women had cried before being relieved of their duties' (1990: 2). Real men/real soldiers don't cry? Mitchell also accused the army of denying 'problems' such as pregnancy, single parenthood and 'fraternisation'.

Meanwhile, supporters and governments quote military assessments and ways around difficulties. Rather than closing down debate, they ask, for example 'What are the needs of and issues raised by a pregnant soldier?' (Carroll and Hall, 1993: 21).

Concern over 'practical difficulties' might disguise profound disquiet at the notion of women trained and armed to kill, and at the challenge to gender relations signalled by this image. Why does it matter so much? What is at stake here? womens' rights? gender power? the military? masculinism? the prerogative state as a site of political power?

The depth of feeling reflects strong investments in social understandings about appropriate roles for men and women, and about women's nature. Resistance can also be framed in terms of a desire to protect women. Then-Brigadier of the Returned and Services League of Australia, Alf Garland, argued 'I would never want my wife, my mother, my sister or my daughter to have to do the sort of things that I have seen in combat'. (Though many others do not want male partners, brother or sons to, either.) He goes on to argue that women are 'too valuable to Australia' to be put in the line of fire. 'Women are too precious. Women are the cradle of civilisation. You need women to populate. Men are expendable, but women aren't' (*Canberra Times*, 2 March 1989). Women are nationalist wombs, with their own—different—job to do for the state.

The distinctions between combat and support roles are hard enough to maintain (and the boundaries keep shifting, according to administrative rule and military and political contingencies). But there seems to be something particularly disturbing to many men in the image of a woman armed with a gun. The Chief of the NZ Defence Force, Vice-Admiral Somerford Teagle, says he does not oppose women in combat roles so long as these do not involve hand-to-hand fighting. 'I can accept the idea of women's involvement in the more clinical aspects—pushing a button marked "kill" or behind a bank of computers—but I guess I am not ready to face the prospect of a woman leading a bayonet charge' (quoted in Phare, 1993: 5).

Is it 'women' that are at issue here, or rather their effects on military men? Critics suggest women will undermine cohesion; men will be more protective of them, and so take more risks; men will fight at more cost, in fear of women being taken prisoner; men will be ashamed to be fighting alongside women, or think that their (less-liberated) enemies or allies will see them as weak and feminised by association; women soldiers will send messages of desperation to the other side. Do these resistances reflect men's fears, including the fear of 'losing their manhood' if women fight for or with them?

> War is man's work. Biological convergence on the battlefield would not only be dissatisfying in terms of what women could do, but it would be an enormous psychological distraction for the male who wants to think that he's fighting for that woman somewhere behind, not up there in the same foxhole with him. It tramples the male ego. When you get right down to it, you have to protect the manliness of war (Former Marine Corps Commandant William Barrows quoted in Williams, 1989: 9–10).

Why is the manliness of war diminished if women participate equally? Is combat still for many men the ultimate test of masculinity, including in defensive assertion against women's childbirthing powers? Why was General Norman Schwarzkopf, commander of the US–Allied forces in the Gulf War, afterwards named Father of the Year?

Feminists on women in combat

'What could be more profoundly gendered than a space said to contain nothing but men, than an activity described as performed by men only?' (Cooke, 1993: 177).

Feminists are deeply divided in these debates, in their under-standings of both gender power and the politics of change, in a mirror of differences over women and peace (chapter 6). A whole set of arguments revolve around the connections between masculinity and militarism, and between militarism and citizenship. The US National Organisation for Women (NOW), while opposed to the draft (conscription) in principle, argued that in the event of a draft, women should be equally liable for call-up (Jones, 1984). Their reasons were associated with equal employment opportunity and good industrial practice (and here there would have to be particular reason to exempt the military). Especially they argued that women's continued exclusion from the right and responsibility to risk their lives for their country reduced them to the status of second-class citizens. This is part of a liberal-feminist argument that sees women's differences used to keep women out of public power, seeks their equal admission to the state and an end to the male monopoly on legitimate violence (Jones, 1984)

Cynthia Fuchs Epstein argues against privileging women's special nature or learnings as women, and rejects special protections for women as always resulting in diminished opportunities. 'Equality for women may mean that some women will become warriors, and some will inevitably die in combat. That is tragic, but it is right so long as men must also die this way' (1991: 422).

There are complex issues here. Sarah Ruddick suggests that 'Since men have created battle and devised the rules of participation, they justifiably bear its burden' (Ruddick, 1983: 474)—though we need to ask which men devise the rules and who actually pay the costs. Yet leaving to men the exclusive right of state violence reinforces both masculinist and militarist constructions of the citizen, which penalise and might endanger women (Ruddick, 1983: 476). Nira Yuval-Davis argues that '[e]mpowering women to play global policemen on equal footing with men is not what feminists (at least not what socialist, anti-racist feminists) should be doing' (1991: 64).

Disrupting the usual men-military and women-protected binary might open up more space to challenge patriarchal power. There are arguments in terms of military women's challenging gender stereotypes, and demonstrating that women can do anything that men can do. We might respond by asking why women would wish to do everything that men currently do; and try to shift the arguments back to when, if ever, anyone should be conscripted or directed by the state to kill on its behalf.

Women in the gulf war

Many women were caught in the Gulf War. Kuwaiti women found the war had come to them, and it came to Iraqi women, some of whom had been mobilised, including in the military. Hundreds of thousands of women from South-East Asia, mostly labour migrants working as domestic servants, were caught in the crossfire. Women were used to mark the boundaries and to carry lessons of hierarchy and status. So the veiled Arab woman who was not even allowed a driving licence (in Saudi Arabia) was contrasted with the liberated US woman tank driver—suddenly approved of by many who had previously expressed strong doubts about the ability or the desirability of women warriors (Enloe, 1990b).

There were 32 340 US servicewomen in the Gulf War, where fifteen women died. For the first time, US officials and the media spoke routinely of 'our service men and women'. The high visibility of state women warriors not only displayed soldier women, but soldier mothers, as young women kissed their babies goodbye, and went off to fight. Some men stayed behind to do the waiting. Debates about fighting women intensified when two US military women were taken prisoner. One released prisoner initially denied that she was raped, for fear of her experience being used against women wishing to fight (Enloe, 1993: 189). At the same time, other US servicewomen began to speak about rapes in the Gulf by their own men, after early reluctance and pressure to remain silent and so preserve the Gulf War as 'a good war' (Enloe, 1993: 191). Danger comes to women in many forms, and often at or close to home. Chivalry and 'protection' never guarantee safety.

Sex and the military

Sexual harassment is an ongoing problem in the US and many other state militaries, now taken more seriously by military administrators for fear of losing too many expensively trained military women and with feminist lobbying in the wider society. A recent Pentagon study reported that 64 per cent of women in the US military say they have been sexually harassed, though many feared reporting it lest there be reprisals or 'unpleasantness'. Embarrassing publicity emerged in the form of the Tailhook 91 when young women were harassed by drunken young officers (Stone, 1993). In Australia a 1987 Australian Defence Force survey found one-quarter of defence-force women regarded sexual harassment as a problem, and more recent incidents and public inquiries saw the military admit to the problem and to not taking it seriously enough.

Sexual harassment is a highly controversial issue, carrying many tensions and ambivalences, as the Anita Hill–Clarence Thomas hearings in the US demonstrated (Morrison, 1992). Women organising and feminist thinking has provided a new language and consciousness of these as well as other 'private' sexual secrets. They also provide evidence of gender relations as power relations and especially the inscribing of sex and sexuality onto women's bodies as objects for and available to men; these relations and inscriptions are part of the construction of everyday compulsory heterosexuality and the reproduction of gender relations, inside and outside the military.

There is a move here from women and gender relations in the military to sexual politics in the military, a source of much contest, confusion and anxiety. If the military is supposed to 'make a man' of you, what kind of man is 'made'? And what happens when some of the soldiers are women? It seems that the masculinity cultivated by most militaries is compulsory or hegemonic masculinity, so dangerous for women, and for sexual-minority men.

Military training and discourse glorify men's bonding and sacrifice for one's mates. This raises questions about how to make young men fight and maybe kill or die. 'Soldiers fight for their pals, not for God, or principle' (Garvey and DiIulio, 1993: 3). What builds solidarity, obedience and sacrifice, and how are soldiers motivated to fight? 'Cohesion' and military morale appear related to male bonding and macho behaviour (Kohn, 1993). Are unresolved and manipulated sexualities a part of it? How then to make young women fight?

The disciplining of military bodies uses certain kinds of masculinity that might make connections between officers and men, and across race and class. Military bodies are both there and denied, feared and desired (Duckworth, 1993). Shaved hair, uniform, control, submission and obedience are part of the institutionalisation and depersonalisation of male recruits. So, too, women's bodies are dressed and disciplined in different ways, including attention to make-up and modification to uniforms to mark soldier women as women still (Enloe, 1988; Williams, 1989). Initiation rituals, bastardisation and feminisation of newer or weaker male recruits, disdain of anyone seen as wimpy, forced 'surrogate heterosexual' sex where those performing penetrative sex on other men would probably deny that they are homosexual, all mark and sexualise bodies and boundaries.

Gay military sex

Official and often popular horror of homosexuality runs alongside intense homo-erotic currents in the barracks and on the ships.

Military men live and train in very close proximity. So the boundary between homo-social and homosexual behaviour is both transgressed and policed. Certain forms of 'play' may only be permissible if the possibility of homosexual desire is not admitted. Many male soldiers who oppose gay soldiers may fear that they might become the object of male desire, and not its purveyor.

Debates over gay men in the military are at least as fierce as debates over women soldiers. The arguments against women in the military are very similar to those against homosexuals in the military. Yet the two debates are mainly kept apart, and conducted as if they are exclusive of one another, as if the debate is either about 'women' or about gay men. So lesbians were practically invisible in the 1993 Rand Report on 'Sexual Orientation and US military Personnel Policy' (D'Amico, 1994).

In 1941 the US military employed psychiatrists to screen out gay men who might 'break down' under fire (Berube, 1990). Some 9000 US soldiers were discharged in World War 2, though manpower shortages later in the war led to efforts to 'rehabilitate' rather than dismiss them. Since then there has been a rigorous exclusion policy. Between 1980 and 1990 16 919 US servicepeople were dishonourably discharged for being gay (Shilts, 1993; D'Amico, 1994).

Despite their usual invisibility in debates about gay soldiers, lesbians have been subjected to more surveillance and punishment in the military than gay men have. In Britain, women made up 40 per cent of all those dismissed for homosexuality between 1978 and 1982, but only about 5 per cent of military personnel (Enloe, 1988). In 1987, one in every 1053 US military men was discharged under the exclusion policy, while one in every 500 women was discharged. There were also rather different rates of discharge for different services, with discharge especially high for women in the marines (0.33 per cent as against 0.4 per cent of men, D'Amico, 1994: 17)

Some women, and men, might be tempted to use 'homosexuality' to get out of the military, but, until very recently, the dreadful cost—in humiliation at the proceedings to difficulties in finding employment—makes this unlikely. 'Lesbian' is a problematic category. Some see military women as lesbians on the basis of their presumed unfemininity simply by joining up. 'Lesbian' is also an accusation that is used to keep women in their place, and available to men. It is a sanction or punishment for not 'coming across', and so is used to extract sexual favours. Military women are caught in a familiar double bind: lesbian if they refuse sex or sluts if they do not. Predatory homophobic male sexual behaviour polices women as much as the military institution and its rules and procedures do.

Why are women's bodies and certain kinds of sexuality or sexual behaviour seen as so dangerous or so disruptive to the military? How do these understandings change over time? Thirty years ago in the US there were furious arguments about racial integration and panics about black soldiers, seen as over-sexed and as disease carriers, with fears about privacy and group cohesion. These debates are echoed in anti-gay sentiments nowadays.

Some states, however, have made significant moves towards ending discrimination on the basis of sexual preference or identification. The Netherlands was the first western state to eliminate the policy of excluding homosexuals in 1974. Sweden followed in 1976, Denmark in 1977, Norway in 1979 and Spain in 1985. In the early 1990s Canada, Australia and Israel did so. In some cases this change flowed on from decriminalising homosexuality in the wider society, though in others there was a time lag, while the military retained exemptions and restrictions no longer permitted outside. Shifts and challenges in society and sexual politics included rising gay-rights movements and anti-discrimination advocacy. Strategic moments saw high-ranking military men and women 'coming out', as did a highly decorated US Vietnam veteran Colonel Margarethe Cammermeyer, whose declaration in a security clearance interview that she was a lesbian was followed by an 'honourable' discharge (Cammermeyer, 1994).

During the US presidential campaign in 1992, candidate Bill Clinton declared he would remove both the exclusion of women from combat, and the gay-exclusion rule. The second especially generated fierce controversy, and a series of Senate Armed Services Committee hearings. The unsatisfactory 'don't ask, don't tell' compromise prevented the official 'hunting out' of gay or lesbian military personnel, but also effectively silenced or closeted them (Doherty, 1993). During the hearings, the suitability or reliability of gay soldiers (seen as male, and feminised) were debated alongside notions of cohesion and morale. So too were 'privacy' concerns, including suggestions that four separate sets of toilet facilities might be required. This again shows sexual unease and heterosexual male fears of becoming an object of desire. In 1993 a US ABC news poll found 57 per cent of men supported the exclusion of gays from the military, while 57 per cent of women opposed it. Women inside and outside the military were more tolerant or less fearful of 'homosexuals' than the equivalent men were.

Recognising homophobia as a military problem, the Netherlands has gone furthest to put in place a 'zero-tolerance' policy, which makes it a punishable offence to discriminate on the basis of sexual orientation. Efforts are made to educate recruits towards non-discrimination, and provide advocacy and support within the organisation for gay and lesbian soldiers (D'Amico, 1994). The Netherlands military is condemned by some for its 'feminisation' and the distance it has moved from old masculinist and homophobic styles. But it may be that different kinds of masculinity or soldiering are required in modern militaries, whether more rational and technological, or more 'feminised' and cooperative in the peacekeeping and other responsibilities of today (Enloe, 1987; Cohn, 1993). It may be going too far, however, to suggest that in this new world, where 'humanitarian' intervention and peacekeeping are part of many militaries' jobs, increasing numbers of women and more inclusive policies within the military and the foreign policy elite 'may actually assist the United States in adapting to the more female approach to foreign policy required by the new world order' (Howes and Stevenson, 1993: 217).

An anti-militarist feminism?

'How then is a woman who is both anti-militarist and feminist to respond to women's claims to equal opportunity and the right to fight?' (Ruddick, 1983: 471).

While many feminists would support women's rights to make career and citizen choices that might include military work, and argue for equal opportunities for women in any workplace, the loaded associations of militaries with violence and the most coercive aspects of the state make this a most difficult issue to pursue. It is further complicated by a first-world–third-world, and now in part second-world, confrontation between those feminists who politic from safer terrains, and those who have been or are associated with struggles in which resistant or revolutionary force appear the only possible responses.

Liberal feminists and others resigned to the necessity for state militaries in existing international relations struggle to come to terms with women's place in the military, and with the high politics of defence and 'security' more generally; hence, Jean Elshain's provocative suggestion (1987) that the good mother and the good soldier share certain characteristics, which many anti-militarist feminists have trouble with. She seeks to domesticate rather than deny the appeal of nationalism and patriotism by advocating the identity of the chastened patriot and a move from sacrifice to responsibility.

Judith Stiehm (1989), in the face of the dangers to women of the protector/protected dichotomy and many women's desire to join state militaries, suggests a shift to citizen–defender, to defuse the aggressive and coercive associations of 'national defence' and to move beyond the gendered associations of soldiering. Urging equal roles, rights and responsibilities becomes part of a strategy for degendering military service and citizenship.

Anti–militarist feminists unable to support such projects focus more on critiques of militarism and the culture that legitimises the use of organised force to resolve conflicts. They stress that political, national and identity security is gendered; as are citizenship practices and militarised or war cultures. Attending to women's different experiences of militarism and political violence also reveals that many women suffer because of their association with particular kinds of identity politics, and not only because of their gender or their membership of aggressive or victim states. Contemporary nationalisms and exclusivist identity politics take their toll in inter-group relations, and often confine and exploit or attack and abuse women. So it is necessary to attempt a more inclusive and gendered definition of security, in terms of the different threats and dangers that confront women, children and men in different political situations.

Attending to different women's experiences of insecurity and danger, and to their attempts to build a safer, more secure world, also widens our definition of security to include material security in economic and environmental terms. It reveals a complex inter-relation between militarism, war, impoverishment and unequal distribution of resources and unequal life choices. These material insecurities are the focus of the next section.

PART 3

THE INTERNATIONAL SEXUAL DIVISION OF LABOUR

8

Women and gender in the international political economy

Women have been largely invisible in debates about states and markets, despite considerable feminist and other writings on women in development (WID), and on women's work in particular states. Women are largely invisible in different paradigms in the international political economy (IPE). Is this because women aren't in the IPE? Alternatively, do women and men play similar roles in and are they affected in similar ways by the IPE? If not, an ungendered IPE is partial at best.

This chapter draws on feminist literature to reveal a gendered IPE, in processes of globalisation, restructuring, labour migration and the changing international division of labour. It interrogates the nature of 'women's work', and brings WID perspectives into the wider IPE debates. It pursues a focus on development, environment and reproductive rights, exploring transnational women's organising in these areas.

An international political economy

In the postwar years, the discipline of International Relations largely excluded 'economics' from its intellectual view and territory. But after the oil shocks of the early 1970s, as state governments and organisations of states such as the G7 focused increasingly on markets as well as states, IPE was reluctantly admitted into the discipline.

IR textbooks usually identify three major 'schools' of IPE—liberal, nationalist and Marxist—but they rarely make women visible or take gender relations or feminist scholarship seriously (Tickner, 1992; R. Pettman, 1991).

Liberalism draws on the familiar model of the rational individual man, driven by self-interest and competitive, in this case, for profit. Liberals argue that wealth-making works best when state-makers let the market flourish and support a separation of states and markets, politics and economics. This free-market rhetoric is evident in the current dismantling of tariffs and restrictive trade practices, in the General Agreement on Tariffs and Trade (GATT) and the North American Free Trade Agreement (NAFTA), for example, and in deregulating banking and finance. Within the growth of the world market, states are no longer willing or able to effect management and control of their economies, but function more as a facilitator or agent of globalisation (Mittelman, 1994; Jenson, 1995). There are tensions here between growing liberalisation of state economies, and continued use of state sovereignty to organise the political relations between states.

Nationalist or mercantilist IPE sees the state as central, and seeks to harness the market for state wealth, power and security. This model, too, is highly competitive, but competition here is between states, to secure the national interest in classic power-politics terms. This view supports protectionism, and reacts fearfully to the US's declining economic position and loss of hegemony, anxiously watching Japan's growth and admission to the G7 as a world powerbroker.

The liberal and nationalist models rest on particular notions of the nature of man, states and markets which are class, culture and gender specific, informed by models of human nature that are masculinist. They ignore fundamental divisions and exploitative relations between capital and labour, men and women, developed and underdeveloped states, which make a mockery of 'free competition'. The nationalist model is a form of Realism in political economy. States are the central units of analysis, so there is little emphasis on people, let alone women; hence, power differences within states—including gender relations—disappear. Both models are profoundly gendered in their notions of power, wealth and the state. Both ignore the vast amount of women's labour—in domestic and subsistence production, in reproduction and community care—motivated not by competition and the profit motive, but by family, local responsibility and 'care' (Tickner, 1992).

Dissident views in IR on the IPE have recognised inequalities between states and regions, for example, between the first and third worlds, the north and south, the haves and the have-nots (Gurtov, 1991); or have gone further to trace structural inequalities and domination relations (Cox, 1987; Gill and Law, 1988; Murphy and Tooze, 1991). There is much debate about different ways of mapping the world, for example, as core and periphery, about the nature of the world system, and the relations between capital and states.

Structural analyses, often Marxist or neo-Marxist, moved beyond both statist IR and states' political economy to identify deep faultlines within and between states, and plot unequal relations of domination, subordination and exploitation that characterise contemporary capitalism. A key factor in structuring the IPE is how states organise their productive relations, and the emergence of a global capitalist political economy. European expansion and imperialism integrated the rest of the world into the system dominated by Western-European, then US, capital and facilitated the exploitation of land, labour and resources in the colonies/third world for the benefit of the rich countries (Lazarus, 1991; Quijano and Wallerstein, 1992).

All states, first, third and the old second world, now in transition, are embedded within global structures and relations, despite different but increasingly similar ways of organising their productive relations. Immanuel Wallerstein (1974) and others track the emergence of this system over the last 500 years. Stephen Gill (1991) prefers a notion of 'world history', and traces shifts in hegemony within a global history shaped by a process of capital accumulation that pre-dates Wallerstein's view. Gill focuses on elites which organise production in order to appropriate a surplus from labour, and identifies coalitions of states and classes which include elites in peripheral states and in socialist and ex-socialist states. Here power and wealth come together, though not without struggle and not beyond challenge. Further explorations attend to the sexual division of labour, or the connections between productive and reproductive labour.

Gender in the IPE?

Some world systems theorists do make women visible. Thus Smith and Wallerstein (1992) move beyond the male breadwinner. In their attempts to make sense of different wages paid in different parts of the world for the same kinds of work, they look to households, including men's, women's and childrens' labour pooled as part of a family's income-earning strategies. But still, gender relations as power relations are not pursued here.

Many aspects of the IPE do not make any sense if we do not gender the account. An ungendered IPE cannot tell us why women are overwhelmingly and everywhere the poorest of the poor, nor why modernisation and development have frequently undermined the lives and status of women. Nor can it explain the current global trend increasing women's employment relative to men's, albeit in temporary, casualised and largely unprotected work. Why do transnational companies increasingly exploit women's labour made cheap (Enloe, 1992) in export-processing zones (EPZs) and cities of third- and first-world countries? Why is women's labour a key element to the 'new' international division of labour? Why does patriarchy, which preceeded capitalism, continue in different forms in 'development', and in socialist and now transition states? Why hasn't women's increasing participation in paid work in many different sectors and states led to equality in the workforce, or to overcoming oppression and exploitation, or relieved most women of their reproductive and domestic labour roles?

A gender-obscuring IPE cannot explain the continued sex segregation of state economies, or the unequal and different impact of the IPE on women compared with men, including those in the same class/country. A concept of labour that theorises from men's work but does not account for women's, ignores the latter's unpaid work in reproduction, including the maintainence and refurbishment of the current labourforce and the raising of the next one, as well as many women's subsistence, farm and informal-sector work, and their unpaid or under-paid community and service work.

Feminist analyses make women visible in the IPE, take account of women's and men's gendered experiences of work, and rethink the international division of labour as a sexual division of labour. They demonstrate that we are all affected by globalisation and the workings of the world market. We cannot make sense of women's everyday lives and choices, or the lack of them, without attention to political economy and the international (Peterson, 1995).

Globalisation and power

Thinking about the IPE means thinking about 'the relations between power and the division of labour' (Mittelman, 1994: 427). The framework for running international capitalist relations after World

War 2 was set up at the Bretton Woods conference, and included international institutions such as the International Monetary Fund (IMF) and the World Bank. Its first decades were dominated by US military and economic power, often called hegemonic (though different users meant very different things when they use this term).

US hegemony was soon threatened by European especially West German recovery, and the growth of new centres of industrial power in East Asia. Some states in the old margins joined the new assembly line (Nash, 1983). The rise of the oil producing states of the Organisation of Petroleum Exporting Countries (OPEC) as international players and a series of economic shocks in the 1970s gave rise to demands for a new international economic order, but the materialising new order was one of world crisis and spectacular third-world debt. This debt placed the IMF and World Bank in a position to dictate terms, or conditionality, in return for funds—needed also in many states for ongoing militarisation and state regime defence. So, through the 1980s, increasing numbers of states were subject to structural adjustment policies, which required the liberalisation and deregulation of their economies, privatisation of state enterprises, reduction of expenditure especially in 'non-productive' social areas, and a focus on export-orientated growth. These were often accompanied by rising unemployment, high inflation, severe reduction of life supporting systems, and growing militarisation and repression as states faced protest movements and organised opposition (Sen and Grown, 1987; Afshar and Dennis, 1992; Brand, 1993).

In the 1990s, ex-state socialist Europe liberalised and 'marketised' (Moghadam, 1994b), with suggestions that parts of Eastern Europe might be becoming 'the new south' (Przeworski, 1991: 91). A feature there and in other areas especially in Latin America was democratisation, though often faltering and notable for its rhetorical 'negative rights' in the face of growing social inequalities (Waylen, 1994). But restructuring has profoundly affected the first world too, especially in terms of liberalisation of trade, deregulation of finance and banking, and moves to 'roll back the state'.

Globalisation means many things (Robertson, 1992). In terms of the IPE, it signals a remarkable mobility of capital, a spread of production processes over many different locations in different states, and a globalised labourforce, as transnational corporations move to cheap labour, in export-processing zones in South-East Asia, for example (known as *maquiladpras* in Mexico and the Caribbean; Marchand, 1996; Runyan, 1996); it also signals labour moving to cities and EPZs, and across state borders. Transnational corporations (TNCs) have also moved into Ireland, Scotland and poorer regions in the European heartlands.

Production is increasingly fragmented and internationalised, as different stages take place in different states, with each particular stage reduced to monotonous, repetitive, 'unskilled' work, in which workers are endlessly disposable and substitutable (K. Ward, 1988; Nash and Fernandez-Kelly, 1983). These shifts and turns reflect the extraordinary mobility of TNCs, of technology and capital, making nonsense of traditional IR understandings of sovereignty and state borders.

The boundaries between the first world and the third, and now the second, and between core and periphery, have become complex and fluid. Often now it is racialised, migrant, minority men and especially women who do work in the core countries, especially their declining inner cities and old industrial areas, very like work being done in some third-world countries, in textiles, clothing and electronics, for example (Enloe, 1992; 1993). Now there is a 'Third World in the midst of the First' (Mitter, 1986: 80), and very rich elites, and often a significant middle class, in many third-world states, too—making mapping and naming of the worlds very difficult.

Migration has become a global labour system, where borders that have been effectively dismantled for free movement of capital become ways of segmenting and exploiting labour. 'Border enforcement emerges as a mechanism facilitating the extraction of surplus value by assigning a status of formal or informal powerlessness to foreign workers generally and criminality to illegal immigrants' (Sassen-Koob, 1983: 183).

Migrant labour is now a key component of the changing international division of labour. The threads between the IPE and the state labour market, between restructuring and cutbacks to welfare and social-right provisioning, generate crises that are often blamed on conspicuously different workers, especially immigrant workers. Scapegoating encourages calls for restrictions on the entry, residence and employment rights of migrant workers. Citizenship politics are racialised, making the super-exploited minority worker even more insecure (Pettman, 1995a).

In many states, economic hardship and state legitimation crises prompt mobilisation of new movements, including the new right/new racism in France and Germany, for example, and rising fundamentalisms in many states, including the Christian right in the US. The IPE reconstitutes identities and citizenship rights along with labour and productive relations. In these circumstances, it is impossible to separate foreign and domestic politics, or the economic from the political or social. This necessitates a rethinking of notions of state, sovereignty and security in IR. It demonstrates, too, that the global political economy segments the changing international division of labour along nationalised, racialised and ethnicised as well as class and gender lines.

The changing international division of labour

Since the 1980s, labour deregulation, increasingly competitive trade and capital's search for cheap labour have generated a global spread of flexible labour practices and an increasing feminisation of labour. Swasti Mitter's *Common Fate, Common Bond* (1986) highlights the global phenomenon of disposable labour, especially women's labour, as capital seeks a 'flexible workforce, undermining organised labour, casualising employment, including increasing rise of part-time and temporary work in the west, leading to the creation of a largely female marginalised workforce in the first and third world, and a core of skilled mainly male workers' (p.139). In these circumstances, increasing numbers of women in paid work do not mean more job security. 'Casualisation' means a shift away from full-time, state regulated and often unionised labour, reducing job rights and disorganising labour (Mitter, 1994). With increasing flexibility and outwork, some women prefer to work from home, but often it means piecemeal payments, very poor conditions and pay, isolation and vulnerablity, including vulnerability to sexual harassment and other unfair demands by middlemen and employers.

The domestication of women

Maria Mies (1986) draws a line between the White Man (elite white men) and women/colonised people/nature, all of whom are feminised. She argues that capital accumulation depends on the systematic exploitation of women, the colonies/underdeveloped regions and nature, using colonising divisions that form the dynamic and destructive system of domination relations. Women, the colonies and nature all become 'natural resources' to be exploited, raw materials for the ongoing accumulation process of capitalist patriarchy.

Mies asks what unites and what divides women in overdeveloped and underdeveloped classes, countries and regions. Like other structuralists, she sees overdevelopment and underdevelopment as related, with the growth and wealth of the former directly dependent on and generated by the underdevelopment of the latter. No part of the world is unaffected by the growth of the world market. This counters 'the limited view of cultural relativism which claims that women are divided by culture worldwide, whereas, in fact, they are both divided and connected by commodity relations' (1986: 3), by their positioning in the global economy.

Mies traces connections between the rise of capitalism and the intensification of both colonisation and housewifisation, beginning with the European witch-hunts and other attacks on women's control of their own bodies and livelihoods. Crucial was the defining of women as housewives, as dependants, against the wage worker, the proletariat, the breadwinner, reproducing the binary public/private, and often the formal/informal economy, too. Developing in the west, women-as-dependants were transferred to the colonies by colonial officials', companies' and missionaries' treatment of colonial women. The notion was consolidated by anticolonial nationalist movements, and by postcolonial governments and development planners' focus on men as the productive workers and heads of households.

So spread 'the specific modern form of forced labour, namely that of the housewife' (Mies et al., 1988: 9). The housewife takes different forms in different cultures, states and classes. Housewifisation means for midddle-class women in first and third worlds that part of their work is consumerism, to maintain the market. Their consumption involves them in complicit relations with the over-exploitation of cheap, now increasingly feminised, labour.

Regardless of class, women everywhere are vulnerable to gender-specific violence, which Mies and others see as formative in domesticating women. They expose the role of violence against women—by individual men and by states—not only to secure women's oppression, but also as intrinsic to the mechanism of primitive accumulation, through direct coercion, to gain control of women's bodies, labour and productive capacities (Omvedt, 1990). This domestication of women (Rogers, 1981) guarantees men's sex right and excludes women from public power, including public economic power.

Domestic labour/women's work

The sexual division of labour continues to marginalise, privatise and exploit women's bodies and labour. There have been fierce debates about domestic labour, and the subsidy that domestic and other unpaid women's work is to men, capital and the state (Molyneux, 1979). Women's work, read as housework, becomes a form of bonded, unpaid work, where her body as well as her labour is given over to others' use. Here 'the housewife' is one side of the appropriation and control of women's bodies, where sexuality and violence is the (related) other. Indeed, much of women's work is sexualised and/or is the business of pleasing men.

A reading of the political economy of women's work means examining ideologies of femininity, marriage and motherhood, which construct and appropriate women's labour in domestic, reproductive and caring work as a labour of love, not work at all. The marriage contract is a work contract (Oakley, 1974). 'In the case of men, labour power becomes a commodity; in the case of women, the whole person becomes a commodity' (Bennholdt-Thomsen in Mies et al., 1988: 121).

The split between men's work and women's work is a gendered division of labour. Within it, certain kinds of work are routinely excluded from notions of productive work, and are literally not counted as well as often not paid for (Waring, 1988; Beneria, 1992). 'Women's work' is universal, even though its particular shape and scope varies over time, place, class, caste, culture and lifecycle.

The gendered nature of domestic work and wage labour involves the dichotomies men/women and public/private. Even though large numbers of women also go 'out' to work, work is primarily associated with the man, and home with the woman. Women are contained within ideologies or discourses of motherhood, marriage and femininity, disguising the work that women do as 'naturally' women's work.

Ideological constructions of women's work link closely with ideas about masculinity and femininity, gendered social practices and social control. Ideologies of control, seclusion, honour and shame in different African, Asian and Middle Eastern states determine women's mobility and access to paid work and productive resources (Afshar and Agarwal, 1989). In South Asia, for example, many women experience freedom from surveillance in inverse proportion to their class or caste economic power. Women from the poorest classes are 'free' to work outside their homes, but are then vulnerable to abuse from other men, as unprotected and therefore inferior women (Ram, 1989). In certain Islamic states or families, the requirements of purdah adversely affect women's access to economic resources or outside employment (Shaheed in Afshar and Agarwal, 1989). Those who are subject to purdah and also need some income are therefore forced to take 'outwork' (which is 'inwork' for women), and are vulnerable to the kinds of exploitation associated with dispersed, fragmented, isolated workplaces. They are either acutely dependent on male kin, and lack any control over their earnings; or face the dangers of communicating with male non-kin and the suspicions that may generate among their 'protectors'.

This is a reminder of the difficulties of separating out neat topics or academic territories for analysis, and the inadequacy of partial and sexless/masculinised models, which dominate in the IPE and the world of work. For while seclusion, chaperonage and segregation are part of the cultural disciplining of women's sexuality and the policing of women's bodies as part of communal or nationalist border patrolling, they also inform constructions of femininity and masculinity that underpin 'women's work' and the more general domestication of women.

So, too, various forms of 'familialism' pressure western women to stay or return to the home, for example, after wars when women's labour is no longer needed, and perhaps now, when nostalgia and right-wing politics around 'the family' valorise 'traditional' gender roles (Leslie, 1993). These ideologies affect social and family practices beyond the west. So in the transition states, where women's labour is discarded in the new market economy and rising unemployment, the nuclear family and the man as worker are growing in favour. In third-world states too, household structure and gender roles are decisive in determining if women go 'out' to work, for example, female-headed family form is a far more significant determining factor than economic need or education levels of women in a recent study of Mexican cities (Chant, 1991).

Ideologies of familialism and gendered roles can also be swung across into factory and other labour, to maintain divisions within the labourforce and to reduce women's wages (C. Lee, 1993; O. Lee, 1993). Ideologies of femininity play a role in the commodification of women's labour, in sex segregating the workforce, and especially in making women's labour cheap.

Women's labour as cheap labour

Women's work cannot be reduced to domestic and reproductive labour, crucial as that is in social as well as physical reproduction. Women are also concentrated in poorly paid work, part-time work and outwork, in the contradictory space between productive and reproductive labour, because of their social construction as dependants. Women are disadvantaged in the labour market because of their double or triple load, and because their often primary or sole home and family care responsibilities restrict the kind of work and income they can get.

'The boundaries between women's formal, informal, and household labour are much more permeable for women than they are for men' (Ward, 1993: 54). Women do different kinds of work at different times, moving from paid work to self-employment and in and out of the informal sector, depending on age, social status, skills, luck, contacts, patronage and the effects of the changing IPE.

Women's labour is also constructed along gendered lines, even where it is paid work. Social constructions of femininity and women's work also underpin the process by which women's labour is commodified as cheap labour (Enloe, 1992). Across very different cultures and states, women are seen as temporary workers, filling in before marriage, or as subsidiary workers, working for extra money, even when they are the only income earners, and with more than one-third of households in the world now female-headed. Women are constructed as good with their hands, hence good at sewing and food preparation, for example, and naturally good at caring, service and support work. Much of women's work is classified as unskilled, even where it is classified as skilled if men do it. Women are projected as patient, submissive, and obedient, less likely to unionise or strike, even though employers and governments in many states forcibly prevent women from organising.

Some employers use small factories or homeworking to avoid concentration of workers in large enough numbers to organise. Control is exercised by piecemeal payments, pressuring women's production and output. There are contradictions here, as employers balance up the dangers of a concentrated workforce against need for close supervision for 'quality control' and convenience (Hutchinson, 1992). This is a reminder of the need to look at the particular productive relations and workplaces in each case.

Shifts in the IPE and related reconstructions of women's work can be seen in the growth of 'pink-collar' work, especially in the transnational information industry. In states such as Barbados, formerly small numbers of women did clerical work and were 'ladies'. Now, many more—reorganised as 'girls'—work in routine and monotonous collation and information-processing tasks, which come to resemble the old factory assembly line (Freeman, 1993).

Women are the vast majority of workers in export-processing zones, where their youth and gender are used alongside coercive and anti-union regulation to keep them in their place (Enloe, 1990a; Nam, 1994). They are exploited as casual, cheap and temporary workers, and often either the firms move on or the women are moved on. But there is evidence that TNCs might provide some better conditions of work than local factory, sweatshop or outwork (Lim, 1983; Standing, 1992). For some, for example, young Muslim women from rural Malaysia, factory work helps support family and brings choices, money of their own, and new friendships and solidarities, even in the face of constraints and dangers. At the same time, their leaving home to work can generate anxiety among parents. It can lead to the young women being seen as disreputable, reducing status at home and damaging marriage chances.

In some circumstances, women and children experience the family firm or home workplace as even more exploitative, amounting to 24-hour-a-day surveillance and control. Other families operate as cooperative and congenial production as well as consumption units. Women's vulnerability also varies with different sectors. They, and men and children, doing plantation work are among the worst paid and most exploited workers in the world.

On the backs of women and children

Structural adjustment and conditionality (the conditions imposed by financial institutions such as the World Bank in return for loans), noted earlier, amount to a transfer of wealth from poor to rich states. They also effect a transfer of many social costs from public to private sectors, from state to household, and from paid to unpaid labour. These transfers are especially damaging to women.

State employment policies affect women differently, because public-sector employment is a major source of women's employment, especially in education, health and social-security areas. Cuts in these areas directly reduce women's employment. Global restructuring is presently being carried out at the expense of women and children'. Structural adjustment policies that reduce social-security expenditure and abolish food subsidies force women, especially poor women, to make an 'invisible readjustment' (UNICEF, 1995) to compensate for the reduction of often already inadequate support. They create a crisis in reproduction that terrorises poorer women and children (Afshar and Dennis, 1992; Imam, 1994). States' attempts to promote export-orientated growth disorganise and feminise the labourforce, removing any protection from casual workers, who become super-exploitable and expendable labour.

One overall effect is the feminisation of poverty, or the global impoverishing of women and their children, though it affects many poorer men, too. Facing state cuts, falling wages, increasing unemployment and growing poverty, household survival strategies include more informal economic activity, taking in lodgers, selling home-made goods or food and providing services on the side, including prostitution (Smith and Wallerstein, 1992). It is difficult to gather and assess information here because of different notions of what 'work' is, and the privatised nature of informal and outwork, which is so often women's work.

Women's experiences of work are also mediated by age and lifecycle changes. The term 'women' is often revealed on closer inspection to include many young women and children of both sexes. The cheap labour of the global assembly line is mainly very young women, 'illeducated teenagers' (Standing, 1992: 368). Child labour is a massive part of the IPE globally, and especially in poorer states, where children as young as six or seven toil in agriculture, factories and sweatshops, in domestic labour and sex work (Fyfe, 1989; Myers, 1991). Within their families, too, girls do considerable house- and childcare work, often compromising any opportunities for schooling. Young children of both sexes contribute essential labour on family farms, plots of land, in seasonal work and household-based production (Kanbargi, 1991; Bonnett, 1993). Often it is children's labour in small factories and businesses that provides the only, though minute, family income. There is much illicit trade in children, for factory and housework, and for sex work. Recruitment procedures include buying children from impoverished parents or those unable to meet debt repayments, making children bonded labourers who are supposed to work to pay off the 'debt'; a trade in bodies with pain for both children and the relinquishing parents. In these circumstances, the conditions under which they work justify the description of child slavery (Lee-Wright, 1990).

Many children and young women are migrant workers, moving from rural areas to towns, cities, factories, EPZs, the streets, bars and brothels. Many more young women are part of the trade in women's bodies across state borders or to oil-rich Middle East or rich western and East Asian states as workers, including as sex workers or mail-order brides. This traffic in women reflects the hierarchy of states and wealth in the IPE. It reflects, too, the growing feminisation of the changing international division of labour, and is part of an emerging international political economy of sex (see chapter 9).

Women's working outside the home and especially travelling away for work disrupts family forms and roles. As many younger women move away, older women acquire more work, including at times responsibility for the care and up-bringing of children of their daughters or nieces. Many female-headed households are now headed by grandmothers. This is especially so where AIDS has devastated those of young and early middle years, as in some parts of Central and East Africa (G. Seidel, 1993).

Not all women in paid employment are super-exploited, though very few anywhere earn the income or have the opportunities of their equivalent men. But class is a crucial dimension of women's lives. Elite and middle-class women everywhere live in conditions of material security that set them apart dramatically from poor women, though in neotraditional families the cost may be heightened surveillance and control. And in many states, some women's freedom to take paid work depends on their employing other women to share their domestic labour and childcare responsibilities. Class, alongside racialised and nationalised differences, are fundamental axes of power and subordination, within as well as between states.

Globalising women

We cannot make sense of productive relations, of the growth and nature of EPZs, of TNCs and the impact of current economic crises if we do not gender our account. We cannot simply add women, for the sexual division of labour is constitutive of the international division of labour. As well, we cannot make sense of different women's lives, their work or their status, if we do not locate those women within the international political economy, and assess the impact on women of the growing crises in much of the world in terms of trade dependency, dependent development and debt dependency (Sen and Grown, 1987). These impacts are not limited to the third world, or to the dramatically restructuring transition states, but shape state labour markets, the welfare state and corporatist labour politics in first-world states as well. Women's different but related location within a global political economy both links and divides women of the world.

So gendering the IPE reveals kinds of work and patterns of exploitation that can be generalised in figures such as: women are half of the world's population and one-third of its official workforce, do two-thirds of its productive work, earn one-tenth of its income and own less than one-hundredth of its property. But we cannot make sense of women's lives if we attend only to gender. For nationality, place of residence and work, class, age, marital status and membership of particular racialised or cultural groups all intersect and constitute the working lives of women.

Development

Boundaries between the first world and the third are reproduced in knowledge-making by the usual separation of IPE and of political-economy studies of women in the first world from women-in-development (WID) literature. This leaves 'development' as a focus of study that constructs 'them', the Other, and 'third-world difference', and so disguises the extent to which all people's lives and livelihoods are contained within global processes and structures.

Through the 1950s and 1960s, as newly independent states were expected to modernise and become more like the developed west, women were usually invisible. Development was supposed to trickle down to them, too. Alternatively, women were occasionally seen as obstacles to development, perceived as more 'traditional' and harder to reach than men.

In 1970 Ester Boserup published *Women's Role in Economic Development*, arguing that women were frequently overlooked by development planners in their roles as workers, owners and entrepreneurs, and in subsistence and communal production. Further, women were often negatively affected by development, which undermined their access to land and resources. Through processes of urbanisation and immigration, women lost kin support and faced new labour demands.

By the 1970s, too, there was growing recognition that development was not 'trickling down'; that development experiences were diverse. Even where growth happened, it could be accompanied by growing poverty. A new language of basic needs entered development discourses, seeing health and education for example as requiring special action. Discovery of the feminisation of poverty suggested women as particularly vulnerable to change, and so a 'target' group for development planning (Jaquette, 1982).

The failure of mainstream models to explain development problems and experiences was paralleled by new emerging political critiques. These included a radical *dependencia* or 'dependent-development' perspective coming out of Latin America from the 1960s; a growing second-wave women's movement that stimulated feminist research, demonstrating that women were positioned differently in all social relations; and especially the growth of third-world women's organisations, protests and theorising about women's lives, including resistance to dominant discourses of development and to policies and programs on the ground. These understandings spread through the 1975 International Women's Year and the UN Decade for Women, which followed it, and through international conferences, transnational networks, and circulating critiques, strategies and conversations since (Newland, 1991).

In these movements, there were complex and at times difficult relations between first- and third-world women and feminists, and between practitioners, academics and activists—though many women moved between or combined these roles (Tinker, 1989; Staudt, 1990). Between them they constituted the WID movement and engaged in contested discourses around the relations between women and development. Often these critiques were policy-orientated, seeking to incorporate 'women', and women's perspectives and interests, into development planning and evaluation, and to persuade policy makers to recognise the different impact of their policies on women.

The UN Decade for Women generated an enormous literature and much research about women, and the development of women's machinery in most states, often feminised rather than feminist (Lycklama à Nijeholt, 1991). Here, women's issues became welfare issues, and associated with policies to do with health, education, children. Alternatively, planners attended to women in the name of good resource management, concerned to increase women's productivity. Women became a category, or a special-needs group, or, occasionally, a constituency. Gender as an analytic category and gender relations as power relations were rarely visible. WID sections were often staffed by women, including some feminist 'guerrillas in the bureaucracy' (Ferguson, 1990: 302), but they remained marginal to the development business. Development planners in first and third worlds were still usually men, who, when they did notice women, often saw development as something to be done to them—still trying to save the third-world woman, as colonial officials and missionaries did before them. The tendency to 'do' development for or to women, not with women, includes some WID practitioners and theorists, too (Mohanty, 1988).

Women in development

Caroline Moser (1991) has classified different approaches to women and development. The first is a welfare approach, which sees women primarily as mothers. Women are treated as passive recipients of development, and as 'targets' for development programs, including population control. This approach is popular with governments and mainstream aid agencies, for it does not challenge existing gender relations or class and political interests.

Growing out of dissatisfaction with welfare approaches and dismay at the negative effects of development was the first WID perspective, an equity approach, seeking to reduce inequalities between men and women. Aiming to integrate women more into development, and to remove discrimination, advocates worked for equal social and citizenship rights. While initially associated with liberal feminism, the implications of this approach are radical, especially when they include claims to equal rights to property, divorce and children. These entail a fundamental transformation of gender relations, and so are often resisted in the name of cultural difference. Despite ongoing rhetorical commitment, equity is rarely a serious policy or political goal of development planners.

A second WID approach is 'anti-poverty', naming women as the poorest of the poor, and so shifting attention to basic needs. Under this rubric are income-generating schemes for women, often run by women's NGOs. Working small miracles in some locales, others often provide only 'pocket money' to women, and even then the women themselves might not retain control of the money. They may reinforce gendered divisions of labour by building on traditional or imposed western notions of women's work, in sewing and handicrafts, for example. Larger processes frequently mean the impoverishment of women and their families, even as the schemes continue.

A third WID approach, that of efficiency, is popular with many donor agencies, governments and international agencies discovering women as workers. This involves a shift of attention from women to development, seeing WID as a resource-management problem. This approach calls for gender-aggregated or gender-sensitive approaches. In the 1980s, the shift in dominant development strategies—from working through states to liberalisation and restructuring in a world market—reduced public support for women's family and community work and intensified women's burdens.

In part in response to the failures and costs of other approaches, a very different approach has emerged. 'Empowerment' is a women-centred approach that is potentially transformative. It has grown out of critiques by third-world activists and their first-world allies, building on grassroots experiences and knowledges. This approach generates a much wider agenda, which attends to women's double or triple load, to gender-specific violence, to ideologies of femininity that entrap women, to women's resistances and strategies for change, and supports women's autonomous organisations.

The empowerment approach signals a strengthening of feminist work in third-world states. While some third-world women's rights activists reject the 'feminist' label as white, western and middle class, growing numbers of activists do name themselves as feminist. In international networks political allegiances across state lines, for example as socialist or materialist feminists, often take precedence over shared nationality (Hendessi, 1986).

Development Alternatives with Women for a New Era (DAWN), a third-world coalition of women's groups, argues:

> [W]e need to reaffirm and clarify our understanding of feminism. Over the last twenty years the women's movement has debated the links between the eradication of gender subordination and of other forms of social and economic oppression based on nation, class, or ethnicity. We strongly support the position in this debate that feminism cannot be monolithic in its issues, goals, and strategies . . . There is and must be a diversity of feminisms, responsible to the different needs and concerns of different women, and *defined by them for themselves* . . .
>
> This heterogeneity gives feminism its dynamism and makes it the most potentially powerful challenge to the status quo. It allows the struggle against subordination to be waged in all arenas—from relations in the home to relations between nations—and it necessitates substantial change in cultural, economic, and political formations (Sen and Grown, 1987: 19).

An empowerment approach recognises that many women's experiences of oppression are in terms of their class, nationality or ethnicity, along with their gender, and that not all men benefit from development. So DAWN activists are attentive to class and other differences, to workers' rights and the need for alliances for change. With a radical politics, cultural differences are recognised but also problematised. Local relations and social practices are not necessarily progressive, or somehow without patriarchy or class. Some development programs reinforce traditional gender roles; others remake them through imposing other gendered readings on them, in assuming men to be the breadwinners and producers, even in those areas, such as agriculture in many African states, where women do most of the farming work.

Avoiding complicity in reproducing or modernising patriarchal power means attending to property and marriage relations, labour laws, and working for women's access to resources and rights over their own bodies (Price, 1993). This then is an argument that 'moral and political priority in making decisions about development should reside with those whose lives are most directly affected by those decisions, and it embraces the self-empowerment of local people as its goal' (Ferguson, 1990: 299).

Engendering development

There are many different approaches to women and development, from massive erasure of women's experiences, interests and learnings, to making women visible as an add-on category, to recognising women's subordination as key. In contesting discourses and battles over naming, some suggest gender in development (GID) to replace WID, focusing on women and men positioned differently in gender relations that must change if women are to be empowered. Far-reaching critiques analyse gender relations connected with and constituted through other power differences, including class, ethnicity and nationality; and all of these as part and parcel of the international political economy. So DAWN's analysis notes

a series of interlinked crises of massive and growing impoverishment, food insecurity and non-availability, financial and monetary disarray, environmental degradation, and growing demographic pressure have worsened the problem. The majority of the world's population finds it increasingly difficult to fulfill even the basic requirements of life and to survive from one day to the next. Rather than channeling available resources into programs aimed at eliminating poverty and the burden of gender and other forms of subordination, nations and the international polity have tended to react to these pressures through increased militarization, domestic repression and foreign aggression (Sen and Grown, 1987: 16).

A fundamental split in current development debates is over whether the struggle is to incorporate women more equally into development planning and programs, or whether it is 'development' that needs problematising and challenging. This latter is especially so for those who critique development within patterns of global domination and subordination; and those who argue that understanding the relations between women and development means listening to and learning from women in different places and different struggles. The problem is not how to bring women into development. Development is already dependent on women's work as cheap labour, in informal and subsistence sectors, in household work and community care.

Contesting women

There is now much local knowledge and situated critiques of development, and examples of good practice, too (for example, Leonard, 1989; Momsen and Kinnaird, 1993). Women's NGOs and networks within poorer third-world states often have national and some international links, including across first-world/third-world boundaries, and feminist critiques and strategies are transnational in exchanges and perspectives. There are deep differences and many contests, but it is probably within development and women's rights groups that there are the most robust internationalism and a multitude of learnings, advocacy, solidarity, and coalition-building.

There are also many examples of appropriation and domestication of women's and feminist learnings. Recently, development discourses have been reworked in state, agency and international forum rhetoric, in ambiguous or contradictory ways. So 'human development' has emerged alongside and in reaction to the devastation wrought on poorer states and people especially through restructuring. *Human Development Reports* cite evidence and social indexes reveal growing disparities and worsening life crises for many, especially women and children (United Nations Development Program, 1995).

'Sustainable development' has emerged as a contested discourse, taken up in official forums in recognition of the environmental costs and dangers of exploitative growth without attention to those resources that are finite and under increasing pressure, and those consequences, especially in terms of global warming and emissions, that threaten future producitivity (Rodda, 1991; Elliott, 1993). Development is now frequently twinned with concern for the environment. The United Nations Conference on the Environment and Development (UNCED) conference in Rio in 1992 reflected severefirst-world/third-world state conflicts over resources and responsibility, internationally, for unequal growth. It was a focus, too, for very different movements and NGOs, including environmentalists and women's groups. It revealed deep tensions around the connections between population, reproduction, environment and development. Once again, women were objects, identified, for example, as responsible for resource management at local and household level in south and north, while women at Rio struggled to be recognised as subjects with interests of their own in environmental issues.

Women and nature

In preparatory committees and in campaigning leading to Rio, women's NGOs worked internationally though not always harmoniously to make women visible and included gendered analyses of environmental needs and strategies. These struggles critiqued dominant views of development, and argued the necessity of engendering development and environment, and recognising connections between them (*Agenda 21*, 1992; Braidotti et al., 1994).

One strand of environmental feminism, ecofeminism, includes a range of views on the connections between women and nature. Its proponents argue that scientific and technological developments from the seventeenth century on led to the conquest and exploitation of women and nature, as resources for (white, western) men. (Rosser, 1991; Mies and Shiva, 1993). There are contests around these connections that resonate with the connections pursued in terms of women and peace (see chapter 6). Many ecofeminists assert women's special skills in nurturing life, calling on women's biological and especially reproductive powers, or on cultural learnings, especially as mothers. Spiritualism, goddess imagery, and valorising women's ways of knowing and learning, challenge masculinist ways of being in the world in much ecofeminist writing, too (Diamond and Orenstein, 1990). Some ecofeminists also draw on tribal, indigenous or traditional ways of knowing, in a women-native-nature connection that is here seen as positive.

Other environmental feminists worry about the appropriation of others' knowings in 'new-age' or essentially spiritualising ways—subversive against dominant ways perhaps, but involving imperialising and colonising moves in some cases, too. There are also concerns about the use of maternalist imagery, for so long used to control and exclude women, or to make them responsible for cleaning up the mess (Plumwood, 1992). There is often a rise in body imagery and pro-family rhetoric at times of social crisis, seen today in widely mobilised conservative rhetoric. Ellen Çronan Rose suggests that ecofeminism and non-feminist use of 'mother-earth' imagery in response to current ecological and developmental crises is a form of 'reproductive anxiety' (1991: 89). She warns against mobilising maternalism in times of strong pro-natal and pro-family right-wing movements globally.

Again echoing women and peace debates, some ecofeminists are accused of essentialism, of homogenising women, and men, when a feminist or gender analysis might reveal power dynamics and more problematic relations between women and 'nature'. Women's choices and use of resources are heavily dependent on local and family political economies and power relations. So Cecile Jackson (1993) argues 'gender/history' as a more useful way of untangling the issues than 'women/nature'. Exploring marriage relations, property rights and the sexual division of labour in Zimbabwe, she outlines women's shifting uses of and felt commitments towards local resources, and differences among women, too; hence, younger women may be exploited by older co-wives or female relatives, too.

Women are frequently portrayed as victims of environmental destruction, because they are primarily responsible for water and fuel gathering and family health, for example (Rodda, 1991). Women often predominate in local environmental protest movements, as they do in political resistances, in response to growing difficulties in carrying out their family and gender responsibilities. Many ecofeminists stress women's agency and their articulation of liberation and holistic values (Shiva, 1989; Bandarage, 1991). So Bina Agarwal (1992) focuses on the materiality of poor women's lives in India, and on the gender-specific consequences of and responses to environmental degradation. She traces a complex play of state action and social or protest movement response, and stresses women as agents, too.

In many states, while women are activists and protesters in environmental struggles, men often occupy positions of leadership. Green movements in the west are seen as white and middle class, with minorities both under-represented in green politics and more likely to be victims in terms of toxic dumping and other environmental burdens (Stabile, 1994). Class compounds with race and other marginalising processes. Here, too, is a new racism, as some environmentalists idealise past imagined spiritual relations with land while simultaneously denying actual indigenous people rights to their land now. In Australia, some 'greens' seek an extension of areas designated as national parks, which would exclude traditional or contemporary use of those lands by local Aboriginal people (Langton, 1995).

Reproductive rights and politics

'Sustainable development' hints at the relations between development and environmental politics and practices. Within these relations lie the highly explosive issues of population and women's reproductive rights.

'Population control' was initially seen as both a condition and a consequence of development, and supported by western international agencies, including the US Agency for International Development (AID). This led to targeting women, especially advocating use of contraceptives, and increasing state intervention in their lives (Jaquette and Staudt, 1988). States of the 'south' won recognition at the 1974 Bucharest conference that 'development is the best contraceptive', but by the 1980s 'development' seemed to elude many states. Population policies made women, once again, objects on other agendas.

States' population policies have taken diverse forms, from the highly coercive one-child policy of China and the forced pregnancy policies of Ceaucescu's Romania, through a range of state-imposed family planning programs in India and Indonesia, and limited and expensive services in many western states, to more inclusive and accessible reproductive rights in the Netherlands for example (Hartmann, 1987). In many states, different policies apply to or resources are discriminately directed at different groups. So Israeli and Malaysian governments, among others, encourage own-group women's fertility to bolster their side in the 'battle of the cradle' (Peterson, 1994).

Women's bodies are frequently disciplined 'in the service of the state' (Kligman, 1992: 365), and in terms of state developmental and nationalist politics. So in complex politics around abortion, for example, women are treated as 'potential "carrying" vessels or "walking wombs" performing a state, religious or society function that they cannot be entirely trusted to determine for themselves'

179

(Hoff, 1994: 621). Women's reproductive behaviour and rights are subject to masculinist power and state surveillance, seriously undermining women's citizenship and social rights.

Against this situation, women's access to contraception and abortion are often claimed as basic human rights. The demand for such rights is indicated in figures of some 38 million abortions taking place annually in the south, many illegal and often a serious risk to women's health (Germain, 1994: 29). Human rights rhetoric now links women's health and reproductive rights with international conventions and declarations, including during the lead-up to the Vienna Human Rights conference in 1993. An international women's health movement has succeeded in articulating a language around women's reproductive rights, to challenge powerful players in the population debate. The 1994 Cairo Population and Development conference was almost hijacked by the Vatican in its opposition to abortion and its temporary alliance with some conservative Muslim leaders. However, the conference did issue a declaration in support of family planning resources and including 'empowerment' as a key strategy in women's reproductive rights.

Contests over language and whether or not it is possible to have state-enabling, not controlling, provision of women's health services, again reveal very different feminist positions on the state. The dangers of appropriation of feminist concerns for nationalist and conservative causes are many. But the shifts in conference discourses also reflect the success of the international women's health movement (Sen et al., 1994). This movement is women centred, and focuses on the relationship between providers and patients. It seeks to address health in ways that women experience it: 'not as a series of isolated biomedical phenomena, but as an integral part of everyday life' (Freedman and Isaacs, 1993: 19).

The movement emerged in rather different circumstances in different states and regions (Garcia-Moreno and Claro, 1994). In Latin America in the 1980s, women's rights were taken up at regional level within a growing feminist movement whose focus included sexuality, reproductive rights and violence against women. In India it grew from responses to authoritarian state population policies and resistance to female foeticide and other abuses of new reproductive technologies. In states as diverse as the Philippines, Ireland and now Poland, women organise to contest official Catholic church teachings that prohibit contraception and abortion choices for women.

Local and state organisers and advocates have increasingly come together in regional and global NGO networks and conferences. In September 1992 an international meeting of women's health representatives issued the Women's Declaration on Population Policies. It argued that 'population policies and programs must be framed within and implemented as a part of broader development strategies that will redress the unequal distribution of resources and power between and within countries, between racial and ethnic groups, and between women and men' (Sen et al., 1994: 31). It asserted fundamental ethical principles, which included treating women as subjects, not objects; respecting the sexual and bodily integrity of girls and women; women's individual right and social responsibility to decide when and how many children to have, and to determine their own sexual relations; men's responsibility for their own sexual behaviour and fertility; principles of equity, non-coercion and mutual respect; opposing violence against women and their being subject to harmful practices, including genital mutilation; asserting women's rights not to be subjected to partners', family, ethnic-group, or religious domination; and the need for women's health activists, practitioners and women themselves to be involved in decision making and program delivery.

Empowerment is multifaceted, a process and a goal, and means locating struggles for women's rights and choices within a wider political economy (Sen et al., 1994). While there are deep divisions within the women's health movement and among feminists more generally on these questions, a feminist approach is by definition women-centred, and aims to enable women's choices. It requires a transformation of gender and other power relations. In the work of many feminist health activists, especially those from or with working knowledge of the south, reproductive rights are more than a matter of 'bodily integrity'. Body rights are one part of a larger whole in which all forms of discrimination against girls and women, on the one hand, and poverty and structural violence, on the other, must be challenged.

Feminist women's health advocates understand reproductive freedom, then, in a much broader framework, as going far beyond 'family planning' provision of contraception, and abortion rights; with a very different focus from top-down population–control policies. 'We define the terrain of reproductive and sexual rights in terms of power and resources: power to make informed decisions about one's own fertility, childbearing, child rearing, gynecologic health, and sexual activity; and resources to carry out such decisions safely and effectively' (Correa and Petchesky in Sen et al., 1994: 107).

Shifting terrain

Reproductive rights are linked back to issues of development and environment, in local struggles and in national and international campaigns. These come together in women's work in different sites, and the complex and changing connections between women's reproductive, productive and community-management work. Many of the changes are being wrought in struggles between increasingly globalised political economy and state regimes' development or structural adjustment policies. They are being played out, too, in contests over ideologies of femininity and family, over sexuality and women's bodies, and in the use of violence against women who appear to challenge existing gender roles, or when some men face development disasters or difficulties, too.

There are ongoing debates over women's autonomous organising, and when, and how, alliances with men are necessary or desirable. The 1979 Convention for the Elimination of Discrimination Against Women (CEDAW) advocated equal rights and responsibilities for men and women in reproductive choices (Reanda, 1991). Most feminists argue rather for women's rights, as women bear the physical and social burdens of childbirth, and sexual and reproductive behaviour is so often under the control of men, and at times older women.

These debates are replayed in many ways, including, for example, in questions about women's spaces. Some feminists argue for equality for men and women, including asking of men a more active role in and commitment to childcare and domestic labour. Others reject what they see as men's incursion into the only space where women can exercise some power (Jaquette, 1982: 280). A women's space might provide some quiet, safety and congenial exchanges with other women. Many households now are female-headed and might include only female adults, but female spaces are largely enclosed within men's power and a male-dominated public sphere. Here, too, violence is often used against those women who attempt to move beyond the women's space.

Differences among women

Many third-world women are not rural and village workers, but work in EPZs, factories, offices and elsewhere in towns and cities. Neither are all third-world women poor. While many are, there are rich elites and large middle classes in most Asian and Latin American states, for example. Nor are all women in the first world middle class—or white. This cautions us against any easy reproduction of first-world/third-world difference, and especially against reproducing 'third-world woman' as passive victim. It also further complicates the question of differences among women.

Dominant IPE and development discourses are powerful devices for 'othering', for holding the centre of white western male knowlege-making (Keyman, 1995). Development discourses are part of the process of 'third-worlding', in which some western and western-educated feminists also participate (Spivak, 1989; Mohanty, 1988; Lazreg, 1988). Learning to listen and to work collaboratively, using difference as a beginning point but not a refusal, has enabled transnational feminist politics, encouraged in some places and subverted in others by academic feminist debates about difference (Goetz, 1991; Parpart, 1993).

'Difference' remains a highly charged political and power issue in women's forums, including in global women's politics. Early UN women's conferences in Mexico in 1975 and Copenhagen in 1980 were marked by first-world/third-world rifts. By the time of the 1985 Nairobi women's conference, many conversations and alliances cut across that divide, and there were also splits between women from the same state, especially between state-sponsored delegates and autonomous, opposition or exile groups (Brah, 1988; Henndessi, 1986). There, too, nationality, class and race came through in complex configurations. The very large US contingent included a number of African-Americans, whose claims to share more with their African than their white US sisters were often rebuffed by African women, while socialist feminist exiles from Iran, for example, had little in common with the Iranian state-sponsored women's delegation.

The divisions among women at international conferences are reminders that by no means are all women's politics feminist; and that feminists from different locations in terms of both global power and political beliefs struggle to assert their own understandings and goals. Since the early 1980s especially, third-world and minority first-world writings and politics have seriously challenged imperialistic feminisms and demanded that power relations between women be attended to, too. Through international networks and conferences, 'third-world women' have become visible, and claimed a voice, or rather, many voices. In so doing they, along with first-world minority feminists, have refused to be spoken for (Bannerji, 1987; Mohanty et al., 1991; Braidotti et al., 1994).

Building international women's networks and transnational alliances has not been easy, but much work has been done. The growing globalisation of power and its gendered consequences have given women some common ground to fight from, and have required transnational coordination against threats and dangers that are now rarely contained within or restricted to a single state.

Many of these dangers, and impetus to women's international action, are in gender-specific violences against women, and in forms of international exploitation of women's bodies and labour, including the international trafficking in women, taken up in the next chapter.

An international political economy of sex

This chapter explores some implications of women's bodies being sexualised, and presumed available for men's sex and service, and of the dangers for women in many combinations of sex and the international (Pettman, 1996b).

Women are especially vulnerable when they are seen to be 'out of place'. This is more likely as a consequence of intensified globalisation and current restructuring of the international political economy. This chapter traces contemporary forms of international traffic in women, including women as migrant labour in internationalised domestic service, as mail-order brides, in sex tourism and militarised prostitution. It does so by utilising the notion of an international political economy of sex. It concludes by tracing women's transnational organising in response to these forms of 'sexploitation'.

Women/out of place

Tracing an international political economy of body politics and women's danger touches on many aspects already raised in previous chapters associated with the domestication of women and women's vulnerablity to violence.

The domestication of women and their containment in the private sphere writes them out of the public–political, such that women's appearance and performance in public space can be read as a transgression, and so 'invite' sexual approach or attack. Security might be sought through the protection of a man, though the cost of protection may be possession and control. In addition, a woman may be (more?) threatened by her protector—there is no necessary safety at home.

The domestication of women naturalises men's sex right to women's bodies, labour and children. This 'right' is related in different ways to the construction of sexuality and of women as the bearers of sex; women are, and are for, (heterosexual) sex (Flax, 1990; Brown, 1987). Women are there to service men, providing domestic and sexual labour, which is assumed to be a labour of love. The close associations of women, bodies, sex, and service to men, means that women are 'seen' as sexed beings; and that women's labour, too, is frequently sexualised.

Women are vulnerable to body policing and to violence if they transgress the public/private boundary or appear unruly or out of (men's) control. Politically organised violence is directed especially against women who are political activists in human rights, women's or workers' rights organisations; or women who may have associated with enemy men (Amnesty International, 1991a,b; Bunster-Burotto, 1994). Especially in more militarised states, state agents are themselves the primary threats to women, and to many men. Male-dominated state agencies are also often second offenders in their complicity with male violence, and in their frequent treatment of women who have experienced violence, especially rape, as somehow suspect, or that the women have 'asked for it'.

Rape and sexual intimidation and harassment are regularly used against women if they are where they are not supposed to be. This recalls the apparent contradiction in the routine invisibility and yet at times hypervisibility of women (and of gay and/or racialised men) who may then experience harassment and violence in public places, such as in the street and on public transport. This suggests that public space is male, heterosexual, and, in first-world states, white. Violence demonstrates the boundaries of belonging, as well as who owns the territory.

There is a close, though by no means fixed or uncontested, connection between social control of women and violence against them, and between these and the wider structures of gender/gendered power. Women are kept resourceless or in their place at least in part, through the threat or act of violence (Mies, 1986; Hanmer et al., 1989; Kelkar, 1992). Violence is a part of the domestication of women, whereby their subordination and service come to seem natural, so guaranteeing men's access to women's bodies and to their labour. Both structural and direct violence and coercion keep women's productive and reproductive labour under the control of men, and so provide a subsidy to states, employers and men's interests. There is some evidence of worsening violences against women, including as a reaction to women's seeking to participate in development or women's rights activities (Carillo, 1993).

Not every woman experiences violence, though in all places many do, and most do because they are women. Not all—hopefully not most—men are violent, but men are overwhelmingly the perpetrators of violence, except against children; and even here men are some half of the perpetrators in western states, despite the overwhelming primacy of women as childcarers (Gordon, 1993). Violence against women can be characterised as a category crime, or as gender-specific violence. The 1995 UNICEF *State of the World's Children* report declared violence against women by male partners as the most common crime in the world. This and other violences against women and girl children amount to a form of gendered terror, which has become increasingly visible internationally from the Nairobi women's conference on.

Many women in very different cultures and social spaces curtail their own movements, clothing and relations in attempts to protect themselves. There is a political geography of gender that appears to be universal, although it takes specific socio-cultural forms in different times and spaces. Some feminist geographers map a geography of women's fear in western states (Pain, 1991). Daphne Spain (1993) argues a direct correlation between women's spatial segregation and their status in different places, and feminist anthropologists and others test these associations. So ideologies of control, seclusion, honour and shame determine women's mobility and access to resources and opportunities (Afshar and Agarwal, 1989). Webs of connection between marriage, kin, community and control recur here, explored in still-productive ways by Gayle Rubin (1975), as a political economy of the sex/gender system (but see also Rubin's rethinking, 1984). The surveillance of women and the disciplining of women's sexuality relate to the maintenance of family and community honour and status, and to competition for resources. Patriarchal policing joins with the border patrols of the nation/race/community, marked on the bodies of women.

Women on the move

Many women and girls are no longer where they are supposed to be, forced or pressured or choosing to move—in some cases doing so to get away from home. Many are displaced by wars, communal or political violence. Women and children make up the vast majority of refugees. Other women move, more or less freely, subject to and acting upon a range of pushes and pulls which constitute another aspect of the international political economy of gender, the changing sexual division of labour.

The globalisation that sees rapid mobility of capital and transnational corporations also rests on cheap labour, including labour migrants (see chapter 8). Many women are on the move, from countryside to town, town to city or capital or military base, to export-processing zone. So labour migrants go from poorer states, such as Sri Lanka or the Philippines to oil-rich Middle Eastern states, to Japan, Hong Kong or Singapore (Heyzer et al., 1994). Many still go from poorer Asian and North-African states to Europe; many others go to the USA from other parts of the Americas. These movements reflect the contemporary international hierarchy of states and regions. They also reflect the impact of international processes and relations, from 'development' to international debt and structural adjustment policies (Afshar and Dennis, 1992). Class and region compound effects of economic dislocation, poverty and changing patterns in the sexual division of labour and the nature of women's work.

The changing international division of labour is also racialised, and women's and children's nationality, ethnicity and citizenship become part of the equation, often placing them at further risk. This is so for older and more recent minority workers in first- and third-world states and for recent labour migrants in many different parts of the globe. Women labour migrants may travel alone or as part of a recruitment package. They often find themselves in situations where women abroad are again beyond the bounds of protection. This is frequently compounded by racialised or culturalised minority status, and insecure residence and employment rights (Bakan and Stasiulis, 1995). This is particularly the case where they are engaged in two of the most significant sectors of women's 'foreign' work, 'domestic service' and 'entertainment'.

Internationalised/domestic service

Domestic service is a problematic arena for feminists, happening as it does within (other people's) homes, where the employer or daily supervisor is often another woman (Wrigley, 1991). The 'domestic' is usually from another class and often from another racialised/culturalised/nationality from the home woman. In situations of unequal power relations and of highly personalised and intimate relations, the question arises whether servants can be sisters (Gaitskell, 1982).

Domestic service has long been the site for 'close encounters' between colonising and coloniser women. Colonised women have provided domestic labour and childcare in white households, and, in the process, gendered and raced boundaries were reproduced in ways that distinguished and privileged whiteness. In Australia, for example, many Aboriginal 'half-caste' girls were seized from their families, institutionalised and trained as domestic servants. Other examples of racialised domestic service include the stereotyped 'mammy' of the slave and post-slavery US south (Rollins, 1985), the black maids of white madams in South Africa (Cock, 1989), the African-American maid and the Chicana or Hispanic nanny in the recent and contemporary US (Jones, 1985; Chaney and Castro, 1989). Their labour makes them party to others' family secrets, and vulnerable to sexual and other abuse and exploitation. Yet much feminist writing on care assumes that domestic and reproductive labour is provided by women of the family working for 'love', so erasing the widespread provision of care and labour in dominant-group or wealthier homes by poorer and/or racialised women (Graham, 1991). White first-world/black third-world dichotomies are misleading here, as, for example, poor Asian domestics allow elite countrywomen and some East Asian and Middle Eastern women certain domestic freedoms.

Nowadays a significant part of international labour migration is in the form of those going to domestic service—largely unnoticed by most IR and IPE commentators until the Iraqi invasion of Kuwait drew international media attention to their plight (Enloe, 1990b). The globalisation of capitalism has created 'an international service class of female employees' (Tinsman, 1992: 42). Shifts in international politics and the IPE are evident in the ebb and flow of this trade. Thus Filipino maids go to Hong Kong, Japan, Jordan, Syria and Saudi Arabia in large numbers, as part of an international trade estimated to involve between 1 and 1.7 million Asian women domestic workers. Here distinctions need to be made in terms of those states and households where home-state women can take up paid work outside the home while foreign domestic workers do family and household labour, and those households, in some Gulf states, for example, where the local woman remains at home, and the use of foreign domestic labour adds to family prestige, as well as supporting local women in their reproductive labour. In both cases, cheap foreign maids have the effect of reinforcing the gendered division of domestic labour and relieve pressure on states to take responsibility for childcare and social reproduction (Heyzer and Wee, 1994: 44). Their support of social reproduction and of particular families in the rich states is at the expense of their own families at home, and a drain of resources, skills and energy from their poorer states.

> Out of the interaction of uneven growth with the existing intra- and inter-household gender division of labour there has emerged a trans-national process in the [Asia-Middle East] region that has become big business. The stakes are high, involving receiving and sending countries, intermediate agencies (such as recruitment agencies, banks, airlines, medical clinics, currency dealers, post offices), employers and their households, the domestic workers' kinship network, and the millions of domestic workers themselves' (Heyzer et al., 1994: xv)

Domestic service is not a marginal or occasional economic category. In 1986 paid household service in Latin American countries accounted for between 30 per cent and 70 per cent of non-agricultural women's work. In the 1980s in the US it was the fastest growing employment sector for immigrant women. Large numbers of women move from Latin America into the United States, and from the Caribbean into Canada as domestic workers. We were reminded of this trade in the recent 'nanny wars' of the Clinton administration (Rosen, 1993) where 'undocumented workers' became an issue between different racialised groups in the suggestion that some African and Hispanic Americans were fearful of losing work to 'aliens'. These incidents also point to the growing significance of a globalised underground economy and of a racialised underclass, whose illegal or temporary status places them in particular dependence on their employers, without union or advocacy support and fearful of state-agent attention (Sivanandan, 1989; Abella, 1991: 73).

In an increasingly regional and globalised market, many women cross state borders in search of work that is simply not available or even more poorly paid at home. Even when states prohibit women from seeking domestic work overseas, as Bangladesh did, the lack of choice in desperate economic circumstances forces many women to move illegally, for example to make the trip to Pakistan and then to Middle East states. But the international traffic in women's labour and bodies is also often sponsored or at least condoned by their home states (Palma-Beltran, 1991). The 'export of women' from states such as the Philippines, Indonesia and Sri Lanka is part of the international politics of debt, and of poorer states' search for hard currency in the form of remittances, as well as reflecting lack of employment opportunities at home. The Philippines receives an estimated US$3 billion per year in remittances from overseas workers; Bangladeshi workers sent US$771 million home in 1989, accounting for 60 per cent of the year's merchandise crop (Heyzer et al., 1994: 13). Poor state dependence on remittances compounds domestic workers' vulnerability through lack of protection from their embassies, whose responsibility to safeguard their citizens' interests is compromised by concern to maintain the wider trade and aid from these richer states (Humphrey, 1991). In addition, lack of labour and women's rights in a number of home states undermines their credibility and political will to defend nationals' rights overseas. The trade in domestic workers also affects the status and image of the sending states, and underlines the growing power and wealth differences between states internationally and in the region. This is dramatically illustrated in relative income per head of those engaged in the international trade in Asian domestic workers in 1992: US$680 for sending countries and US$10 376 for receiving countries (Heyzer et al., 1994: xxiii).

While their states may benefit from the remittances, used to underwrite development and militarisation, the women themselves may not benefit. The costs of recruitment and travel, and loans from recruiters to enable women to move, are heavy expenses that are difficult to repay. The remitted money may not get back safely, especially where women are working illegally or are restricted to the house. What does get through might allow a family to survive, or it may be spent on consumer items, which do not extend to children or other women in the family. But some women do enjoy their earnings, and the choices they might not have had at home.

Domestic service is internationalised not only in the origins and different backgrounds of the 'serving' women, but in the construction of different racialised gendered stereotypes of women from different countries. Hence preferences in the US for maids from Central and South American states rather than African-American and local Hispanic communities; and in Jordan for the lighter-skinned and more likely English-speaking Filipinas over Sri Lankan maids (Humphrey, 1991). Recruitment agencies in Canada work to 'match' worker and household, often predicting and reproducing racialised and gendered stereotypes according to national origin (Bakan and Stasiulis, 1995). Women from sending countries are associated with servant status, and are locked into racialised stereotypes as passive, accommodating or exotic, aggravating the already sexualised nature and associations of domestic work.

Connections are frequently made between domestic service and sexual availability, where the domestic labourer is seen to have sold her body and not just her labour, and where male domination asserts authority over dependants and servants, especially women (Tinsman, 1992). While some households are warm and supportive, others are oppressive or abusive. Privacy, respect or care for domestic workers is capriciously dependent on the good will of the men and, often, the women of the house. Racialised gender stereotypes that construct women as promiscuous or exotic heighten the danger and are mobilised to blame the victim. Tensions may be caused between the worker and a jealous or fearful wife, who may be a complicit or active policer of raced sexual boundaries.

These relations are complicated still further where significant numbers of women appear to opt for a decline in class status for more money. So former nurses and teachers go from the Philippines as domestics, and may be better educated than their mistresses, especially in some Gulf states. Some are married, and/or have children of their own, at home. At the other end of the spectrum, large numbers of home-state domestic workers in poorer states may be children, for example, in Peru some domestic workers are under ten, and usually average between fourteen and sixteen years of age; in Bangladesh some are as young as six or seven and they will often be dismissed at puberty, for fear of their becoming 'sexual' (Ennew, 1993).

Such fears are reportedly one reason white women preferred 'houseboys' (not necessarily young) as domestic servants in colonial Northern Rhodesia and Papua New Guinea, for example, though local women's and men's reluctance about women living away from their own families contributed too. In the early to mid-1980s male domestic workers were the largest single occupation in urban Zambia—even larger than mining—working for elite black as well as white families (Hansen, 1990). But globally, domestic work remains overwhelmingly female, whether paid or unpaid.

Feminised domestic labour mantains 'men as masters'. '[T]he fact that it is still *women* who continue to be employed in service reproduces the unequal sexual division of labour that devalues women's work and entitles men to female services' (Tinsman, 1992: 55)—and presumably feminises those poorer and racialised men who sometimes also labour at 'women's work'.

Domestic service is one of the arenas where power relations between women are problematic. As usual, there is no inevitable or transparent shared interest or good will between women. Some, especially middle- or upper-class women, gain mobility and support from live-in help. An Australian newspaper report suggested that (elite) 'Asian' women were doing better than Australian women in professions and business because of the availability of cheap domestic servants in Asian states, enabling other women to go out to work without needing to negotiate changes in men's roles in childcare or housework (Williams, 1993). But some Australian women, like other women in rich states and classes, can buy services out of the house, such as childcare, fast food and laundry services. Other women, especially poorer and single mothers also engage others to care for their children where they lack kin support. Their race, culture, age and class are likely to be different from the usual image of domestic-employer or childcare arrangement.

Male/mail-order brides

There are fascinating writing and feminist contests over domestic labour in general, the marriage contract as a work contract, and the (universal?) assumption that women's work in the care and servicing of men and children is a 'labour of love'. While many wish to retain notions of a marriage or household based on love and fair work practices, marriage's dubious sexual politics and the usual choice of wives as younger, smaller and generally having less power and status does not make for equality. This is especially so when marriages are not only across racialised/nationality lines, but deliberately sought by men looking for 'other' women as better wives.

There is now a significant international trade in wives, another part of the international traffic in women, captured in the phrase mail-order brides. Here again women become tradeable commodities, as evidenced by the book *War of the Sexes* (1993), in which an Australian author offers advice on 'How to marry a virgin, where to find them, how to meet them and how much it will cost to bring them to Australia' from the Philippines (Centre for Philippine

Concerns, Media Release, 2 March 1993). Some who have acquired 'brides' assume rights that may trample any rights or choices for those women. The international lies in the fact that women are brought from outside the man's state across international borders. This affects women's citizenship status if they enter as fiancées or recent wives, for example, who may be threatened with deportation if they are 'ungrateful'. (Lack of knowledge of immigration rules, resources and support available to them, and being without trusted kin or women's networks means this threat can be effective regardless of the legal niceties.)

The international is evident, too, in the ways that some countries become acquirers of brides and others supply them, roughly reflecting their relative positioning in the international political economy. In Australia, mail-order brides were read as Filipinas, now extending to Thai and Malaysian women. Lately personal and agency advertisements for Russian and East European 'wives' have appeared in local papers. Mail-ordering husbands are stereotyped as older white often rural men, presumed to be 'purchasing' a wife because no 'Australian' woman would have them, or because they fear and reject Australian women as 'too feminist'. But a significant part of the trade involves migrant and minority men, including those whose rural or remote working place does not encourage meeting local women, or who lack a community or social network of their own.

Many Filipinas married to Australian men bitterly resent those who see them as mail-order brides, a stereotype that encourages their treatment as exotic/available Asian women, or as passive victims. Filipinas, indeed non-refugee third-world women generally in Australia, are on average better educated with higher-level occupations than many Australian-born women (Price, 1990), and it is Filipinas who have the highest proportion of parents residing with them. Some women did enter Australia as part of the trade, seeking an Australian husband for better opportunities for themselves and their children, and resources for family at home, including sponsorship of others to migrate. In this they were acting as agents and making what they could of arrangements that are quite satisfactory in many of their tellings (Cahill, 1990). However, compounding male domestic power with being out-of-place and isolated makes these marriages deadly for some women and difficult for others.

The trade marks danger to women who come into Australia under its terms, and in situations of acute dependence on their new husband. There has recently been some media attention to violence against them. Since 1980 eighteen Filipino women and four children have died at the hands of their husbands, and four women and a child have disappeared. As in the different but similarly sex-ualised/racialised situation of international child prostitution, this has led to pressure on the Australian government to take some respon-sibility, to deny serial sponsors and those with a history of domestic violence permission to sponsor again, and to counsel and advise prospective migrant/brides about both domestic violence and the provision and support available against it. These moves are part of new international exchanges and alliances between 'white' Austra-lian, 'migrant'—including Filipino-Australian—and Filipino feminists (Marginson, 1992).

There is another trade in wives developing, itself the result of devaluing girls, which in its more violent forms includes female foeticide and infanticide (Batou, 1991; Oldenburg, 1992). Routine son preference discriminates against girls' access to resources, including good health. In some areas, especially in parts of South Asia and China, there is a growing preponderance of males, which is beginning to materialise in a related shortage of wives, so women are being trafficked from Thailand and Vietnam, for example, into China. There are suggestions that this trade, together with the trades in domestic servants and sex workers, may enhance the use and sale value of girls, and so encourage their survival and better treatment. But to be valued as commodities offers little in the way of rights to girls or women.

International services/sex tourism

Cynthia Enloe (early in feminist IR times) prompted us to ask how Asian women's sexuality is being packaged and sold internationally, and how this feeds off and into representations of colonial and third-world women as passive/exotic (1990a). In reaction to feminist challenges in western states, Asian women can be used to stand for essential femininity, the essence of service and sex. Particular representations of 'the Asian woman' circulate globally, reproducing racialised and gendered difference. Media images, tourist brochures and airline advertising such as the Singapore 'girl', or Thailand as the Land of (young women's) Smiles associate the Asian woman with male adventure and female availability . These kinds of images are used to sell third-world tourism, and make 'other' women available to the tourist/predatory sexed gaze. They join the colonial/third-world scenery as unspoiled and natural resources, there for the taking.

International tourism is now an enormous business. Some 500 million tourists cross state boundaries each year and tourist earnings make up significant proportions of some states' revenue. International sex tourism is a significant part of this trade, but even short of actual sex, third-world tourism relies on certain commodified notions of nature, culture, difference and sex. Tourism is part of a huge international hospitality and service trade that connects the objectification of Asian women with widespread associations between women, femininity, sex and service.

Internationalised and racialised domestic service and mail-order brides are examples of traffic across state borders where the woman leaves home, by choice or in response to various kinds of family, political or economic coercion. But the international traffic in women also manifests itself in rich-state men crossing borders to purchase 'other' women's bodies (though large numbers of poor-state women also leave home to work in the sex trade in rich states, too). Why are the purchasers so often men? Though they may use women or boy or girl children. Eighty-five per cent of tourists to the Philippines are men. Why do some countries, richer and more powerful in the IPE, 'send' the men, and why do poorer countries and regions 'sell' women, young men and children to these men? Why do some states become sex-tourist destinations, and others supply those tourists (Enloe, 1990a)? There is an international political economy of sex here, as sex tourism and the relations between clients and prostitutes mirror relations of domination, subordination and exploitation between first and third worlds (Hall, 1992: 74).

The 'fiction documentary' film *The Good Woman of Bangkok* sparked controversy when it was released in 1992. Dennis O'Rourke, an Australian film maker, begins the film with the declaration that, on his marriage break-up, he headed for Bangkok in search of a prostitute for sex and a script (Souter, 1992). The film constructs a sexualised and exploitative relationship that reproduces even while it attempts to critique first-world/third-world power relations.

International sex tourists are mainly western and Japanese men going especially to South-East Asian states for adventures and services not available, or not so cheaply or anonymously available, at home. Sex tourism reenacts colonial and contemporary power relations, which are 'raced' as well as gendered. Sex tourism becomes a metaphor for relations between men and women under capitalism, and in colonisation and racism. Some western men reassert their privileged position in times now formally postcolonial. The battle between different men for possession of women is underlined by the near-absence of Thai men in the film, except as patriarchal despots/betrayers (gambling father, violent husband and pimp), who force Aoi into prostitution. Critiquing the film, Jeannie Martin observes 'The Master is the West. Thailand/Asia gives up its women to the Master . . . "Woman" functions as a metaphor in an allegory of relations among men in a global battle about the control of resources' (1992: 35).

There are debates about agency, as the prostituted Aoi, though dreadfully exploited and caught in power relations loaded against her, does resist and subvert within the film and beyond it (Berry, 1992/3). The film maker plays a familiar role as exploiter/saviour, which includes his purchase of a rice farm for Aoi to buy her out of prostitution; but we learn that she has sold the farm and returned to the trade. Implied is the binary dangerous city/sheltered rural village, which ignores the ways village male behaviour coerced Aoi's earlier choices, and the ways that global and state political economy impact on rural areas, too. Capitalism and globalised development policies are worked on the bodies of women (Ansara, 1992: 36).

In the film, several young Australian men argue the sexual servicing attractions of Thai women, and represent the bar girls as victims of poverty who are 'being helped out' by the men/'s trade. There is a political economy of sex pushing many young women, and young men, into the cities and often into hospitality, entertainment and prostitution work. Their movement is shaped by relations of colonialism, development, urbanisation, industrialisation, the growing internationalisation of state economies, indebtedness and the conditionality and structural-adjustment policies of IMF and World Bank propelled policies. These materialise in the growing impoverishment of rural and urban poor in many third-world states and regions, and in increasing numbers of women who are heads of households and/or the only family income earner. Once in the trade it may be very hard to go home, through fear and shame and unmarriageability when there are few options, and now HIV/AIDS. Alternatively, those who do go home may become part of an AIDS track, in the circulatory traffic between urban and rural areas (Ford and Koetsawang, 1991).

An international political economy of sex operates in terms of demand—in sex tourism and militarised prostitution—and supply—including the impact of development and restructuring, rural impoverishment and urban unemployment, the low status of women, and poor states' search for foreign exchange (Truong, 1990; C. Hill, 1993). Thailand's sex tourism can be traced back through local forms of prostitution and concubinage, and colonial sex trading. Its scope and numbers dramatically changed in the face of another international process, that of militarisation, linked especially to the use of Bangkok for rest and recreation during the Vietnam War, which involved some 700 000 United States military personnel between 1962 and 1976. It has been compounded by the exponential growth in sex tourism, often supported or overlooked in Thailand's search for foreign currency in the face of the debt crisis. A class and racialised hierarchy reveals special dangers and devastation for poorer prostitutes, including those trafficked across the Thai–Burma border, displaced and impoverished through military action and discrimination on both sides of the border (*Asia Watch*, 1993).

Untangling these threads, indigenous prostitution presents its own history in different states and often in different classes too. Colonial histories in many states (though not officially Thailand) included provision of sex for colonial officials, soldiers and settlers. White women were actively discouraged from settling in tropical colonies, in particular, early on, and there was some official tolerance of concubinage, longer-term cohabitation between coloniser men and colonised women. These women remained vulnerable to abuse or abandonment, with few, if any, legal or social rights. As the nineteenth century advanced and racist discourses became more 'scientific' and infused with eugenics and fears of pollution and danger, colonised boundaries were solidified, and colonised women, especially those seen as prostitutes, came under heightened surveillance and control. Much attention was directed to sexual relations, where the boundary lines between coloniser and colonised were transgressed, and in determining who could claim white/coloniser privileges, especially in regard to children of mixed parentage (Baustad, 1994).

Sexual domination is often used as a metaphor for and privilege of other forms of domination, including colonisation. Dominant-group men expected sexual access to colonised women, while their states worked to construct and reproduce racialised orders and boundaries. While now formally dismantled, these colonial relations live on in racialised power differences and continuing, sometimes intensifying, relations of dominance, subordination and exploitation.

These relations are meshed with global processes of militarisation and restructuring. Coloniser and now-independent states' development and export-orientated development policies undermined subsistence farming and local access to land, and contemporary world-trade policies have destroyed the agriculture bases of many rural peasants, farmers and workers. Many women from rural areas, and those who moved to the cities with their men folk or for other jobs, shuttle between work as petty traders, factory workers, labourers, domestic workers and sex workers (Murray, 1991; C. Hill, 1993). Sex workers might service local men, though often in spatially and socially different locations from those for 'foreign' sex. Some move on to service foreign men, while others, including children, are forced by debt peonage or false promises into recruiters' nets, and delivered directly to the foreign sex trade. Usually though, they still have to deal with local men in or protecting the trade, and often with boyfriends too. In these circumstances, they find themselves negotiating between two different sets of men, and with different definitions of masculinity and expectations of sex, too (Sturdevant and Stoltzfus, 1993; Enloe, 1993).

The boundaries between casual and full-time sex workers is not always clear, though once into bars or brothels, escape may be hard. Distinctions between free and unfree or coerced sexual labour are also unclear, as the political economy of sex is not so different from that which prospers on cheap feminised and young labour in other kinds of work. In those workplaces, too, sex may be the price of staying employed.

> [S]ex tourism is like any other multinational industry, extracting enormous profits from grotesquely underpaid local labour and placing the immediate experience of the individual worker—what happens to the body of a 15-year-old from a village in Northeast Thailand—in the context of global economic policy. From the perspective of First World customers, the international inequalities translate into a great bargain, while their personal experiences of cut-rate ecstasy combine to make up those totals in the billions' (Robinson, 1993: 496; see also Truong, 1990).

Here, another boundary—between women and children—is blurred. In conditions of desperate poverty and family dislocation, many children are forced to take up adult roles, including as workers and quite often as families' only income earner. The End Child Prostitution in Asian Tourism organisation (ECPAT) estimates that some one million children are working as prostitutes in South and South-East Asia, where a 'new colonialism pillages Asia for children' (Kempton, 1992: 39). They work for paedophiles, with the Philippines and Thailand again especially noted, including for 'sexpatriates' who have settled locally for the sex, though many who use child prostitutes deny the paedophile label and claim local cultural differences as permission. While presumably there needs to be a recognised age of consent for prosecuting child sex, the prevalence of exploitative and dangerous forms of child labour more generally mean the issue of children's rights is far wider than the sex trade alone. And reaching the age of sixteen or even eighteen does not necessarily change the situation. Many young women, in the face of organised crime, local and police corruption, and client and manager violence are also powerless, imprisoned in a potentially deadly trade.

The lethal combination of poverty, powerlessness and poor health shows in the figures. Many prostitutes know little or nothing of AIDS, but even if they did they would be in no position to demand that their clients use condoms. Indeed, their clients' fear of AIDS has had the apparent effect of sending them in search of younger and younger girls and boys, in the hope that they are newer and therefore cleaner. In the Thai city of Chiang Mai 72 per cent of prostitutes tested HIV positive among those charging 30–50 baht (about A$2) for sex, 30 per cent of those charging 50–100 baht, and 16 per cent among those charging over 100 baht tested positive (Linter and Hseng Noung, 1992). The incidence was especially high among those who had been working for more than a year, and among young women from the hill tribes and from across the Burmese border (Eddy and Walden, 1992: 18).

What sex tourism requires is women economically desperate enough, men affluent enough to travel and willing to pay for it, local governments in search of foreign currency, and foreign businessmen (and women?) selling sexualised travel (Enloe, 1990a). States and local authorities play crucial roles in organising tourism or in turning a blind eye to it. 'The Thai state functions as the pimp and procurer for the pleasure world of advanced capitalism' (Petras and Wongchaisuwan, 1993: 442). The industry is propelled by local business owners, bar managers and pimps. The local traders include men from the 'client' states. Some US men stayed or came back to Thailand after the Vietnam War and ran bars in Patpong and Pattaya. Australian men have interests in many of the bars in the Philippines, reflected along with the targeted clients in names such as Ned Kelly and Crocodile Dundee (Hall 1992: 73). In both these states there is an elaborate bar system of drinks and 'fines' paid to the bar by men taking the women, which means that most sex workers see very little return for their labours. They are also subject to gruelling and controlling surveillance, including the need for them to have access to certificates of clean health to continue working.

Keeping in mind the different sites and configurations of this political economy of sex shifts us beyond a simple first-world/third-world and men/women dichotomy. Rich-state men or rich men from other poorer states move across borders as sex tourists. Japanese men used to go to Taiwan for sex, until establishing Chinese-Japanese relations closed off that track; they then increasingly went for Kisaeng sex tourism in South Korea, and later to Thailand and the Philippines too, often in organised, including employer-sponsored, tours. They used to go to Patpong Rd in Bangkok, but reacted aginst the noise, the shows and especially the large numbers of western men, and so now frequent their own particular areas (Matsui, 1993; C. Hill, 1993).

While sex tourism is understood to be for foreign men from rich states in search of cheap and exotic racialised sex, there are locations in North and West Africa, the Caribbean and South Asia where single women go in search of the exotic/erotic, including 'affairs' with local men, so inverting the usual gendered, but not racial, politics of international sex. Like male sex tourists, they transgress and reproduce racialised, sexualised difference. But the language around these exchanges is somewhat different, and its sites usually less organised and commercialised. In Bali's 'economy of pleasure' (Jennaway, 1993), young men 'hang around' the beach, and act as guides, often becoming 'boyfriends' of particular tourist women, who in turn give gifts and cover 'expenses' for them. A somewhat different dynamic appears in the so-called 'yellow cabs', the derisive label given to young single Japanese women who go overseas, or make contact with western men in Japan, expressly for the purpose of sex (Kelsky, 1994). In these examples, the usual compounding effects of sex, class, culture, race and age are played out in more ambiguous ways; though not so different in some cases from the stereotypic, and sometimes actual, lonely and vulnerable tourist or military man and the sex worker who can translate the relationship into that of girlfriend or wife.

Militarised sex

Much of the 'foreign sex' is not so much individual or group sex tourism as militarised prostitution, grown up especially around huge foreign military bases such as those, until recently, in the Philippines. There is the international here, too, in the close connections between the Cold War and foreign-base sex (Enloe, 1993; Godrej, 1995).

Militarised prostitution is seen as providing for the (hetero)sexual needs of the (male) soldier, rationalised in different ways as 'boys will be boys', as maintaining morale and rewarding long overseas service, and (less explicitly) as protecting and defusing the intense and intimate homo-social living of the base by providing a 'safe' outlet. There is often a racialised, as well as sexualised, subtext here. The soldiers' use of foreign (to them; local, actually) women may also play a role in the elaboration of their own identities as American, and so consolidate the very boundary of national difference that they are crossing for sex (Baustad, 1994: 13).

The connections between militarisation and sex tourism, and between bodies and danger, are illustrated in the Philippines, where some children born of US servicemen and local women become street children or grow up to service more white, western or Japanese men who come often through organised tours and networks. As in racialised domestic service, there is often a hierarchy of 'military' children, where Filipino–black boys are much cheaper than Filipino–white boys (Enloe, 1990a: 87). With the closure of the US bases, many women and children have been left destitute and without alternative means of survival—prompting some, doubtless, to join another international traffic in women going to the Gulf or Japan in various guises. Other ex-prostitutes took action to try to force the US government and navy to take responsibility for the 'children of the Cold War', born to women servicing the bases (Godrej, 1995).

In March 1992 women of Olongapo led by the Coalition for the Rights and Welfare of the Filipino Amerasian Children marched on the US embassy and called for recognition of the extent of their sexual labour and the difficulties faced by those raising Amerasian children. They sued for financial support for 8600 children (those still under the age of eighteen), on the basis of an 'implied-in-fact' contract between the US naval authorities and the women. The US defended the case on the grounds that it was beyond the court's jurisdiction, but at no stage did it deny that US authorities had been intimately involved in the base sex industry.

> For the first time, those in authority have actually acknowledged the existence of an officially sanctioned and supported system around the US military bases, which thrived on the sale of sexual labour. The women's claims and the ensuing response from the US authorities steer the issue away from simple financial compensation, towards notions of accountability and political responsibility—possibly even toward a

recognition of the significance of sexual labor within the framework of international relations (Godrej, 1995: 16).

There is a long and now well-documented international politics around military prostitution, from colonial times to the present, as colonial authorities and now foreign military commanders and local government officials negotiate to make sex available to soldiers, while reducing the local political impact. Managing the base is a foreign-policy issue, a community-relations issue and a law-and-order issue. It is also a public-health issue, with familiar antecedents in terms of earlier troublesome sexually transmitted diseases, from the UK *Contagious Diseases Acts* of the 1860s to the present, especially since AIDS came to threaten 'our [US] men' and military security itself (Bonacci and Luce, 1992).

HIV/AIDS compounds the stigmatisation of prostitutes as bad women, who are seen as responsible for its spread. It is extremely difficult for young women and children to negotiate safe sex in situations of powerlessness and potential coercion and violence, and in the knowledge that the bar or owner can easily acquire more cheap replacements. At the same time, AIDS panics provide the excuse for heightening surveillance and control of women. So in the Philippines, sex workers from Olongapo and Angles responded to the introduction of mandatory AIDS testing for them with a petition that stated 'We are in agreement that AIDS comes from the Americans', and demanded that US military personnel also be tested and carry evidence that they are not carrying the virus (Sturdevant and Stoltzfus, 1993: 340).

So, too, Filipino feminists in GABRIELA (General Assembly Binding Women for Reforms, Integrity, Equality, Leadership and Action) give a different reading to AIDS as a threat to national security, seeing US military men and foreign tourists as invading national sovereignty and infecting the body politic. Their politicisation of prostitution and violence against women locates these within the international political economy, in relations both dependent and militarised. The impact of a politics of unequal trade and debt, World Bank conditionality, restructuring and the government's search for hard currency are linked with a feminist analysis of patriarchy and the eroticisation of women's bodies.

AIDS itself is conspicuously a part of this international political economy of sex, demonstrating how permeable state borders and people's bodies are to certain kinds of international traffic. It is also internationalised in its construction in terms of sex, body and danger and of particular kinds of racialised difference. Distinctions between the pattern of AIDS in western states as primarily associated with gay sex and drug use as against more heterosexual, and especially sex-trade related, patterns in many third-world states is open to racialised readings. So 'African AIDS' is complicit in representations of Africans as deviant and over-sexed, with odd cultural practices (Patton, 1990). Bringing in a political-economy perspective includes recognising the shattering effects of AIDS in Central and East Africa, for example, on those of young working and reproductive ages, and reflects the lack of power and the poor health of so many African women, as well as the impoverishment and sex demand that pushes many women into prostitution (G. Seidel, 1993).

Women organising/transnational coalitions

In these international boundary trades, women are constructed as objects, used and abused in men's and states' competitions and conflicts. But many women do act, though within a range of constraints. Women have sought to make sense of and to resist the uses made of them, symbolically and materially, and some of those struggles are now being theorised and informing theory in feminist IR (for example, Sylvester 1993, Peterson and Runyan, 1993).

Women's and feminist organisations and coalitions, such as GABRIELA, ECPAT, Education Means Protection of Women Engaged in Recreation (EMPOWER), and the Third World Movement Against the Exploitation of Women (TW-MAE-W), work in support of women and children caught up in these powerful international sexual politics. Their analyses frequently link feminist and IPE knowledges, building theory from women's own experiences, and developing strategies for change on the ground (Sen and Grown, 1987; Heyzer et al., 1994). Their campaigns and those of other women's NGOs in poorer and richer states have succeeded in naming and publicising international sex tourism and child prostitution and pornography. They have directed public-education campaigns, demonstrations and boycotts aimed at the clients and at the network of interests and businesses that service them, including travel agents, airlines and advertisers. They have brought considerable pressure on states, including those that 'send' the men. As a result some states such as Australia and Germany have legislated to make their citizens liable for prosecution on return from using child prostitutes, a distinct departure from conventional understandings of sovereignty. These campaigns deny the inside/outside and international/domestic separations so long used to organise IR. They are informed by an understanding of the international as personal, and the personal as international (Enloe, 1990a), 'worlding' the everyday of feminist politics.

Transnational NGOs and their feminist academic allies also lobby rich-state aid agencies for funding and support to go directly to women-run NGOs, which work at the grassroots level. Their advocacy work is informed by the myriad of personal differences, choices and difficulties behind the larger patterns and structural relations that generate the trades. So while some families seek assistance in locating and recovering their children, others are reluctant or hostile when the sporadic crackdowns on child prostitution, for example, summarily return the child to them and eliminate their only source of income. Working with families and communities of origin and return must be done alongside supporting women and children in the workplace and sex place, too.

They work, too, to empower women and to dismantle the gender relations that currently so devalue women and girl children. They do so in the face of complex debates about women's agency. There is a danger of representing all third-world sex workers as innocent and passive victims, although many are indeed victimised, and work within powerful structural constraints and exploitative relations (Murray, 1994; *Asia Watch*, 1993). But young women and children do develop strategies and pursue choices to varying degrees within those constraints. While the circumstances might not promote choice or solidarity, there are stories of subversion and resistance, and of mutual support. There are also many examples of women from inside and outside the trade organising in support of sex workers (Enloe, 1993).

Sex and feminisms

Women's NGOs and campaigns within states often draw on and tap into transnational and international links and understandings. These connections are complicated by the politics around prostitution in western states, where women have organised and campaigned as sex workers for deregulation and rights, which jars against the stories of many so young and powerless and the relentless forces shaping the sex trade in poorer states. But in poor states, other forms of work are also exploitative, dangerous and underwritten in regimented and health-endangering ways, and in rich states there are poor and racialised sex workers who are subject to extreme coercion and violence. So the specificity of different women's work, status and rights, or their lack, needs to be attended to carefully.

Guarding against imperialising feminisms and replicating first-world agency and third-world victimhood is complicated more by the 'sex wars' in and between feminisms about pornography, prostitution and sexual politics, and about the merits or threats of state intervention (Kaufmann, 1993; Shrage, 1994). In the US especially, there are strong splits between different feminists. Some oppose criminalisation or regulation of prostitution, seeing the state and control of women's sexuality as part of women's oppression. Others see sexual violence and exploitation, and sometimes heterosexual sex itself, as damaging to the women involved and to all other women, in its degradation and confirmation of the sex-object use of women, and so they oppose all prostitution and pornography (Vance,1984; Segal and McIntosh, 1989; MacKinnon, 1993a). Different strategies and alliances emerge from different analyses of the bases of women's oppression or subordination. In most states, too, local and national political and enforcement personnel are part of the problem. The gross social and economic inequalities that underwrite the international sex trade are often enforced through state repression and militarisation. In such circumstances, addressing women's concerns to and claims against the state is extremely difficult.

There is a need, too, to analyse the different discourses around women and children's sexual labour, and the ways in which these issues enter the international agenda. An older language about the international traffic in women was often associated with moral and racial panics about white slavery, especially suggestions of white prostituted women in brothels providing sex for 'other' men (Reanda, 1991). Now other kinds of trafficking in women include a vast trade of 'cheap' and vulnerable young women and children across state borders, especially from Burma into Thailand, but also, for example, from Nepal into India. Illegal, isolated and unsupported, they face police and military involvement in the trade and fear deportation. Other border crossings leave many women stranded in refugee camps, where disorder and the predatory behaviour of guards and some other refugees combine with lack of access to basic resources, and force women into providing sex in return for food or 'protection' (Pittaway, 1991; Bhabha, 1993).

At the same time, there is a growing traffic in 'exotic' women from sex destination states to rich states, mainly western but including Japan. The term 'entertainers' is often a transit category or euphemism for prostitution. Some 286 000 Filipinas and some 50 000 Thai women entered Japan as entertainers between 1988 and 1992. They are particularly vulnerable as young women, in jobs that are sex related, who frequently become overstayers, in a country that is both largely unknown to them and where they are subjected to gendered, racialised stereotyping and treatment (David, 1992). This in turn affects labour migrants in more 'respectable' jobs, as, for example, Filipino maids avoid the company of 'entertainers'.

There are an estimated 200 000 Thai women in Western European brothels, and many more in other states, often they are on temporary or tourist visas or they are overstayers, caught in the familiar binds of debt, poverty, violence and control. These forms of traffic make the international/internal state distinction even more problematic. What is the difference between sex tourism that takes Australian and Japanese men to Thailand and the Philippines, and that which takes poor racialised women from South-East Asia to the brothels of Amsterdam, Tokyo or Sydney? Might it make more sense to talk of globalisation and localisation to tell these stories?

The international impacts upon the everyday life of people everywhere. Those caught up in different forms of international traffic in women are especially vulnerable to racialisation and eroticisation of their bodies and labour. While gender relations are part of international relations, so is sexuality. Women's bodies become quite literally a part of making 'the international'.

Worlding women

The preceding chapters trace gender relations in the international, through the politics of identity, war and peace, and the globalised political economy. Women are players in these international politics, and are affected by them in ways different from men, even men of their own class and state.

Women's responses to these gendered international politics include resistance to exploitation and victimisation, and organising in NGOs, social movements and campaigns to change these politics. These struggles are especially evident around women's rights issues, and in transnational feminist networks and understandings.

What can we learn from these struggles and from a feminist project that seeks to incorporate them into IR?

Are women's rights human rights?

Women are slowly becoming visible internationally and in the changing international agenda, whose 'new items' include issues raised here. In the process, feminist analysis has revealed human rights and international law to be gendered.

> Human rights are defined by the criterion of what men fear will happen to them . . . From conception to old age, womanhood is full of risks: of abortion and infanticide because of the social and economic pressure to have sons in some cultures; of malnutrition because of social practices of giving men and boys priority with respect to food; of less access to health care than men; of endemic violence against women

in all states. The great level of documented violence against women around the world is unaddressed by the international legal notion of the right to life because the legal system is focussed on 'public' actions by the state (Charlesworth, 1994: 122).

Women's equality with men was asserted in the United Nations Charter in 1945 and by the UN Commission on the Status of Women set up in 1946 (Wright, 1993). The growing mobilisation of women and the declaration of 1975 as the International Women's Year, with the Decade for Women to follow, included negotiations that secured the Convention on the Elimination of All Forms of Discrimination Against Women (CEDAW) in 1979. CEDAW sought equality for women, but did not pursue issues to do with direct violence against women. Since then, there has been ongoing debate about whether women have been overlooked or excluded from human rights, in which case the struggle is to extend those rights to women; or whether women's rights need to be women-centred, and focus especially on gender-specific violence and gender relations that position women differently in relation to the state, to violence and to productive relations generally.

Human rights are often identified in terms of generational rights—first-generation political and civil rights; second-generation social and economic rights; and third-generation or people's rights, including cultural and minority rights (James, 1994). Women's membership of many other groups mean that strengthening human rights or the rights of workers or refugees, for example, benefit women, too. But a feminist analysis reveals the gendered nature of human-rights abuses, even within this mainstream frame (Bunch, 1990). Women's ambiguous citizenship prevents full political participation, and women suffer gender-specific violence in custodial and war rape, for example. In addition, women are over-represented among the poor. Girls and women also suffer gendered structural violence, which routinely denies them access to economic and health resources. And while women experience much discrimination and violence as a result of their social or community identity, they are also often trapped within a reading of 'culture' that disguises gender power and gendered violence against women within particular families and communities.

Violence against women appears to be a universal characteristic of patriarchy, although its form, extent and intensity vary. Questioning certain kinds of masculinity and gender oppression in particular locations is a key here (Alder, 1992). Some violence takes 'cultural' or spatial forms, for example, *sati* and dowry murders in India, female genital mutilation in some North African states and female foeticide, especially in South Asia and China. While each carries its own gender politics, all stem from devaluation of women and masculinist power to define abuses against women as cultural, natural or private, not political. Women's rights are often not treated as human rights; nor have states or international human rights bodies assumed serious responsibility for abuses against women.

Human rights have long been associated with a western, liberal and individualistic approach to rights (Peterson, 1990; Charlesworth, 1994), though some anti-democratic states use this association to deny both internal and international demands for people's rights. Cultural and other differences are important in trying to answer questions about What rights? and whose rights? At the same time, women have been as disadvantaged by 'culture' as by 'nature'. In the name of a respect for culture, women's rights have often been appropriated in a struggle between different men, to define what is culture and what is right (Razack, 1994; Winter, 1994).

Organising and campaigning for women's rights require careful theorising about the causes of abuse, and of women's subordination; and finding a language, strategies and allies to strengthen women's chances and choices. So Indian feminists renamed 'bride burning' as dowry murder (Katzenstein, 1989); Filipino feminists refer to 'prostituted women' and call military-base sex 'institutionalised rape'; and in the US forced sex on dates is named acquaintance rape. Feminists in different states call violence against women a health issue, and a development issue. Other feminists suggest a focus on men's advantage rather than women's disadvantage (Eveline, 1994).

Part of the work is addressing differences among women, for there is no automatic or transparent interest or identity among women, despite the many commonalities that women do experience as women. This is often as much an issue between elite or middle-class women and poorer women within a state or region, as it is between women from different states. It is also a problem of politics and different women's ways of interpreting their own experiences. While it seems obvious to urge women to listen to other women, this can mean collaborating in strategies or decisions that go against the grain. The Indian Forum against the Oppression of Women called a national meeting on rape in Bombay in 1990, to redefine the issue in the light of the experiences of different women's organisations in fighting against rape. They grappled with contradictions on the ground between individual women's situations and the wider campaign. Some raped women sought support to force their rapist to marry them, seeing this as their only possible future option, while other poor women rated their rape as less important and damaging than their everyday struggle to survive (Davies, 1994: 72). Contesting discourses and making private secrets public mean unsettling those responses that have grown out of patriarchy. So women ask Is rape really a fate worse than death? Others seek to focus on men's or states' crime in ways that do not reproduce or require women's victimhood (Bush, 1992; Mikhailovich, 1990). So, too, feminists ask questions about why some kinds of violence are legitimated or privatised while others are condemned and punished. Why, for example, is 'the right to life' so often associated with arguments about capital punishment, or the rights of the foetus, rather than rights against state use of militarised force or survival rights (Poonacha, 1993)?

Violence against women has often been the catalyst for women organising within and between states. But women's rights have also been asserted in the context of other social movements, especially where women have been leaders and members in significant numbers. So in India, feminist critiques of and strategies against violence have grown especially in urban areas against gender-specific violence, but feminist theorising and campaigns are informed by learnings and alliances coming out of anti-caste and -communalist, development, worker and environmental movements as well (Omvelt, 1990).

Transnational feminisms?

There are now strong links across state and social-movement borders in support of women's rights. In the process, connections and networks are built internationally, through women's NGOs and international women's conferences, rethinking the impact of the international on all women's lives, and the gendered power of international political relations and processes generally.

Women's NGOs worked towards Rio in 1992, bringing together women's concerns to widen the development–environment agenda to include, for example, militarisation and violence against women (*Agenda 21*, 1992). Women' issues became visible in the lead-up to the second international human rights conference in Vienna in 1993, including through intensive preparatory committees and women's NGO forums. The Bangkok regional forum determined five priority areas to take to Vienna: violence against women, the international traffic in women, the resurgence of fundamentalisms, military rape as a crime, and women's reproductive rights. At the Vienna official forum, women's rights were overshadowed by a split characterised as first world/third world. But human rights were declared universal and indivisible, and women's rights, including rights to development and health, and freedom from discrimination and violence, were asserted.

In 1985, the UN General Assembly adapted a resolution on domestic violence. In 1993, it adopted the Declaration on Violence Against Women, which represents a significant step forward in the international politics of women's rights. It acknowledges the structural roots of violence against women in their subordination and a gender analysis that goes well beyond the anti-discrimination rhetoric. It refers to violence as gender-based, and covers public and private life, calling on states to punish perpetrators of violence in both cases. It also gives prominence to women's groups, and it recognises that culture and religion cannot be used as excuses for violence against women. There are still profound difficulties in terms of implementation, especially in an international system that depends so heavily on states—often the worst offenders—to act. But it does incorporate feminist and NGO understandings into the public international arena (Charlesworth, 1993). There are currently transnational campaigns, including to make war rape a war crime, against the international traffic in women, and in support of women's rights as migrant labourers or refugees. The international exploitation of women's and children's bodies, labour and sex, and their vulnerability to sexual abuse and violence are often the motivating force and shared experience behind feminist politics and alliances.

Transnational feminist understandings are not monolithic and many differences, on the ground and in theory, need negotiating. But connections between women's productive and reproductive lives, their political and other identities and their experiences of different kinds of violence are now being drawn and theorised. Within the globalised political economy, and its characteristic 'forced march' of women (Grewal and Kaplan, 1994; Runyan, 1996), what are the possibilities of a more internationalised and multilayered feminist politics, all the stronger for the criss-crossing of ideas, networks, and moving women themselves?

A postscript

The world of international relations as a discipline is still largely a world without women. At the same time, many feminisms are also state based, and address claims to or resist their particular state.

In this book, I argue that we cannot make sense of the world without gendering the account, without taking women's views and experiences of the world seriously, and applying a feminist lens to those topics and forms of relation that IR aims to understand. I argue, too, that we cannot make sense of women's lives without attending to 'the international', and its impact on women and gender relations more generally. 'Worlding' women means recognising that women are in the world and in world politics, which, in turn, are profoundly gendered.

Gender relations are constructed as power relations through dichotomies within which women and the feminine are inferiorised. (Elite) men are associated with mind and reason; women are associated with body and emotion. IR makes itself a disembodied discipline, colluding with political theory and philosophy in displacing the body and sex onto women, who are in turn displaced into the private, away from IR's view (Brown, 1987; cf Grosz, 1994).

Transnational relations are frequently sexualised in ways that endanger women and some men. Women's bodies are caught up, symbolically and physically, in a range of international and global processes. Women are relegated away from state and political power in ways that mark them as transgressing public/male space. Women's bodies are used to mark the boundaries of belonging in colonial and nationalist power relations and in other identity conflicts. Military women's bodies unsettle understandings of state security, as do women peace demonstrators. Women workers, including sex workers, negotiate across dangerous terrain, as race, class and nationality connect with other axes of power, inscribed on the bodies of women. In each case, the international and the personal come together in the bodies of actual women.

Running like a thread through this book, then, is the female body—marking the physicality of people's experiences of the international—and the strange absence of real bodies, especially female bodies, in IR. These bodies are not stable or transparent in their meanings or affiliations. Bodies become the site of contestation, and of negotiation of multiple identities in relations that are increasingly globalised in implication and effect.

The personal and physical cannot be separated from the

international. It is only through a resistance to hegemonic and disciplinary mapping that we can unearth the real bodies that the nation-state and mainstream IR have buried.

This book, then, is part of a feminist attempt to expose the certainties and absences of IR's masculinist discourse, and of a dangerously masculinist world. It seeks ways to look at the world that can incorporate women's experiences and make visible the gender politics of its construction and reproduction. It disrupts IR by telling other stories, stories inscribed upon the bodies of real women, across borders and time, which speak also of resistance, action, and inevitably, change.

Bibliography

Abdo, Nahla 1991, 'Women of the Intifada: Gender, Class and National Liberation', *Race and Class*, vol. 2, no. 4, pp.20–34.

Abella, Manolo 1991, 'Recent Trends in Asian Labour Migration', *Asian Migrant*, vol. 4, no. 3, pp.72–7.

Accad, Evelyne 1990, *Sexuality and War: Literary Masks of the Middle East*, New York University Press, New York.

Adam–Smith, Patsy 1984, *Australian Women at War*, Nelson, Melbourne.

Adelman, Howard ed. 1993, *Immigration and Refugee Policy: Australia and Canada Compared*, vol. 1, Melbourne University Press, Melbourne.

Afray, Janet 1992, 'The Debate on Women's Liberation in Iran' in *Expanding the Boundaries of Women's History*, eds C. Johnson-Odim and M. Strobel, Indiana University Press, Bloomington.

Afshar, Haleh ed. 1985, *Women, Work and Ideology in the Third World*, Tavistock, New York.

Afshar, Haleh ed. 1987, *Women, State and Ideology—Studies from Africa and Asia*, State University of New York Press, Albany.

Afshar, Haleh ed. 1991, *Women, Development and Survival in the Third World*, Longman, London.

Afshar, Haleh and Agarwal, Bina eds 1989, *Women, Poverty and Ideology in Asia*, Macmillan, London.

Afshar, Haleh and Dennis, Carolyne eds 1992, *Women and Structural Adjustment Policies in the Third World*, Macmillan, London.

Afshar, Haleh and Maynard, Mary eds 1994, *The Dynamics of 'Race' and Gender: Some Feminist Interventions*, Taylor and Francis, London.

Agarwal, Bina ed. 1988, *Structures of Patriarchy: the State, the Community and the Household in Modernizing Asia*, Zed Books, London.

Agarwal, Bina 1992, 'The Gender and Environment Debate: Lessons from India', *Feminist Studies*, vol. 18, no. 1, pp.119–30.

Agenda 21: Women, Environment Development 1992, United Nations

Development Fund for Women/United Nations Conference on Environment and Development, New York.

Aird, John 1990, *Slaughter of the Innocents*, The American Enterprise Institute Press, Washington.

Alcoff, Linda 1988, 'Cultural Feminism and Post Structuralism: the Identity Crisis in Feminist Theory', *Signs*, vol. 13, no. 3, pp.405–36.

Alder, Christine 1992, 'Violence, Gender and Social Change', *International Social Science Journal*, vol. 44, no. 132, pp.267–76.

Alexander, Meena 1993, 'Piecemeal Shelter: Writing, Ethnicity and Violence', *Public Culture*, vol. 5, no. 3, pp.621–5.

Alexander, M. Jacqui 1994, 'Not Just (Any)Body Can Be a Citizen: the Politics of Law, Sexuality and Postcoloniality in Trinidad, Tobago and the Bahamas', *Feminist Review*, no. 48, pp.5–23.

Alexiyevich, S. 1988, *War's Unwomanly Face*, Progress Publishers, Moscow.

Alternatives 1993, special issue 'Feminists Write International Relations', vol. 18, no. 1.

Alvarez, Sonia 1990, 'Contradictions of a Women's Space in a Male-Dominated State: the Political Role of Commissions on the Status of Women in Postauthoritarian Brazil', in *Women, International Development and Politics: the Bureaucratic Mire*, ed. K. Staudt, Temple University Press, Philadelphia.

Alvarez, Sonia E. 1990, *Engendering Democracy in Brazil: Women's Movements in Politics*, Princeton University Press, New York.

Amnesty International 1991a, *Rape and Sexual Abuse: Torture and Ill-Treatment of Women in Detention*, London.

Amnesty International 1991b, *Women in the Front Line: Human Rights Violations against Women*, London.

Amos, Valerie and Parmar, Pratibha 1984, 'Challenging Imperial Feminism', *Feminist Review*, no. 17, pp.3–20.

Anderson, Benedict 1991, *Imagined Communities: Reflections on the Origin and Spread of Nationalism*, 2nd edn, Verso, London.

Anderson, Benedict 1992, 'The New World Disorder', *New Left Review*, no. 193, pp.3–14.

Ansara, Martha 1992, 'A Man's World', *Australian Left Review*, no. 139, May, pp.36–37.

Anthias, Floya and Yuval-Davis, Nira 1992, *Racialized Boundaries: Race, Nation, Gender, Colour and Class and the Anti-Racist Struggle*, Routledge, London.

Anzaldua, Gloria 1987, *Borderlands/la frontera*, Spinsters, San Francisco.

Appadurai, Arjun 1990, 'Disjuncture and Difference in the Global Cultural Economy', *Public Culture*, vol. 2, no. 2, pp.1–24.

Appadurai, Arjun 1993, 'Patriotism and Its Futures' *Public Culture*, vol. 5, no. 3, pp.411–29.

Ardener, Shirley ed. 1993, *Women and Space: Ground Rules and Social Maps*, Berg, Oxford.

Arditti, Rita and Lykes, M. Brinton 1992, ' "Recovering Identity": the Work of the Grandmothers of Plaza de Mayo', *Women's Studies International Forum*, vol. 15, no. 4, pp.461–71.

Arena 1991, special issue on Post Colonialism, no. 96.

Arendt, Hannah 1970, *On Violence*, Harcourt, Brace and World, New York.

Aron, Adrianne, Corne, Shawne, Fursland, Anthea and Zelwer, Barbara 1991, 'The Gender-Specific Terror of El Salvador and Guatemala', *Women's Studies International Forum*, vol. 14, nos 1/2, pp.37–47.

Ashley, Rick 1989, 'Living on Border Lines: Man, Poststructuralism and War' in *International/Intertextual Relations*, eds J. Der Derian and M. Shapiro, Lexington Books, Lexington.

Ashley, Rick and Walker, Rob. 1990, 'Speaking the Language of Exile: Dissident Thought in International Studies', *International Studies Quarterly*, vol. 34, no. 3, pp.259–68.

Asia Watch and The Women's Rights Project 1993, *A Modern Form of Slavery: Trafficking of Burmese Women and Girls into Brothels in Thailand*, Human Rights Watch, New York.

Asian Migrant 1991, special issue on Asian Women Migrant Workers vol. 4, no. 2.

Asian Migrant, 1993, 'Trends in Asian Labour Migration,1992', vol. 6, no. 1, pp.4–16.

Atkinson, Judy 1990, 'Violence in Aboriginal Communities: Colonisation and Its Impact on Gender', *Refractory Girl*, no. 36, pp.21–4.

Australian Asia Worker Links 1992, *Hard Labour: Women Workers in the Asia Pacific Region*, Melbourne.

Australian Feminist Studies 1989, special issue on Sex/Gender, no. 10.

Australian Feminist Studies 1993, special issue on Gender and Ethnicity, no. 18.

Australian Feminist Studies 1994, special issue on Women and Citizenship, no. 19.

Bacchi, Carol 1986, *Women and Peace through the Polls*, Working Paper No. 8, Peace Research Centre, Australian National University, Canberra.

Bacchi, Carol 1990, *Same Difference: Feminism and Sexual Difference*, Allen & Unwin, Sydney.

Badram, Margot and Cooke, Miriam eds 1990, *Opening the Gates: a Century of Arab Feminist Writing*, Virago, London.

Bakan, Abigail and Stasiulis, Daiva 1995, 'Making the Match: Domestic Placement Agencies and the Racialization of Women's Household Work', *Signs,* vol. 20, no. 2, pp.303–35.

Baker Cottrell, Ann 1990, 'Cross-National Marriage: a Review of the Literature', *Journal of Comparative Family Studies*, vol. 21, no. 2, pp.151–70.

Balen, Ivana 1993, 'Using Women for War Propaganda: Responding to War-Time Rapes', *Women's Studies International Forum*, vol. 16, no. 5, pp.x–xiii.

Bandarage, Asoka 1991, 'In Search of a New World Order', *Women's Studies International Forum*, vol. 14, no. 4, pp.345–55.

Bannerji, Himani 1987, 'Introducing Racism: Notes Towards an Anti-Racist Feminism', *Resources for Feminist Research*, vol. 16, no. 1, pp. 10–12.

Barbalet, Jack 1988, *Citizenship: Rights, Struggle and Class Inequality*, Open University Press, Milton Keynes.

Baron, Beth 1993, 'The Construction of National Honour in Egypt', *Gender and History*, vol. 5, no. 2, pp.244–55.

Barrett, Michele 1988, *Women's Opression Today: the Marxist/Feminist Encounter*, Verso, London.

Barrett, Michele and Phillips, Anne eds 1992, *Destabilizing Theory: Contemporary Feminist Debates*, Polity, Cambridge.

Barry, Brian and Goodin, Robert eds 1992, *Free Movement: Ethical Issues in the Transnational Migration of People and Money*, Harvester Wheatsheaf, London.

Barsotti, Odo and Lecchini, Laura 1991, 'The Case of Asian Female Migrants' *Asian Migrant*, vol. 4, no.2, pp.40–5.

Barton, Jane 1993, 'Women Soldiers Tell of Rape', *Womanspeak*, December-January, pp.4–5.

Batou, Jean 1991, '100 Million Women are Missing', *International Viewpoint*, no. 206, 13 May, pp.26–8.

Baubock, Rainer 1991, 'Migration and Citizenship', *New Community*, vol. 18, no. 1, pp.27–48.

Baustad, Suzanne 1994, 'Sex and Empire Building: Prostitution in the Making and Resisting of Global Orders', paper for the Citizenship, Identity, Community conference, York University, Ontario.

Beckett, Jeremy 1988, 'Aboriginality, Citizenship and the Nation-State', *Social Analysis*, no. 24, pp.3–18.

Beckman, Peter and D'Amico, Francine eds 1994, *Women, Gender and World Politics*, Bergin and Garvey, Westport.

Bell, Di and Nelson, Topsy 1989, 'Speaking about Rape Is Everyone's Business', *Women's Studies International Forum*, vol. 12, no. 4, pp.406–16.

Beneria, Lourdes 1992, 'Accounting for Women's Work: the Progress of Two Decades', *World Development*, vol. 20, no. 11, pp.1547–61.

Bennholdt-Thomsen, Veronika 1988, 'The Future of Women's Work and Violence against Women', in *Women: the Last Colony*, eds M. Mies, V. Bennholdt-Thomsen and C. von Werlhof, Zed Books, London.

Bernard, Cheryl 1994, 'Rape as Terror: the Case of Bosnia', *Terrorism and Political Violence*, vol. 6, no. 1, pp.29–43.

Berry, Chris 1992/3, 'Exploitation or Dennis O'Rourke's The Good Woman of Bangkok', *Metro*, no. 92, pp.36–9.

Bérubé, Allan, 1990, *Coming out under Fire: the History of Gay Men and Women in World War Two*, The Free Press/Macmillan, New York.

Bhabha, Homi ed. 1990, *Nation and Narration*, Routledge, London.

Bhabha, Homi and Parekh, Bhikhu 1989, 'Identities on Parade', *Marxism Today*, June, pp.24–9.

Bhabha, Jacqueline 1993, 'Legal Problems of Refugees', *Women: A Cultural Review*, vol. 4, no. 3, pp.240–49.

Bhattacharjee, Anannya 1992, 'The Habit of Ex-Nomination: Nation, Woman, and the Indian Immigrant Bourgeoisie', *Public Culture*, vol. 5, no. 1, pp.19–44.

Bhavnani, Kum-Kum 1993, 'Towards a Multicultural Europe? "Race", Nation and Identity in 1992 and beyond', *Feminist Review* no. 45, pp.30–45.

BIR (Bureau of Immigration Research) 1991, *Australia's Population Trends and Prospects*, AGPS, Canberra.

Blake, Fred 1994, 'Foot-Binding in Neo-Confucian China and the Appropriation of Female Labour', *Signs*, vol. 19, no. 3, pp.676–712.

Bloul, Rachael 1993, 'Engendering Muslim Identities: De-territorialization and the Ethnicization Process in France', Gender Relations project, Australian National University, Canberra.

Bock, Gisela 1992, 'Equality and Difference in National Socialist Racism', in *Beyond Equality and Difference: Citizenship, Feminist Politics and Female Subjectivity*, eds G. Bock, and S. James, Routledge, London.

Bock, Gisela and James, Susan eds 1992, *Beyond Equality and Difference: Citizenship, Feminist Politics and Female Subjectivity*, Routledge, London.

Bombay Women's Centre 1992, 'Supporting Maltreated Women', *Manushi*, no. 68, pp.19–22.

Bonacci, Mark and Luce, Don, 1992, 'The AIDS Threat to South East Asians and US Military Personnel', *Bulletin of Concerned Asian Scholars*, vol. 24, no. 3, pp.48–9.

Bonnet, Michel 1993, 'Child Labour in Africa', *International Labour Review*, vol. 132, no. 3, pp.371–90.

Booth, Ken 1991, 'Security and Emancipation', *Review of International Studies*, vol. 17, pp.313–26.

Boserup, Ester 1970, *Women's Role in Economic Development*, Allen & Unwin, London.

Bottomley, Gill and de Lepervanche, Marie eds 1988, *The Cultural Construction of Race*, Sydney Association for Studies in Society and Culture, Sydney.

Bottomley, Gill, de Lepervanche, Marie and Martin, Jeannie eds 1991, *Intersexions: Gender/Class/Culture/Ethnicity*, Allen & Unwin, Sydney.

Boulding, Elise 1982, 'The Role of Women in Peace Research', *Unesco Yearbook on Peace and Conflict Studies*, Paris, pp.24–35.

Bourne, Jenny 1987, 'Homelands of the Mind: Jewish Feminism and Identity Politics', *Race and Class*, vol. 29, no. 1, pp.1–24.

Boyden, Jo 1994, 'Children's Experience of Conflict Related Emergencies', *Disasters*, vol. 18, no. 3, pp.254–67.

Bradshaw, York, Noonan, Rita and Gash, Laura 1993, 'Borrowing against the Future: Children and Third World Indebtedness', *Social Forces*, vol. 71, no. 3, pp.629–56,

Brah, Avtar 1988, 'A Journey to Nairobi', in *Charting the Journey: Writings by Black and Third World Women*, ed. S. Grewal, Sheba Feminist Publishers, London.

Brah, Avtar 1992, 'Difference, Diversity, Differentiation', *'Race', Culture and Difference*, eds J. Donald and A. Rattansi, Sage/Open University, London.

Brah, Avtar 1993, 'Re-framing Europe: En-gendering Racisms, Ethnicities and Nationalisms in Contemporary Western Europe', *Feminist Review*, no 45, pp.9–29.

Braidotti, Rosi 1994, *Nomadic Subjects: Embodiment and Sexual Difference in Contemporary Feminist Theory*, Columbia University Press, New York.

Braidotti, Rosi 1992, 'On the female feminist subject, or: from 'she-self to she-other' in *Beyond Equality and Difference: Citizenship, Feminist Politics and Female Subjectivity*, eds G. Bock and S. James, Routledge, London.

Braidotti, Rosi, Charkiewicz, Ewa, Häusler, Sabine and Wieringa, Saskiz 1994, *Women, the Environment and Sustainable Development: Towards a Theoretical Synthesis*, Zed Books/INSTRAW, London.

Brand, H. 1993, 'The World Bank, the International Monetary Fund and Poverty', *Dissent*, vol.40, Fall, pp.497–504.

Brandes, Lisa 1993, 'Who Cares? Interest, Concern and Gender in International Security Policy' International Studies Association conference paper, Acapulco.

Braybon, Gail and Summerfield, Penny 1987, *Out of the Cage: Women's Experiences in Two World Wars*, Pandora Press, London.

Brock-Utne, Birgit 1983, 'Symmetric Peace Education as advanced by Pikas, Anatol, a critique and analysis', *International Review of Education*, vol. 29, no. 3, pp.345–52.

Brock-Utne, Birgit 1985, *Educating For Peace*, Pergamon, Oxford.

Brock-Utne, Birgit 1989, *Feminist Perspectives on Peace and Peace Education*, Pergamon, New York.

Brock-Utne, Birgit 1990, 'Listen to Women—For a Change', *Peace Review*, vol. 2, no. 4, Fall, pp.32–4.

Brown, Christopher 1992, *International Relations Theory*, Harvester Wheatsheaf, Hemel Hempstead.

Brown, Laura 1993, *Ends of Empire: Women and Ideology in Early Eighteenth-Century English Literature*, Cornell University Press, Ithaca.

Brown, Wendy 1987, 'Where is the Sex in Political Theory?' *Women and Politics*, vol. 7, no. 1, pp.3–23.

Brown, Wendy 1992, 'Finding the Man in the State', *Feminist Studies*, vol. 18, no. 1, pp.7–34

Bryan, Beverly, Dadzie, Stella and Scafe, Suzanne 1985, *The Heart of the Race: Black Women's Lives in Britain*, Virago, London.

Brydon, Lynne and Chant, Sylvia 1989, *Women in the Third World: Gender Issues in Rural and Urban Areas*, Rutgers University Press, New Brunswick.

Bryson, Valerie 1992, *Feminist Political Theory: an Introduction*, Macmillan, London, 1992.

Bulbeck, Chilla 1988, *One World Women's Movement*, Pluto, London.

Bulbeck, Chilla 1991, 'New Histories of the the Memsahib and Missus: the Case of Papua New Guinea', *Journal of Women's History*, vol. 3, no. 2, pp.82–105.

Bull, Hedley, 1977, *The Anarchical Society*, Macmillan, London.

Bunch, Charlotte 1987, *Passionate Politics*, St. Martin's Press, New York.

Bunch, Charlotte, 1990, 'Women's Rights as Human Rights: towards a Re-Vision of Human Rights', *Human Rights Quarterly*, vol. 12, no. 4, pp.486–98.

Bunch, Charlotte 1992, 'A Global Perspective on Feminist Ethics and Diversity' in *Explorations in Feminist Ethics: Theory and Practice*, eds E. Browning Cole and S. Coultrap-McQuin, Indiana University Press, Bloomington.

Bunster-Burotto, Ximena 1986, 'Surviving Beyond Fear: Women and Torture in Latin America', in *Women and Change in Latin America*, eds J. Nash and H. Safa, Bergin and Garvey, New Jersey.

Bunting, Annie 1993, 'Theorizing Women's Cultural Diversity in Feminist International Human Rights Strategies', *Journal of Law and Society*, vol. 20, no. 1, pp.6–22.

Burguieres, Mary K. 1990, 'Feminist Approaches to Peace', *Millennium*, vol. 19, no. 1, pp.1–18.

Burman, Erica 1994, 'Innocents Abroad: Western Fantasies of Childhood and the Iconography of Emergencies', *Disasters*, vol. 18, no. 3, 238–53.

Burton, Antoinette 1990, 'The White Woman's Burden: British Feminists and the Indian Woman, 1865–1915', *Women's Studies International Forum*, vol. 13, no. 4, pp.295–308.

Burton, Antoinette 1991, 'The Feminist Quest for Identity: British Imperial Suffrage and "Global Sisterhood", 1900–1915', *Journal of Women's History*, vol. 3, no. 2, pp.46–81.

Bush, Diane 1992, 'Women's Movements and State Policy Reform Aimed at Domestic Violence against Women: A Comparison of Movement Mobilization in the US and India', *Gender & Society*, vol. 6, no. 4, pp.587–608.

Butler, Judith and Scott, Joan eds 1992, *Feminists Theorize the Political*, Routledge, New York.

Bynum, Victoria 1992, *Unruly Women: The Politics of Social and Sexual Control in the Old South*, University of North Carolina Press, Chapel Hill.

Bystydzienski, Jill ed. 1992, *Women Transforming Politics: Worldwide Strategies for Empowerment*, Indiana University Press, Bloomington.

Bystydzienski, Jill 1993, 'Women in Groups and Organizations: Implications for the Use of Force' in *Women and the Use of Military Force*, eds R. Howes and M. Stevenson, Lynne Rienner, Boulder.

Cagatay, Nilufer, Grown, Caren and Santiago, Adia 1986, 'The Nairobi Women's Conference: towards Global Feminism?', *Feminist Studies*, vol. 12, no. 2, pp.401–12.

Cahill, Desmond 1990, *Intermarriage in International Contexts*, Scalabrini Migration Centre, Quezon City.

Callaway, Helen 1987, *Gender, Culture and Empire: European Women in Colonial Nigeria*, Macmillan, London.

Cambridge Women's Peace Collective 1984, *My Country Is the Whole World: an Anthology of Women's Work on Peace and War*, Pandora Press, London.

Campbell, David 1992, *Writing Security: United States Foreign Policy and the Politics of Identity*, Manchester University Press, Manchester.

Campbell, David 1993, *Politics Without Principle: Sovreignty Ethics and the Narratives of the Gulf War*, Lynne Rienner, Boulder.

Cammermeyer, Margarethe 1994, *Serving in Silence*, Viking Penguin, New York.

Carby, Hazel 1982, 'White Woman Listen! Black Feminism and the Boundaries of Sisterhood' in *The Empire Strikes Back*, ed. Centre for Contemporary Cultural Studies, Hutchinson, London.

Carby, Hazel 1986, 'Lynching, Empire and Sexuality in Black Feminist Theory' in *Race, Writing and Difference*, ed. H. Gates, Chicago University Press, Chicago.

Carrillo, Roxanna, 1993, 'Violence against Women: an Obstacle to Development' in *Women's Lives and Public Policy*, eds M. Turshen and B. Halcomb, Greenwood Press, Westport.

Carroll, Berenice 1972, 'Peace Research: the Cult of Power', *Conflict Resolution*, vol. 16, no. 4, pp.591–616.

Carroll, Berenice and Hall, Barbara Welling 1993, 'Feminist Perspectives on Women and the Use of Force', in *Women and the Use of Military Force*, eds R. Howes and M. Stevenson, Lynne Rienner, Boulder.

Carter, April 1992, *Peace Movements: International Protests and World Politics since 1945*, Longman, London.

Carter, Susanne 1992, *War and Peace through Women's Eyes: a Selective Bibliography of Twentieth Century American Women's Fiction*, Greenwood Press, Westport.

Carty, Linda and Brand, Dionne 1988, ' "Visible Minority" Women—A Creation of the Canadian State', *Resources for Feminist Research*, vol. 17, no. 3, pp.39–42.

Castles, Stephen, Cope, Bill, Kalantzis, Mary and Morrissey, Michael eds 1988, *Mistaken Identity: Multiculturalism and the Demise of Australian Nationalism*, Pluto, Sydney.

Castles, Stephen 1993, 'International Movements of People and Their Relevance for Australia', *Bureau of Immigration Research Bulletin*, Australian Government Publishing Service, Canberra, pp.32–3.

Cavarero, Adriana 1992, 'Equality and sexual difference: amnesia in political thought', in *Beyond Equality and Difference: Citizenship, Feminist Politics and Female Subjectivity*, eds G. Bock and S. James, Routledge, London.

Centre for Contemporary Cultural Studies ed. 1982, *The Empire Strikes Back*, Hutchinson, London.

Chakravati, Uma 1990, 'What Happened to the Vedic *Dasi?* Orientalism, Nationalism and a Script for the Past', in *Recasting Women: essays in Indian Colonial History*, eds K. Sangari, and S. Vaid, Rutgers University Press, New Brunswick.

Chaney, Elsa and Castro, Mary eds 1989, *Muchachas No More: Domestic Workers in Latin America and the Caribbean*, Temple University Press, Philadelphia.

Chant, Sylvia 1991, *Women and Survival in Mexican Cities: Perspectives on Gender, Labour Markets and Low-Income Households*, Manchester University Press, Manchester.

Charlesworth, Hilary 1993, 'The Draft Declaration on Violence against Women', *Inkwel*, no. 5, pp.7–8.

Charlesworth, Hilary 1994, 'Women and International Law', *Australian Feminist Studies*, no. 19, pp.115–28.

Charlton, Sue Ellen, Everett, Jana and Staudt, Kathleen eds 1989, *Women, the State and Development*, State University of New York Press, Albany.

Chatterjee, Partha 1990, 'The Nationalist Resolution of the Women's Question', in *Recasting Women: essays in Indian Colonial History*, eds K. Sangari, and S. Vaid, Rutgers University Press, New Brunswick, New Jersey.

Chatterjee, Partha 1991, 'Whose Imagined Community?', *Millennium*, vol. 20, no. 3, pp.251–5.

Chattopadhyay, Kunal 1993, 'The Politics of Hate', *International Viewpoint*, no. 244, pp.28–32.

Chaudhuri, Nupur and Strobel, Margaret 1992, *Western Women and Imperialism: Complicity and Resistance*, Indiana University Press, Bloomington.

Chavez, Linda 1993, 'Just Say Latino', *New Republic*, 22 March, pp.18–19.

Chazan, Naomi 1989, 'Gender Perspectives on African States' in *Women and the State in Africa*, eds J. Parpart and K. Staudt, Lynne Rienner, Boulder.

Cherifati-Merabtine, Doria 1994, 'Algeria at a crossroads: national liberation, Islamization and women', in *Gender and National Identity: Women and Politics in Muslim Societies*, ed V. Moghadam, Zed Books, London.

Chinchilla, Norma 1989, 'Women in Revolutionary Movements: The Case of Nicaragua', in *Revolution in Central America*, ed Stanford Central American Action Network, Westview, Boulder.

Chodorow, Nancy 1978, *The Reproduction of Mothering: Psychoanalysis and the Sociology of Gender*, University of California Press, Berkeley.

Chow, Rey 1990, *Women and Chinese Modernity: the Politics of Reading Between West and East*, University of Minnesota Press, Minneapolis.

Chowdry, Prem 1990, 'Customs in a Peasant Economy: Women in Colonial Haryana, in *Recasting Women: essays in Indian Colonial History*, eds K. Sangari, and S. Vaid, Rutgers University Press, New Brunswick.

Chuchryk, Patricia 1989, 'Subversive Mothers: the Women's Opposition to the Military Regime in Chile' in *Women, the State and Development*, eds S. E. Charlton, J. Everett and K. Staudt, State University of New York Press, Albany.

Cleaver, Tessa and Wallace, Marion 1990, *Namibia: Women in War*, Zed Books, London.

Cock, Jacklyn 1989, *Maids and Madams*, The Women's Press, London.

Cock, Jacklyn 1992, *Women and War in South Africa*, Open Letters, London.

Cock, Jacklyn 1994, 'Women and the Military: Implications for Demilitarization in the 1990s in South Africa', *Gender & Society*, vol. 8, no. 2, pp.152–69.

Coe, Paul 1994, 'The Struggle for Aboriginal Sovereignty', *Social Alternatives*, vol. 13, no. 1, pp.10–12.

Cohen, Robin 1991, 'East-West and European Migration in a Global Context', *New Community*, vol. 18, no. 1, pp.9–26.

Cohen, Robin 1992, 'Migrants in Europe: Processes of Exclusion and Inclusion', *New Community*, vol. 18, no. 2, pp.332–6.

Cohn, Carol 1987, 'Sex and Death in the Rational World of Defence Intellectuals', *Signs*, vol. 12, no. 4, pp.687–718.

Cohn, Carol 1993, 'War, Wimps and Women: Talking Gender and Thinking War' in *Gendering War Talk*, eds M. Cooke and A. Woollacott, Princeton University Press, Princeton.

Cole, Eve Browning and Coultrap-McQuin, Susan eds 1992, *Explorations in Feminist Ethics: Theory and Practice*, Indiana University Press, Bloomington.

Collinson, Helen ed. 1990, *Women and Revolution in Nicaragua*, Zed Books, London.

Connell, R.W. 1985, 'Masculinity, Violence and War', *Intervention*, no. 19, pp.4–11.

Connell, R.W. 1990, 'The State, Gender and Sexual Politics: Theory and Appraisal', *Theory and Society*, vol. 19, no. 5, pp.507–44.

Connell, R.W. 1993, 'The big picture: Masculinities in Recent World History', *Theory and Society,* vol. 22, no. 5, pp.597–623.

Connell, R.W. 1995, *Masculinities*, Allen & Unwin, Sydney.

Connell, John 1991, 'The New Diaspora: Migration, Social Change, the South Pacific and Australia', *Asian Migrant*, vol. 4, no. 4, pp.pp.108–13.

Connell, John 1992, 'The Implications of Warfare for Asian Migration', *Australian Geographer*, vol. 23, no. 1, pp.44–50.

Connolly, Clara 1993, 'Culture or Citizenship', *Feminist Review*, no. 44, pp.104–111.

Conway, Jill, Bourque, Susan and Scott, Joan eds 1989 *Learning about Women: Gender, Power and Politics*, University of Michigan Press, Ann Arbor.

Cook, Rebecca 1993, 'International Human Rights and Women's Reproductive Health', *Studies in Family Planning*, vol. 24, no. 2, pp.73–86.

Cooke, Miriam 1988, *War's Other Voices: Women Writers on the Lebanese Civil War*, Cambridge University Press, New York.

Cooke, Miriam 1993, 'WØ-man, Retelling the War Myth' in *Gendering War Talk*, eds M. Cooke, and A. Woollacott, Princeton University Press, Princeton.

Cooke, Miriam and Woollacott, Angela eds 1993, *Gendering War Talk*, Princeton University Press, Princeton.

Coole, Diana 1993, *Women in Political Theory*, 2nd edn Lynne Rienner, Boulder.

Cooper, Annabel 1993, 'Textual Territories: Gendered Cultural Politics and Australian Representations of the War of 1914–1918', *Australian Historical Studies*, vol. 25, no. 100, pp.403–21.

Cooper, Helen, Munich, Adrienne and Squier, Susan Merrill 1989, *Arms and the Woman: War, Gender and Literary Representation*, University of North Carolina Press, Chapel Hill.

Cox, Robert 1987, *Production, Power and World Order: Social Forces in the Making of History*, Columbia University Press, New York.

Curry, Kate 1992, 'Child Labour in the Indian Subcontinent', *Journal of Contemporary Asia*, vol. 22, no. 4, pp.576–83.

Curthoys, Ann 1993a, 'Feminism, Citizenship and National Identity', *Feminist Review*, no. 44, pp.19–38.

Curthoys, Ann 1993b, 'Identity Crisis: Colonialism, Nation and Gender in Australian History', *Gender and History*, vol. 5, no. 2, pp.165–76.

Daly, Mary 1984, *Pure Lust: Elemental Feminist Philosophy*, The Womens Press, London.

D'Amico, Francine and Beckman, Peter eds 1994, *Women in World Politics*, Bergin and Garvey, Westport.

D'Amico, Francine 1994, 'Military Gay Exclusion and Gender: a Comparative Analysis', International Studies Association conference paper, Washington.

Damousi, Joy 1992, 'Marching to Different Drums: Womens Mobilisations 1914–1939' in *Gender Relations in Australia: Domination and Negotiation*, eds K. Saunders & R. Evans, Harcourt Brace Jovanovich, Sydney.

Dankelman, Irene and Davidson, Joan 1988, *Women and the Environment in the Third World: Alliance for the Future*, Earthscan Publications, London.

David, Randolf 1992, 'Filipino Workers in Japan: Vulnerability and Survival', *Kasarinlan*, vol. 6, no. 3, pp.9–23.

Davies, Miranda 1994, *Women and Violence*, Zed Books, London.

Davion, Victoria 1990, 'Pacifism and Care', *Hypatia*, vol. 5, no. 1, pp.90–100.

Davion, Victoria 1992, 'Caring and Violence', *Hypatia*, vol. 7, no. 1, pp.135–37.

Davis, Angela 1990, 'We Do Not Consent: Violence against Women in a Racist Society' in *Women, Culture and Politics*, Vintage Books, New York.

Davis, Kathy 1992, 'Towards a Feminist Rhetoric: the Gilligan Debate Revisited', *Women's Studies International Forum*, vol. 15, no. 2, pp.219–31.

de Groot, Joanna 1993, 'The Dialectics of Gender: Women, Men and Political Discourses in Iran c.1890–1930', *Gender and History*, vol. 5, no. 2, pp.256–68.

de Ishtar, Zohl 1994, *Daughters of the Pacific*, Spinifex, Melbourne.

de Lauretis, Teresa ed. 1988, *Feminist Studies/Critical Studies*, Indiana University Press, Bloomington.

de Lepervanche, Marie 1989, 'Breeders for Australia: a National Identity for Women?', *Australian Journal of Social Issues*, vol. 24, no. 3, pp.163–81.

de Lepervanche, Marie 1991, 'Holding It All Together: Multiculturalism, Nationalism, Women and the State in Australia', *International Review of Sociology*, no. 2, pp.73–95.

der Derian, James and Shapiro, Michael eds 1989, *International/Intertextual Relations*, Lexington Books, Lexington.

di Leonardo, Michaela 1985, 'Morals, Mothers and Militarism: Anti-Militarism and Feminist Theory', *Feminist Studies*, vol. 11, no. 3, pp.599–617.

di Leonardo, Michaela ed. 1991, *Gender at the Crossroads of Knowledge*, University of California Press, Berkeley.

di Stefano, Christine 1982, 'Masculinity as Ideology in Political Theory: Hobbesian Man Reconsidered', *Women's Studies International Forum* vol. 6, no. 6, pp.633–44.

di Stefano, Christine 1991, 'Who the Heck are We? Theoretical Turns against Gender', *Frontiers*, vol. 12, no. 2, pp.86–107.

Diamond, Irene and Orenstein, Gloria eds 1990, *Reweaving the World: the Emergence of EcoFeminism*, Sierra Club Books, San Francisco.

Dietz, Mary 1985, 'Citizenship with a Feminist Face,' *Political Theory*, vol. 13, no. 1, pp.19–37.

Dietz, Mary 1989, 'Context is All: Feminism and Theories of Citizenship' in *Learning about Women: Gender, Power and Politics*, eds J. Conway, S. Bourque, and J. Scott, University of Michigan Press, Ann Arbor.

Dimock, Liz 1993, 'Bridges across Activism and the Academy: Conference on Women in Africa and the African Diaspora', *Australian Feminist Studies*, no. 18, pp.215–27.

Disasters, 1994, Special Issue on Children and Childhood in Emergency Policy and Practice 1919–1994, vol. 18, no. 3.

Doherty, Carroll 1993, 'Heated Issue is off to Cool Start as Hearings on Gay Ban Begin', *Congressional Quarterly*, 3 April, pp.851–3.

Dolgopol, Ustinia 1994, 'Women's Views, Women's Pain', Peace Research Centre Working Paper no. 152, Australian National University, Canberra.

Donaldson, Laura 1992, *Decolonizing Feminism: Race, Gender and Responsibility*, University of North Carolina Press, Chapel Hill.

Donaldson, Mike 1993, 'What Is Hegemonic Masculinity?' *Theory and Society*, vol. 22, no. 5, pp.643–57.

Donato, Katherine 1993, 'Current Trends and Patterns of Female Migration:

Evidence from Mexico', *International Migration Review*, vol. 27, no. 4, pp.748–71.

Doty, Roxanne Lynn 1993, 'The Bounds of "Race" in International Relations', *Millennium*, vol. 22, no. 3, pp.443–62.

Drakulić, 'Slavenka 1993, *Balkan Express: Fragments from the Other Side of War*, Hutchinson, London.

Duckworth, Penny 1993, 'Frontline: (M)others in the Politics of Militarism and Identity', Honours Thesis, Women's Studies, Australian National University.

East German Feminists 1990, 'The Lila Manifesto', *Feminist Studies*, vol. 16, no. 3, pp.621–34.

Eddy, Paul and Walden, Sara 1992, 'Deadly Business', *The Australian Magazine*, 19–20 September, pp.12–18.

Einhorn, Barbara 1993, *Cinderella Goes to Market: Citizenship, Gender and the Women's Movement*, Verso, London.

Eisenstein, Hester and Jardine, Alice eds 1987, *The Future of Difference*, Rutgers University Press, New York.

Elliott, Lorraine 1993, 'Women, Gender, Feminism and the Environment' Australian Political Science Association conference, Monash University, Melbourne.

El Saadawi, Nawal 1982, *The Hidden Face of Eve*, Beacon Press, Boston.

Elshtain, Jean Bethke 1981, *Public Man, Private Woman: Women in Social and Political Thought*, Princeton University Press, Princeton.

Elshtain, Jean Bethke 1985, 'Reflections on War and Political Discourse', *Political Theory*, vol. 13, no. 1, pp.39–57.

Elshtain, Jean Bethke 1987, *Women and War*, Basic Books, New York.

Elshtain, Jean Bethke ed. 1990, *Power Trips and Other Journeys: Essays in Feminism as Civic Discourse,* University of Wisconsin Press, Madison.

Elshtain, Jean Bethke ed. 1992a, *Just War Theory,* Blackwell, Oxford.

Elshtain, Jean Bethke 1992b, 'Making Peace with Justice: the Story of Las Madres de Plaza de Mayo', *International Review of Sociology* no. 1, pp.51–94.

Elshtain, Jean Bethke 1992c, 'Sovereignty, Identity and Sacrifice' in *Gendered States: Feminist (Re)Visions of International Relations,* ed. V. S. Peterson, Lynne Rienner, Boulder.

Elshtain, Jean Bethke and Tobias, Sheila 1990, *Women, Militarism and War,* Rowman and Littlefield, Savage, Maryland.

Engels, Dagmar 1989, 'Limits of Gender Ideology: Bengali Women, the Colonial State and the Private Sphere, 1890–1930', *Womens Studies International Forum*, vol. 12, no. 4, pp.425–37.

Enloe, Cynthia 1983, 'Women Textile Workers in the Militarization of Southeast Asia' in *Women and Men in the International Division of Labour,* eds J. Nash and P. Fernandez-Kelly, State University of New York Press, Albany.

Enloe, Cynthia 1987, 'Feminist Thinking About War, Militarism and Peace' in *Analyzing Gender,* eds B.B. Hess and M. Marx Ferree, Sage, Newbury Park.

Enloe, Cynthia 1988, *Does Khaki Become You? The Militarisation of Women's Lives,* Pandora, London.

Enloe, Cynthia 1990a, *Bananas, Bases and Beaches: Making Feminist Sense of International Politics,* Pandora, London.

Enloe, Cynthia 1990b, 'The Gulf Crisis: Making Feminist Sense of It', *Pacific Research,* November, pp.3–5.

Enloe, Cynthia 1992, 'Silicon Tricks and the Two Dollar Woman', *New Internationalist,* January, pp.12–14.

Enloe, Cynthia 1993, *The Morning After: Sexual Politics at the End of the Cold War,* University of California Press, Berkeley.

Ennew, Judith 1993, 'Maids of All Work', *New Internationalist,* February, pp.11–13.

Epstein, Cynthia Fuchs 1991, 'In Praise of Women Warriors', *Dissent,* vol.38, Summer, pp.421–2.

Evans, David 1993, *Sexual Citizenship: the Material Construction of Sexualities,* Routledge, New York.

Evans, Judith ed. 1986, *Feminism and Political Theory,* Sage, London.

Evans, Raymond 1992, 'A Gun in the Oven: Masculinism and Gendered Violence' in *Gender Relations in Australia: Domination and Negotiation,* eds K. Saunders and R. Evans, Harcourt Brace Jovanovich, Sydney.

Eveline, Joan 1994, 'The Politics of Advantage', *Australian Feminist Studies,* no. 19, pp.129–54.

Evita, Elizabeth Uy 1992, *The Political Economy of Gender: Women and the Sexual Division of Labour in the Philippines,* Zed Books, London.

Featherstone, Mike ed. 1990, *Global Culture: Nationalism, Civilization and Modernity,* Sage, London.

Feminist Review 1991, special issue on Shifting Territories: Feminisms and Europe, no. 39

Feminist Review 1993a, special issue on Ethnicities, no. 43.

Feminist Review 1993b, special issue on Nationalisms and National Identities, no. 44.

Feminist Review 1994, special issue on Sex and the State, no. 48.

Feminist Review 1995, special issue on Feminist Politics—Colonial/Postcolonial Worlds, no. 49.

Ferguson, Ann 1989, *Blood at the Root: Motherhood, Sexuality and Male Dominance,* Pandora, London.

Ferguson, Kathy 1987, 'Male-Ordered Politics: Feminism and Political Science' in *Idioms of Inquiry,* ed. T. Ball, State University of New York Press, Albany.

Ferguson, Kathy 1990, 'Women, Feminism and Development' in *Women, International Development and Politics: the Bureaucratic Mire,* ed. K. Staudt, Temple University Press, Philadelphia.

Ferguson, Moira 1992, *Subject to Others: British Women and Colonial Slavery 1670–1834,* Routledge, London.

Finch, Sue et al 1986, 'Socialist Feminists and Greenham', *Feminist Review*, no 23, pp.93–101.

Fincher, Ruth 1993, 'Gender and Migration Policy' in *Immigration and Refugee Policy: Australia and Canada Compared*, vol. 1, ed. H. Adelman, Melbourne University Press, Melbourne.

Fisher, Jo 1989, *Mothers of the Disappeared*, Zed Books, London.

Fisher, Jo 1993, *Out of the Shadows: Women, Resistance and Politics in South America*, Latin American Bureau, London.

Fishman, Sarah 1992, *We Will Wait: Wives of French Prisoners of War, 1940–45*, Yale University Press, New Haven.

Flax, Jane 1987, 'Post-modernism and Gender Relations in Feminist Theory', *Signs*, vol. 12, no. 4, pp.621–43.

Flax, Jane 1990, *Thinking Fragments: Psychoanalysis, Feminism and Postmodernism in the Contemporary West*, University of California Press, Berkeley.

Florence, Mary, Marshall, Catherine and Ogden, C.K. 1987, *Militarism Versus Feminism: Writings on Women and War*, edited by Margaret Kamester and Jo Vellacott, Virago, London.

Forbes Martin, Susan 1991, *Refugee Women*, Zed Books, London.

Forcey, Linda ed. 1989, *Peace: Meanings, Politics, Strategies*, Praeger, New York.

Forcey, Linda 1994, 'Women in India Thinking about Peace: an Outsider's Reflections' International Studies Association conference paper, Washington.

Ford, Nicholas and Koetsawang, Suporn 1991, 'The Socio-cultural Context of the Transmission of HIV in Thailand', *Social Science and Medicine*, vol. 33, no. 4, pp.405–14.

Frankenberg, Ruth 1993, *White Woman, Race Matters*, University of Minnesota Press, Minneapolis.

Freedman, Lynne and Isaacs, Stephen 1993, 'Human Rights and Reproductive Choice', *Studies in Family Planning*, vol. 24, no. 1, pp.18–30.

Freeman, Carla 1993, 'Designing Women: Corporate Discipline and Barbados's Off-Shore Pink-Collar Sector', *Cultural Anthropology*, vol. 8, no. 2, pp.169–86.

French, Marilyn 1992, *The War against Women*, Summit Books, New York.

Friedman, Marilyn 1993, 'Beyond Caring: the De-Moralization of Gender' in *An Ethic of Care*, ed. M. Larrabee, Routledge, New York.

Fyfe, Alex 1989, *Child Labour*, Polity Press, Cambridge.

Gaitskell, Deborah, 1982, 'Are Servants Ever Sisters?', *Hecate*, vol. 7, no. 1, pp.102–12.

Gallagher, Nancy 1993, 'The Gender Gap in Popular Attitudes Toward the Use of Force', in *Women and the Use of Military Force*, eds R. Howes and M. Stevenson, Lynne Rienner, Boulder.

Galtung, Johan 1975, *Peace: Research Education Action*, Ejlers, Copenhagen.

Galtung, Johan 1990, 'Cultural Violence', *Journal of Peace Research*, vol. 27, no. 3, pp.291–305.

Galtung, Johan 1991, 'Woman: Man = Peace:War?' Australian Political Science Association Conference paper, Brisbane.

Garvey, Gerald and DiIulio, John 1993, 'Only Connect? Cohesion vs Combat Effectiveness', New Republic, 26 April, pp.18–21.

Gatens, Moira, 1991, Representation in/and the Body Politic' in Cartographies: Poststructuralism and the Mapping of Bodies and Spaces, eds R. Diprose and R. Ferrell, Allen & Unwin, Sydney.

Geiger, Susan 1990, 'Women and African Nationalism', Journal of Women's History, vol. 2, no. 1, pp.227–44.

Gender and History 1992, special issue on Motherhood, Race and the State in the Twentieth Century vol. 4, no. 3.

Gender and History 1993, special issue on Gender, Nationalism and National Identities vol. 5, no. 2.

Gender and Society 1990, special issue on Women and Development in the Third World vol. 4, no. 3.

George, Jim 1989, 'International Relations and the Search for a Thinking Space', International Studies Quarterly, vol. 3, no. 3, pp.269–79.

George, Jim 1994, Discourses of Global Politics: a Critical (Re)Introduction to International Relations, Lynne Reinner, Boulder.

George, Rosemary 1992, 'Travelling Light: of Immigration, Invisible Suitcases, and Gunny Sacks', Differences, vol. 4, no. 2, pp.72–99.

Germain, Adrienne et al. 1994, 'Setting a New Agenda: Sexual and Reproductive Health and Rights', in Population Policies Reconsidered; Health, Empowerment, and Rights, eds G. Sen, A. Germain and L. Chen, Harvard University Press, Boston.

Giacaman, Rita and Johnson, Penny, 1990, 'Palestinian Women Breaking Barriers', Peace Review, Fall, pp.39–42.

Gibbs, Sara 1994, 'Post-War Reconstruction in Mozambique: Re-Framing Children's Experiences of Trauma and Healing', Disasters, vol. 18, no. 3, 268–77.

Gibson, Suzanne, 1993, 'On Sex, Horror and Human Rights', Woman: a Cultural Review, vol. 4, no. 3, pp.250–61.

Gill, Stephen 1991, 'Reflections on Global Order and Sociohistorical Time', Alternatives, vol. 16, no. 3, pp.275–314.

Gill, Stephen and Law, David. 1988, The Global Political Economy: Perspectives, Problems and Policies, Johns Hopkins University Press, Baltimore.

Gilligan, Carol 1982, In a Different Voice: Psychological Theory and Women's Development, Harvard University Press, Cambridge.

Gilligan, Carol 1993, 'Reply to Critics' in An Ethic of Care, ed. M. Larrabee, Routledge, New York.

Gilroy, Paul 1987, There Ain't No Black in the Union Jack, Hutchinson, London.

Gilroy, Paul 1993, Black Atlantic: Modernity and Double Consciousness, Verso, London.

Godrej, Farah 1995, 'Women and Post-Cold War US Foreign Policy: Filipina

Prostitutes as Participants in the Cold War', International Studies Association Conference paper, Chicago.

Goetz, Anne Marie 1991, 'Feminism and the Claim to Know: Contradictions in Feminist Approaches to Women in Development' in *Gender and International Relations*, eds R. Grant and K. Newland, Open University Press, Milton Keynes.

Goldman, Emma 1991 [1911], 'Patriotism: A Menace to Liberty' reprinted in *Freedom, Feminism and the State*, ed. Wendy McElroy, Holmes and Meier, New York,

Gordon, Linda 1990, 'The Peaceful Sex? On Feminism and the Peace Movement', *NWSA Journal*, vol. 2, no. 4, pp.624–34.

Gordon, Linda 1993, 'Family Violence, Feminism and Social Control' in *Gender and American History Since 1890*, ed. B. Melosh, Routledge, London.

Grace, Felicity 1994, 'Do Theories of the State Need Feminism?' *Social Alternatives*, vol. 12, no. 4, pp.17–20.

Graham, Hilary 1991, 'The Concept of Caring in Feminist Research: the Case of Domestic Service', *Sociology*, vol. 25, no. 1, pp.61–78.

Grant, Rebecca 1991, 'The Sources of Gender Bias in International Relations Theory', in *Gender and International Relations*, eds R. Grant and K. Newland, Open University Press, Milton Keynes.

Grant, Rebecca 1992, 'The Quagmire of Gender and International Security', in *Gendered States: Feminist (Re)Visions of International Relations*, ed. V. Peterson, Lynne Rienner, Boulder.

Grant, Rebecca and Newland, Kathleen eds 1991, *Gender and International Relations*, Open University Press, Milton Keynes.

Grewal, Inderpal and Kaplan, Caren eds 1994, *Scattered Hegemonies: Postmodernity and Transnational Feminist Practices*, University of Minnesota Press, Minneapolis.

Grewal, Shabnam ed 1988, *Charting the Journey: Writings by Black and Third World Women*, Sheba Feminist Publishers, London.

Grosz, Elizabeth 1994, *Volatile Bodies: towards a Corporeal Feminism*, Allen & Unwin, Sydney.

Guidieri, Remo and Pellizzi, Francesco eds 1988, *Ethnicities and Nations*, University of Texas Press, Austin.

Gunew, Sneja and Mahyjuddin, Jan 1988, *Beyond the Echo: Multicultural Women's Writing*, University of Queensland Press, St Lucia.

Gunew, Sneja and Yeatman, Anna eds 1993, *Feminism and the Politics of Difference*, Allen & Unwin, Sydney.

Gurtov, Mel 1991, *Global Politics in the Human Interest*, 2nd edn, Lynne Rienner, Boulder.

Gutek, Barbara, Stromberg, Ann and Larwood, Laurie eds 1988, *Women and Work*, vol. 3, Sage, Newbury Park.

Guy, Donna 1992, *Sex and Danger in Buenos Aires: Prostitution, Family and Nation in Argentina*, University of Nebraska Press, Lincoln.

Hackstaff, Karla and Pierce, Jennifer 1985, 'Is Sisterhood Global?', *Berkeley Journal of Sociology,* vol. 30, pp.189–204.

Haggis, Jane 1990, 'Gendering Colonialism or Colonising Gender?', *Women's Studies International Forum,* vol. 13, nos 1/2, pp.105–15.

Haggis, Jane 1992, 'Good Wives and Mothers or Dedicated Workers: Contradiction of Domesticity in the Mission of Sister Hood' Gender Relations Project paper, Australian National University, Canberra.

Haley, Eileen 1988/9, 'El Salvador Women Guerillas', *Scarlet Woman,* no. 25, pp.10–13.

Hall, Catherine 1993, 'Gender, Nationalisms and National Identities', *Feminist Review,* no. 44, pp.97–103.

Hall, C. Michael 1992, 'Sex Tourism in South-East Asia' in *Tourism and the Less Developed Countries,* ed. D. Harrison, Belhaven Press, London.

Hall, Stuart 1988, 'New Ethnicities' in *Black Film, British Cinema,* ed K. Mercer, Institute of Contemporary Arts, London.

Hall, Stuart and Held, David 1989, 'Left and Rights', *Marxism Today,* vol. 36, no. 6, June, pp.16–21.

Halliday, Fred 1990, 'International Relations: Is There a New Agenda?', *Millennium,* vol. 20, no. 1, pp.249–59.

Hammond, Jenny 1990, *Sweeter Than Honey: Ethiopian Women and Revolution: Testimonies from Tigrayan Women,* Red Sea Press, New Jersey.

Hancock, Eleanor 1993, 'Women, Combat and the Military', *Journal of Australian Studies,* no. 37, pp.88–98.

Handler, Richard and Segal, Daniel 1993, Introduction to "Nations, Colonies and Metropols", *Social Analysis,* no. 33, pp.3–8.

Hanmer, Jalna, Radford, Jill and Stanko, Elizabeth eds 1989, *Women, Policing and Male Violence: International Perspectives,* Routledge, London.

Hansen, Karen 1990, 'Body Politics: Sexuality, Gender and Domestic Service in Zambia', *Journal of Women's History,* vol. 2, no. 1, pp.120–42.

Harding, Sandra 1986, 'The Instability of the Analytical Categories of Feminist Theory', *Signs,* vol. 11, no. 4, pp.645–60.

Harrington, Mona 1992, 'What Exactly Is Wrong with the Liberal State as an Agent of Change?', in *Gendered States: Feminist (Re)Visions of International Relations,* ed. V. Peterson, Lynne Rienner, Boulder.

Harris, Adrienne and King, Ynestra 1989, *Rocking the Ship of State: Towards a Feminist Peace Politics,* Lynne Rienner, Boulder.

Harris, Ruth 1993, 'The "Child of the Barbarian": Rape, Race and Nationalism in France During the First World War', *Past and Present,* no. 141, pp.170–206.

Hartmann, Betsy 1987, *Reproductive Rights and Wrongs: Global Politics of Population Control and Contraceptive Choices,* Harper and Row, New York.

Hartsock, Nancy 1983, *Money, Sex and Power: Towards a Feminist Historical Materialism,* Longman, New York.

Hartsock, Nancy 1984, 'Prologue to a Feminist Critique of War and Politics' in *Women's Views of the Political World of Men,* ed. J. Stiehm, Transnational Publishers, Dobbs Ferry, New York.

Hassim, Shireen and Walker, Cherryl 1993, 'Women's Studies and the Women's Movement in South Africa', *Women's Studies International Forum,* vol. 16, no. 5, pp.523–34.

Hatem, Mervat 1989, 'Through Each Other's Eyes: Egyptian, Levantine-Egyptian and European Women's Images of Themselves and Each Other', *Women's Studies International Forum,* vol. 12, no. 2, pp.183–98.

Hawkesworth, Mary 1989, 'Knowers, Knowing, Known: Feminist Theory and Claims of Truth', *Signs,* vol. 14, no. 3, pp.533–57.

Hearn, Jeff 1987, *The Gender of Oppresssion: Men, Masculinity and the Critique of Marxism,* Harvester Wheatsheaf, Brighton.

Hearn, Jeff and Morgan, David 1990, *Men, Masculinities and Social Theory,* Unwin Hyman, London.

Heise, Lori 1989, 'Crimes of Gender', *World Watch,* March-April, pp.12–21.

Hendessi, Mandana 1986, 'Fourteen Thousand Women Meet: Report from Nairobi', *Feminist Review,* no. 23, pp.147–56.

Hendessi, Mandana 1990, *Armed Angels,* Change International Reports, London.

Hennayake, Shantha 1992, 'Interactive Ethnonationalism: an Alternative Explanation of Minority Ethnonationalism', *Political Geography,* vol. 11, no. 6, pp.526–49.

Hernes, Helga 1988, 'The Welfare State Citizenship of Scandinavian Women', in *The Political Interests of Gender: developing theory and research with a feminist face,* eds K. Jones and A. Jónasdóttir, Sage, London.

Heschel, Susannah 1995, 'Feminists Gain at Cairo Population Conference', *Dissent,* vol. 42, Winter, pp.15–19.

Heyzer, Noeleen, Lycklama à Nijeholt, Geertje and Weerakoon, Nedra eds 1994, *The Trade in Domestic Workers: Causes, Mechanisms and Consequences of International Migration,* Zed Books, London.

Heyzer, Noeleen and Wee, Vivienne 1994, 'Domestic Workers in Transient Overseas Employment: Who Benefits, Who Profits?', in *The Trade in Domestic Workers,* eds N. Heyzer, N. Geertje & N. Weerakoon, Zed Books, London.

Higgonnet, Margaret 1989, 'Civil Wars and Sexual Territories', in *Arms and the Woman: War, Gender and Literary Representation,* eds H. Cooper, A. Squier and S. Merrill, University of North Carolina Press, Chapel Hill.

Higgonet, Margaret, Jenson, Jane, Michel, Sonya and Wietz, Margaret eds 1987, *Behind the Lines: Gender and the Two World Wars,* Yale University Press, New Haven.

Higgott, Richard and Richardson, Jim eds 1991, *International Relations: Australian Perspectives on an Evolving Discipline,* Australian National University, Canberra.

Hill, Catherine, 1993, 'Planning for Prostitution: an Analysis of Thailand's

Sex Industry' in *Women's Lives and Public Policy*, eds M. Turshed and B. Halcomb, Greenwood Press, Westport.

Hill, Helen 1994, 'Developing Women?', *Arena Magazine*, February-March, pp.6–7.

Hill, Peter 1993 'National Minorities in Europe', *Journal of Intercultural Studies*, vol. 14, no. 1, pp.33–48.

Hilsdon, Anne-Marie 1993, 'Martyrdom and Militarism in the Philippines', Regimes of Sexuality conference paper, ANU, Canberra.

Hiltermann, Joost 1991, *Behind the Intifada: Labour and Women's Movements in the Occupied Territories*, Princeton University Press, Princeton.

Hirsch, Marianne and Fox Keller, Evelyn eds 1990, *Conflicts in Feminism*, Routledge, New York.

Hodes, Martha 1993, 'The Sexualization of Reconstruction Politics: White Women and Black Men in the South after the Civil War', *Journal of the History of Sexuality*, vol. 3, no. 3, pp.402–17.

Hoff, Joan 1994, 'Comparative Analysis of Abortion in Ireland, Poland, and the United States', *Women's Studies International Forum*, vol. 17, no. 6, pp.621–46.

Hollinsworth, David 1992, 'Discourses on Aboriginality and the Politics of Identity in Urban Australia' and Comments, *Oceania*, vol. 63, no. 2, pp.137–55.

hooks, bell 1984, *Feminist Theory: from Margin to Centre*, South End Press, Boston.

hooks, bell 1989, *Talking Back: Thinking Feminist, Thinking Black*, South End Press, Boston.

hooks, bell 1991, *Yearning: Race, Gender and Cultural Politics*, South End Press, Boston.

Howe, Renata ed. 1993, 'Women and the State: Australian Perspectives', *Journal of Australian Studies*, special issue, no. 37.

Howes, Ruth and Herzenberg, Caroline 1993 'Women in Weapons Development: The Manhattan Project', in *Women and the Use of Military Force*, eds R. Howes and M. Stevenson, Lynne Rienner, Boulder.

Howes, Ruth and Stevenson, Michael eds 1993, *Women and the Use of Military Force*, Lynne Rienner, Boulder.

Human Rights and Equal Opportunity Commission 1991, *Racist Violence: a Report of the National Inquiry into Racist Violence in Australia*, Australian Government Publishing Service, Canberra.

Huggins, Jackie 1987, 'Firing on in the Mind: Aboriginal Domestic Servants in the Interwar Years', *Hecate*, vol. 13, no. 2, pp.5–23.

Huggins, Jackie 1992, 'A Contemporary View of Aboriginal Women's Relationship to the White Women's Movement' in *A Woman's Place in Australia*, eds L. Johnson et al, Deakin University, Geelong.

Huggins, Jackie 1993, 'Always Was, Always Will Be', *Australian Historical Studies*, vol. 25, no. 100, pp.459–64.

Huggins, Jackie et al 1991, 'Letters to the Editor', *Women's Studies International Forum*, vol.14, no.5, pp.506–7.

Huggins, Jackie and Huggins Rita 1994, *Auntie Rita*, Aboriginal Studies Press, Canberra.

Humm, Maggie ed. 1992, *Feminisms: A Reader*, Harvester Wheatsheaf, New York.

Humphrey, Michael 1991, 'Asian Women Workers in the Middle East: Domestic Servants in Jordan', *Asian Migrant*, vol. 4, no. 2, pp.53–60.

Hune, Shirley 1991, 'Migrant Women in the Context of the International Convention on the Protection of the Rights of All Migrant Workers and Members of their Families', *International Migration Review*, vol. 25, no. 4, pp.800–17.

Hutchinson, Jane 1992, 'Women in the Philippines Garments Export Industry', *Journal of Contemporary Asia*, vol. 22, no. 4, pp.471–89.

Hypatia 1990, special issue on Feminist Ethics and Care, vol.5, no.1.

Imam, Ayesha 1994, 'SAP is really sapping us', *New Internationalist*, July, pp.12–13

Inayatullah, Sohail 1992, 'Introducing the Futures of South Asia', *Futures*, vol. 24, no. 9, pp.951–7.

Inglis, Amirah 1974, *'Not a White Woman Safe': Sexual Anxiety and Politics in Port Moresby 1920–34*, Australian National University Press, Canberra.

International Migration Review 1991, special issue on Migrant Workers, vol.25, no. 4.

Isaksson, Eva ed. 1988, *Women and Military Systems*, Harvester Wheatsheaf, Brighton.

Ivekovoc, Rada 1993, 'Women, Nationalism and War: "Make Love Not War"' *Hypatia*, vol. 8, no. 4, pp.113–26.

Jackson, Cecile 1993, 'Women/Nature or Gender/History? A Critique of Ecofeminist "Development" ', *The Journal of Peasant Studies*, vol. 20, no. 3, pp.389–419.

Jacobs, Sylvia 1990, 'African-American Women Missionaries and European Imperialism in Southern Africa', *Women's Studies International Forum*, vol. 13, no. 4, pp.381–94.

James, Stanlie 1994, 'Challenging Patriarchal Privilege through the Development of International Human Rights', *Women's Studies International Forum*, vol. 17, no. 6, pp.563–78.

Janeway, Elizabeth 1987, 'Women and the Uses of Power', *The Future of Difference,* eds H. Eisenstein & A. Jardine, Rutgers University Press, New York.

Jaquette, Jane 1973, 'Women in Revolutionary Movements in Latin America', *Journal of Marriage and the Family*, vol. 35, no. 2, pp.344–54.

Jaquette, Jane 1982, 'Women and Modernization Theory: a Decade of Feminist Criticism', *World Politics*, vol. 34, no. 2, pp.267–84.

Jaquette, Jane and Staudt, Kathleen 1988, 'Politics, Population and Gender: a Feminist Analysis of US Population Policy in the Third World' in *The Political Interest of Gender: Developing Theory and Research with a Feminist Face* eds K. Jones and A. Jónasdóttir, Sage, London.

Jayawardena, Kumari 1986, *Feminism and Nationalism in the Third World*, Zed Books, London.

Jeffords, Susan 1989, *The Remasculinization of America: Gender and the Vietnam War*, Indiana University Press, Bloomington.

Jennaway, Megan 1993, 'Strangers, Sex and the State in Paradise: the Engineering of Balinese Tourism and its Economy of Pleasure', The State Sexuality and Reproduction in Asia and the Pacific Conference paper, Gender Relations Project, Australian National University, July.

Jenson, Jane 1995, 'Mapping, Naming and Remembering: Globalisation at the End of the Twentieth Century', *Review of International Political Economy*, vol. 2, no. 1, pp.96–116.

Johnson-Odim, Cheryl and Strobel, Margaret eds 1992, *Expanding the Boundaries of Women's History: Essays on Women in the Third World*, Indiana University Press, Bloomington.

Jolly, Margaret 1992, 'Other Mothers: Material Insouciance and the Regulation Debate in Fiji and Vanuatu 1890–1930', Gender Relations Project paper, Australian National University, Canberra.

Jolly, Margaret 1993, 'Colonising Women: the Maternal Body and Empire' in *Feminism and Politics of Difference*, eds S. Gunew and A. Yeatman, Allen and Unwin, Sydney.

Jolly, Margaret and McIntyre, Martha eds 1989, *Family and Gender in the Pacific: Domestic Contradictions and the Colonial Impact*, Cambridge University Press, Cambridge.

Jones, Adam 1994, 'Gender and Ethnic Conflict in Ex-Yugoslavia', *Ethnic and Racial Studies*, vol. 17, no. 1, pp.115–29.

Jones, Jacqueline 1985, *Labor of Love, Labor of Sorrow: Black Women, Work and the Family from Slavery to the Present*, Basic Books, New York.

Jones, Kathleen 1984, 'Dividing the Ranks: Women and the Draft', *Women and Politics*, vol. 4, no. 4, pp.75–88.

Jones, Kathleen 1988, 'Towards a Revision of Politics' in *The Political Interests of Gender: developing theory and research with a feminist face*, eds K. Jones and A. Jónasdóttir, Sage, London.

Jones, Kathleen 1990, 'Citizenship in a Woman-Friendly Polity', *Signs*, vol. 15, no 4, pp.781–812.

Jones, Kathleen and Jónasdóttir, Anna eds 1988, *The Political Interest of Gender: Developing Theory and Research with a Feminist Face*, Sage, London.

Kanbargi, Ramesh ed. 1991, *Child Labour in the Indian Sub-continent: Dimensions and Implications*, Sage, New Delhi.

Kandiyoti, Deniz ed. 1991a, *Women, Islam and the State*, Macmillan, London.

Kandiyoti, Deniz 1991b, 'Identity and Its Discontents: Women and the Nation', *Millennium*, vol. 20, no. 3, pp.429–43.

Kapadia, Karin 1995, 'Where Angels Fear to Tread?: "Third World Women" and "Development"', *The Journal of Peasant Studies*, vol. 22, no. 2, pp.356–68.

Kapferer, Bruce 1989, 'Nationalist Ideology and a Comparative Anthropology', *Ethnos*, vol. 54, nos 3–4, pp.161–99.

Kardam, Nuket 1991, *Bringing Women in: Women's Issues in International Development Programs*, Lynne Rienner, Boulder.

Katzenstein, Mary 1989, 'Organizing against Violence: Strategies of the Indian Women's Movement', *Pacific Affairs*, vol. 62, no. 1, pp.53–71.

Kaufmann, Linda 1993, *American Feminist Thought at Century's End: a Reader*, Blackwell, Cambridge MA.

Kelkar, Govind 1992, 'Violence against Women in India' Gender Studies Paper no. 1, Asian Institute of Technology, Bangkok.

Kelsky, Karen 1994, 'Intimate Ideologies: Transnational Theory and Japan's "Yellow Cabs"', *Public Culture*, vol. 6, no. 3, pp.465–78.

Kempton, Murray, 1992, 'A New Colonialism', *New York Review of Books*, 19 November, p.39.

Keyman, E. Fuat 1995, 'Articulating Difference: the Problem of the Other in International Political Economy', *Review of International Political Economy*, vol. 2, no. 1, pp.70–95.

Khalife, Lashar 1991, 'Women and the Intifada', *International Viewpoint*, no. 215, pp.20–3.

Khamsin 1987, *Women in the Middle East*, Zed Books, London.

King, Deborah 1988, 'Multiple Jeopardy, Multiple Consciousness', *Signs*, vol. 14, no. 1, pp.42–71.

King, Katie 1993, 'Local and Global: AIDS Activism and Feminist Theory, *Camera Obscura*, no. 28, pp.79–98.

Kishor, Sunita 1993, ' "May God Give Sons to All": Gender and Child Mortality in India', *American Sociological Review*, vol. 58, no.2, pp.247–65.

Klein, Bradley 1989, 'The Textual Strategies of Military Strategy: Or Have You Read Any Good Defence Manuals Lately' in *International/Intertextual Relations*, eds J. Der Derian and M. Shapiro. Lexington Books, Lexington.

Kligman, Gail 1992, 'The Politics of Reproduction: Ceauçescu's Romania', *East European Politics and Societies*, vol. 6, no. 3, pp.364–418.

Klusacek, Allan and Morrison, Ken eds 1992, *A Leap in the Dark: AIDS, Art and Contemporary Cultures*, Artextes, Montreal, Quebec.

Knapman, Claudia 1986, *White Women in Fiji 1835–1930: the Ruin of Empire?* Allen & Unwin, Sydney.

Knapman, Claudia 1992, 'From Missionary Wives to Development Workers: Western Women in Colonial and Postcolonial Societies', Australian Sociology Association conference paper, University of South Australia, Adelaide.

Kobayashi, Audrey 1993, 'Multiculturalism: Representing a Canadian Institution' in *Place/Culture/Representation*, eds J. Ducan and D. Ley, Routledge, London.

Kofman, Eleonore and Sales, Rosemary 1992, 'Towards Fortress

Europe?', *Women's Studies International Forum*, vol. 15, no. 1, pp.29–39.

Kofman, Eleonore and Youngs, Gillian eds 1996, *Globalization: Theory and Practice*, Pinter Press, London.

Kohn, Richard 1993, 'Women in Combat, Homosexuals in Uniform' *Parameters*, vol. 23, no. 1, pp.2–4.

Koso-Thomas, Olayinka 1987, *The Circumcision of Women: a Strategy for Eradication*, Zed Books, London.

Krause, Jill 1994, 'The International Dimension of Gender Inequality and Feminist Politics: a "New Direction for IPE?" ',Global Agendas conference paper, Nottingham.

Lake, Marilyn 1992, 'Mission Impossible: How Men Gave Birth to the Australian Nation', *Gender and History*, vol. 4, no. 3, pp.305–22.

Lake, Marilyn 1993, 'Colonised and Colonising: the White Australian Feminist Subject', *Women's History Review*, vol. 2, no. 3, pp.377–86.

Lake, Marilyn 1994, 'Between Old World "Barbarism" and "Stone Age" Primitivism: the Double Difference of the White Australian Feminist' in *Australian Women: Contemporary Feminist Thought*, eds N.Grieve and A. Burns, Oxford University Press, Melbourne.

Lamare, James 1989, 'Gender and Public Opinion: Defense and Nuclear Issues in New Zealand', *Journal of Peace Research* vol. 26, no. 3, pp.285–96.

Langer, Beryl 1990, 'From History to Ethnicity: El Salvadoran Refugees in Melbourne', *Journal of Intercultural Studies*, vol. 11, no. 2, pp.1–13.

Langer, Beryl 1991, 'Multicultural Fictions: Salvadoran Women in Australia', *Arena*, no. 96, pp.135–44.

Langton, Marcia 1981 'Urbanising Aborigines: the Social Scientists' Great Deception', *Social Alternatives*, vol. 2, no. 2, pp.16–22.

Langton, Marcia 1995, Reconciliation series, ABC Radio National, 12 April.

Lapid, Josef 1993, 'Nationalism, Identity and Security: Global Threats and Theoretical Challenges', International Studies Association conference paper, Acapulco.

Larrabee, Mary Jean ed. 1993, *An Ethic of Care*, Routledge, New York.

Larbalestier, Jan 1990, 'The Politics of Representation: Australian Aboriginal Women and the Feminist Encounter', *Refractory Girl*, no. 20/21, pp.31–9.

Lattas, Andrew 1990, 'Aborigines and Australian Nationalism', *Social Analysis*, no. 27, pp.50–69.

Lazarus, Neil 1991, 'Doubting the New World Order: Marxism, Realism and the Claims of Postmodernist Social Theory', *Differences*, vol. 3, no. 3, pp.94–138.

Lazreg, Marina 1988, 'Feminism and Difference: the Perils of Writing as a Woman on Women in Algeria', *Feminist Studies*, vol. 14, no. 1, pp.81–107.

Leacock, Eleanor and Safa, Helen eds 1986, *Women's Work: Development and the Division of Labour by Gender*, Bergin and Garvey, South Hadley Massachusetts.

Lee, Ching Kwan 1993, 'Familial Hegemony: Gender and Production Politics on Hong Kong's Electronics Shopfloor', *Gender & Society*, vol. 7, no. 4, pp.529–47

Lee, Ok-Jie 1993, 'Gender-Differentiated Employment Practices in the South Korean Textile Industry', *Gender & Society*, vol. 7, no. 4, pp.507–28

Leech, Marie 1994, 'Women, the State and Citizenship: "Are Women in the Building or in a Seperate Annex?" ', *Australian Feminist Studies*, no.19, pp.79–91.

Lee-Wright, Peter 1990, *Child Slaves*, Earthscan, London.

Leonard, Ann ed. 1989, *Seeds: Supporting Women's Work in the Third World*, Feminist Press, New York.

Lerner, Adam J. 1991, 'Transcendence of the Imagination', International Studies Association conference paper, Vancouver.

Leslie, D. A. 1993, 'Femininity, Post-Fordism and the "New Traditionalism", *Environment and Planning/Society and Space*, vol. 11, no. 6, pp.689–708.

Levy, Diane E. and Lerch, Patricia B. 1991, 'Tourism as a Factor in Development: Implications for Gender and Work in Barbados', *Gender & Society*, vol. 5, no. 1, pp.67–85.

Lewis, Desiree 1993, 'Feminisms in South Africa', *Womens Studies International Forum*, vol. 16, no. 5, pp.535–42.

Liddle, A. Mark 1989, 'Feminist Contributions to an Understanding of Violence against Women—Three Steps Forward and Two Steps Back', *Canadian Review of Sociology and Anthropology*, vol. 26, no. 5, pp.759–75.

Lightfoot-Klein, Hanny 1989, *Prisoners of Ritual: an Odyssey into Female Genital Circumcision in Africa*, Haworth Press, New York.

Lim, Linda 1983, 'Capitalism, Imperialism and Patriarchy: the Dilemmas of Third World Women in Multinational Companies' in *Women and Men in the International Division of Labour*, eds J. Nash and Fernandez-Kelly, State University of New York Press, Albany.

Linter, Vertil and Linter, Hseng Noung 1992, 'Immigrant Viruses', *Far Eastern Economic Review*, 20 February, p.31.

Lister, Ruth 1993, 'Tracing the Contours of Women's Citizenship', *Policy and Politics*, vol. 21, no.1, pp.3–16.

Lobao, Linda 1990, 'Women in Revolutionary Movements: Changing Patterns in Latin American Struggle' in *Women and Social Protest*, eds G. West and R. Blumberg, Oxford University Press, New York.

Lucashenko, Melissa 1994, 'No Other Truth? Aboriginal Women and Australian Feminism', *Social Alternatives*, vol. 12, no. 4, pp.21–4.

Luciak, Ilja 1993, 'The Struggle Goes On: Female Peasants in the Nicaraguan Transition', International Studies Association conference paper, Acapulco.

Lui, Tessie 1991, 'Race and Gender in the Politics of Group Formation', *Frontiers*, vol. 12, no. 2, pp.155–65.

Lycklama à Nijeholt, Geertje ed. 1991, *Towards Women's Strategies in the 1990s*, Macmillan, London.

McAllister, Pam ed. 1982, *Reweaving the Web of Life: Feminism and Non-Violence*, New Society Publishing, Philadelphia.

McClintock, Ann 1993, 'Family Feuds: Gender, Nationalism and the Family', *Feminist Review*, no. 44, pp.61–80.

MacDonald, Eileen 1991, *Shoot the Women First*, Fourth Estate, London.

MacDonald, Sharon, Holden, Pat and Ardener, Shirley eds 1987, *Images of Women in Peace and War: Cross Cultural and Historical Perspectives*, Macmillan, London.

McDowell, Linda and Pringle, Rosemary eds 1992, *Defining Women: Social Institutions and Gender Divisions*, Polity Press/Open University Press London.

McEachern, Charmaine 1992, 'Wild Men', *Refractory Girl*, no. 43, pp.25–8.

McGlen, Nancy and Sarkees, Meredith 1993, *Women in Foreign Policy: the Insiders*, Routledge, Chapman and Hall, New York.

McHugh, Siobhan 1993, *Minefields and Miniskirts: Australian Women and the Vietnam War*, Doubleday, Sydney.

McIntyre, Martha, 1993, 'Virtuous Women and Violent Men: Salvadoran Women and the Sexual Politics of Machismo', Humanities Research Centre paper, Australian National University, Canberra.

McKay, Nellie 1991, 'Alice Walker's "Advancing Luna—and Ida B. Wells": a Struggle Toward Sisterhood' in *Rape and Representation*, eds L. Higgins and B. Silver, Columbia University Press, New York.

MacKinnon, Catherine 1993a, *Only Words*, Harvard University Press, Cambridge, MA.

MacKinnon, Catherine 1993b, 'Turning Rape into Pornography: Postmodern Genocide', *Ms.*, July–August, pp.24–30.

MacLeod, Arlene 1991 *Accomodating Protest: Working Women, the New Veiling, and Change in Cairo*, Columbia University Press, New York.

Madood, Tariq 'British Asians and the Rushdie Affair', in *Race, Culture and Difference*, eds J. Donald and A. Rattansi, Sage/Open University, London.

Mani, Lata 1989, 'Contentious Traditions: The Debate on Sati in Colonial India', In *Recasting Women in India: essays in Colonial History*, eds K. Sangari and S. Vaid, Rutgers University Press, New Jersey.

Mani, Lata 1990, 'Multiple Mediations: Feminist Scholarship in the Age of Multinational Reception', *Feminist Review*, no. 35, pp.24–41.

Marchand, Marianne and Parpart, Jane eds 1995, *Feminism/ Postmodernism/ Development*, Routledge, London.

Marchand, Marianne 1996, 'Selling NAFTA: Gendered Metaphors and Silenced Gender Implications', in *Global Politics: Setting Agendas for the Year 2000*, eds E. Kofman and J. Youngs, Polity Press, London.

Marcus, Jane 1989, 'Corpus/Corps/Corpse: Writing the Body in/at War', *Arms and the Woman: War, Gender and Literary Representation*, eds H.

Cooper, A. Squier and S. Merrill, University of North Carolina Press, Chapel Hill.

Marginson, Melba, 1992, 'Filipina Migration and Organisation in Australia', *Lilith*, no. 7, pp.11–24.

Martin, Jeannie 1986, 'Non-English Speaking Migrant Women in Australia' in *Australian Women: New Feminist Perspectives*, eds N. Grieve and A. Burns, Oxford University Press, Melbourne.

Martin, Jeannie 1992, 'Missionary Positions', *Australian Left Review*, no. 139, May, pp.35–6.

Mason, David 1992, 'Women's Participation in Central American Revolutions', *Comparative Political Studies*, vol. 25, no. 1, pp.63–89.

Mathur, Kanchan 1992, 'Bhateri Rape Case: Backlash and Protest', *Economic and Political Weekly*, vol. 27, no. 41, 10 October, pp.2221–4.

Matsui, Yayori 1993, 'The Sex Tourist's Yen', *New Internationalist*, July, pp.16–17.

Matthews, Irene 1993, 'Daughtering in War: Two "Case Studies" from Mexico and Guatemala' in *Gendering War Talk*, eds M. Cooke and A. Woollacott, Princeton University Press, Princeton.

Mayall, James 1990, *Nationalism and International Society*, Cambridge University Press, Cambridge.

Mazumdar, Sucheta 1995, 'Women on the March: Right-Wing Mobilisation in Contemporary India', *Feminist Review*, no. 49, pp.1–28.

Meekosha, Helen and Pettman, Jan 1991, 'Beyond Category Politics', *Hecate*, vol. 17, no. 2, pp.75–92.

Melman, Billie 1992, *Women's Orients: English Women and the Middle East 1718–1918: Sexuality, Religion and Work*, Macmillan, Basingstoke.

Menchu, Rigoberta 1984, *I, Rigoberta Menchu: an Indian Woman in Guatemala*, Verso, London.

Menon, Rita and Bhazin, Kamla 1993, 'Abducted Women, the State and Questions of Honour', Gender Relations Project no. 1, Australian National University, Canberra.

Mercer, David 1993, 'Terra Nullius, Aboriginal Sovereignty and Land Rights in Australia', *Political Geography*, vol. 12, no. 4, pp.299–318.

Mercer, Kobena 1988, 'Recoding Narratives of Race and Nation', in *Black Film, British Cinema*, ed. K. Mercer, Institute of Contemporary Arts, London.

Mercer, Kobena and Julien, Isaac 1988, 'Race, Sexual Politics and Black Masculinity' in *Male Order: Unwrapping Masculinity*, eds R. Chapman and J. Rutherford, Lawrence and Wishart, London.

Meznaric, Silva 1994, 'Gender as an Ethno-Marker: Rape, War, and Identity Politics in the Former Yugoslavia' in *Identity Politics and Women: Cultural Reassertions and Feminism in International Perspective*, ed. V. Moghadam, Westview, Boulder.

Midgley, Clare 1992, *Women against Slavery: The British Campaigns 1780–1870*, Routledge, London.

241

Mies, Maria 1986, *Patriarchy and Accumulation on a World Scale*, Zed Books, London.

Mies, Maria, Bennholdt-Thomsen, Veronika and Von Werlhof, Claudia 1988, *Women: the Last Colony*, Zed Books, London.

Mies, Maria and Shiva, Vandana 1993, *Ecofeminism*, Spinifex Press, Melbourne.

Migration Action 1989, special issue on Migrant and Refugee Women, vol. 11, no. 3.

Mikhailovich, Katja 1990, 'The Social Construction of the Victim—Women as Victims of Male Violence', National Association of Women conference, Canberra.

Miles, Robert 1987, *Capitalism and Unfree Labour: Anomaly or Necessity?* Tavistock Publications, London.

Millennium 1988, special issue on Women and International Relations. vol. 17, no. 3.

Millennium 1991, special issue on Reimagining the Nation, vol. 20, no. 3.

Millennium 1993, special issue on Culture and International Relations, vol. 22, no. 3.

Miller, Francesca 1991, *Latin American Women and the Search for Social Justice*, University Press of New England, Hanover.

Miller, Jane 1991, *Seductions: Studies in Reading and Culture,* Harvard University Press, Cambridge.

Misztal, Barbara 1991, 'Migrant Women in Australia', *Journal of Intercultural Studies*, vol. 12, no. 2, pp.15–31.

Mitchell, Brian 1989, *Weak Link: the Feminization of the American Military*, Regnery Gateway, New York.

Mitchell, Brian 1990, 'Women in Arms: What Happened in Panama', *Defense Media Review*, vol. 3, no. 1, pp.1–3.

Mitchell, Sonya 1992, 'Danger on the Home Front: Motherhood, Sexuality, and Disabled Veterans in American Postwar Films', *Journal of the History of Sexuality*, vol. 3, no. 2, pp.109–28.

Mittelman, James 1994, 'The Globalisation Challenge: Surviving at the Margins', *Third World Quarterly*, vol. 15, no.3, pp.427–44.

Mitter, Swasti 1986, *Common Fate, Common Bond: Women in the Global Economy*, Pluto, London.

Mitter, Swasti 1994, 'On Organising Women in Casualised Work: a Global View' in *Dignity and Daily Bread; new forms of economic organizing among poor women in the Third World and the First*, eds S. Rowbotham and S. Mitter, Routledge, New York.

Miyoshi, Masao 1993, 'A Borderless World? From Colonialism to Transnationalism and the Decline of the Nation-State', *Critical Inquiry*, vol. 19, no. 4, pp.726–51.

Mladjenovic, Lepa and Litricin, Vera 1993, 'Belgrade Feminists 1992: Separation, Guilt and Identity Crisis', *Feminist Review*, no. 45, pp.113–19.

Moghadam, Valentine 1992, 'Development and Women's Emancipation: Is

There a Connection?', *Development and Change*, vol. 23, no. 3, pp.215–55.

Moghadam, Valentine ed. 1994a, *Gender and National Identity: Women and Politics in Muslim Societies*, Zed Books, London.

Moghadam, Valentine 1994b, 'Economic Restructuring, Identity Politics and Gender: Parallels and Constrasts in Eastern Europe and the Middle East', International Political Science Association conference, Berlin.

Moghadam, Valentine 1995, 'Women, Revolution and National Identity in the Middle East' in *The Women and International Development Annual*, vol. 4, eds R. Gallin and A. Ferguson, Westview, Boulder.

Mohanty, Chandra 1988, 'Under Western Eyes: Feminist Scholarship and Colonial Discourses', *Feminist Review*, no. 30, pp.61–88.

Mohanty, Chandra and Mohanty, Satya 1990. 'Contradictions of Colonialism', *Women's Review of Books*, vol. 7, no. 6, pp.19–21.

Mohanty, Chandra, Russo, Ann and Torres, Lourdes eds 1991, *Third World Women and the Politics of Feminism*, Indiana University Press, Bloomington.

Molyneux, Maxine 1979, 'Beyond the Domestic Labour Debate', *New Left Review*, no. 116, pp.1–27.

Molyneux, Maxine 1985, 'Mobilisation without Emancipation? Women's Interests, the State and Revolution in Nicaragua', *Feminist Studies*, vol. 11, no. 2, pp.227–54.

Molyneux, Maxine 1989, 'Some International Influences on Policy-Making: Marxism, Feminism and "the Woman Question" in Existing Socialism', *Millennium*, vol. 18, no. 2, pp.255–63.

Molyneux, Maxine 1991, 'Marxism, Feminism and the Demise of the Soviet Model' in *Gender and International Relations*, eds R. Grant and K. Newland, Open University Press, Milton Keynes.

Molyneux, Maxine and Stienberg, Deborah 1995, 'Mies and Shiva's Ecofeminism: a New Testament?', *Feminist Review,* no. 49, pp.86–107.

Momsen, Janet and Kinnaird, Vivian eds 1993, *Different Places, Different Voices: Gender and Development in Africa, Asia and Latin America*, Routledge, London.

Momsen, Janet and Townsend, Janet eds 1987, *Geography of Gender in the Third World*, Hutchinson, London.

Moreton-Robinson, Aileen 1992, 'Masking Gender and Exalting Race: Indigenous Women and Commonwealth Employment Policies', *Australian Feminist Studies*, no. 15, pp.5–10.

Morgan, David 1992, *Discovering Men*, Routledge, London.

Morgan, Robin 1984, *Sisterhood Is Global*, Anchor Press, New York.

Morgan, Robin 1989, *The Demon Lover: the Sexuality of Terrorism*, Norton, New York.

Morgenthau, Hans 1978, *Politics Among Nations: the Struggle for Power and Peace*, 5th rev. edn, Alfred A. Knopf, New York.

Morokvasic, Mirjana 1991, 'Fortress Europe and Migrant Women', *Feminist Review*, no. 39, pp.69–84.

Morris, Lydia 1993, 'Migrants and Migration', *Work, Employment and Society*, vol. 7, no. 3, pp.473–92.

Morrison, Toni 1992, *Race-ing Justice, En-gendering Power: Essays on Anita Hill, Clarence Thomas and the Construction of Social Reality*, Pantheon Books, New York.

Moser, Caroline 1991, 'Gender Planning in the Third World: Meeting Practical and Strategic Needs' in *Gender and International Relations*, eds R. Grant and K. Newland, Open University Press, Milton Keynes.

Moser, Caroline 1993, *Gender and Development: Theory, Practice and Training*, Routledge, London.

Mosse, George 1985, *Nationalism and Sexuality: Respectability and Abnormal Sexuality in Modern Europe*, Howard Fertig, New York.

Mouffe, Chantal 1992, 'Feminism, Citizenship and Radical Democratic Politics' in *Feminists Theorize the Political*, eds J. Butler and J. Scott, Routledge, New York.

Murphy, Craig and Tooze, Roger eds 1991, *The New International Political Economy*, Lynne Rienner, Boulder.

Murphy, Craig and de Ferro, Cristina Rojas 1995, 'The Power of Representation in International Political Economy: Introduction', *Review of International Political Economy*, vol. 2, no. 1, pp. 63–9.

Murray, Alison 1991, *No Money No Honey: a Study of Street Traders and Prostitutes in Jakarta*, Oxford University Press, Singapore and New York.

Murray, Alison 1994, 'Globalising Sexualities and Urban Identity Politics', Global-Local Relations in Pacific Rim Development conference paper, Australian National University, Canberra.

Murray, Kay 1993 'The Asia Pacific Regional Human Rights Conference', *Womanspeak*, June–July, pp.29–31.

Myers, William ed. 1991, *Protecting Working Children*, Zed Books/UNICEF, London.

Nain, Gemma Tang 1991, 'Black Women, Sexism and Racism', *Feminist Review*, no. 37, pp.3–22.

Nair, Janaki 1992, 'Uncovering the *Zenana*: Visions of Indian Womanhood in Englishwomen's Writing' in *Expanding the Boundaries of Women's History: Essays on Women in the Third World*, eds C. Johnson-Odim and M. Strobel, Indiana University Press, Bloomington.

Nair, Janaki 1994, 'On the Question of Agency in Indian Feminist Historiography, *Gender and History*, vol. 6, no. 1, pp.82–100.

Nam, Jeong-Lim 1994, 'Women's Role in Export Dependence and State Control of Labour Unions in South Korea', *Women's Studies International Forum,* vol. 17, no. 1, pp.57–67

Nash, June 1983, 'The Impact of the Changing International Division of Labour on Different Sectors of the Labour Force', in *Women and Men in the International Division of Labour*, eds J. Nash and P. Fernandez-Kelly, State University of New York Press, Albany.

Nash, June and Fernandez-Kelly, Patricia eds 1983, *Women and Men in the*

International Division of Labour, State University of New York Press, Albany.

New Community 1991, special issue on Migration, Racism and European Integration, vol. 18, no. 1.

Newland, Kathleen 1991, 'From Transnational Relationships to International Relations: WID and the International Decade for Women', in *Gender and International Relations*, eds R. Grant and K. Newland, Open University Press, Milton Keynes.

Nicaragua Today 1989, special issue: A Woman's Place is in the Revolution, no. 34.

Nicolson, Linda ed. 1990, *Feminism/Postmodernism*, Routledge, New York.

Nordstrom, Carolyn 1994a, *Warzones: Cultures of Violence, Militarisation and Peace*, Working Paper no. 145, Peace Research Centre, Canberra.

Nordstrom, Carolyn 1994b, *Rape: Politics and Theory in War and Peace*, Working Paper no. 146, Peace Research Centre, Canberra.

Northrup, Terrell 1994, 'Getting to Maybe: the Uneasy Partnership Between Conflict Theory and Feminist Theory', International Studies Association conference paper, Washington.

O'Connor, Julia 1993, 'Gender, Class and Citizenship in the Comparative Analysis of Welfare State Regimes', *British Journal of Sociology*, vol. 44, no. 3, pp.503–18.

O'Lincoln, Tim 1984, 'What's Wrong with Disarmament Feminism?', *Hecate*, vol. 10, no. 1, pp.86–97.

Oakley, Ann, 1974, *The Sociology of Housework*, Robertson, London.

Odeh, Lama Abu 1993, 'Post-Colonial Feminism and the Veil: Thinking the Difference', *Feminist Review*, no. 43, pp.26–37.

Oldenburg, Philip, 1992, 'Sex Ratio, Son Preference and Violence in India', *Economic and Political Weekly*, pp.2657–62, December 5–12.

Omvedt, Gail 1990, *Violence against Women: New Movements and New Theories in India*, Kali, New Dehli.

Ong, Aihwa, 1987, *Spirits of Resistance and Capitalist Discipline: Factory Women in Malaysia*, State University of New York Press, Albany.

Ostergaard, Lise ed 1992, *Gender and Development: a Practical Guide*, Routledge, London.

Pain, Rachael 1991, 'Space, Sexual Violence and Social Control', *Progress in Human Geography*, vol. 15, no. 4, pp. 415–31.

Palley, Marian Lief 1991, 'Women's Rights as Human Rights: an International Perspective', *Annals*, no. 515, pp.163–71.

Palma-Beltran, Ruby 1991, 'Filipino Domestic Helpers Overseas', *Asian Migrant*, vol. 4, no. 2, pp.46–52

Pandlan, M.S.S. 1993, ' "Denationalising" the Past: "Nation" in E.V. Ramasamy's Political Discourse', *Economic and Political Weekly*, 16 October, pp.2282–7

Parker, Andrew, Russo, Mary, Sommer, Doris and Yaeger, Patricia eds 1992, *Nationalism and Sexualities*, Routledge, London.

Parmar, Pratibha 1989, 'Other Kinds of Dreams', *Feminist Review*, no. 31, pp.55–65.

Parpart, Jane 1993, 'Who is the "Other"? A Postmodern Feminist Critique of Women and Development Theory and Practice', *Development and Change*, vol. 24, no. 4, pp.439–64.

Parpart, Jane and Staudt, Kathleen eds 1989, *Women and the State in Africa*, Lynne Rienner, Boulder.

Pateman, Carole 1988, *The Sexual Contract*, Basil Blackwell, Oxford.

Pateman, Carole 1992, 'Equality, difference, subordination: the politics of motherhood and women's citizenship', in *Beyond Equality and Difference: Citizenship, Feminist Politics and Female Subjectivity*, eds G. Bock and S. James, Routledge, London.

Patton, Cindy 1990, *Inventing AIDS*, Routledge, New York.

Paxton, Nancy 1990, 'Feminism under the Raj—Complicity and Resistance in the Writings of Flora Annie Steel and Annie Besant', *Womens Studies International Forum*, vol. 13, no. 4, pp.333–46.

Pedraza-Bailey, Silvia 1990, 'Immigration Research: A Conceptual Map', *Social Science History*, vol. 14, no. 1, pp.43–67.

Peteet, Julie 1991, *Gender in Crisis: Women and the Palestinian Resistance Movement*, Columbia University Press, New York.

Peterson, V. Spike, 1990, 'Whose Rights? A Critique of the "Givens" in Human Rights Discourse', *Alternatives*, vol. 15, no. 3, pp.303–44.

Peterson, V. Spike ed. 1992a, *Gendered States: Feminist (Re)Visions of International Relations*, Lynne Rienner, Boulder.

Peterson, V. Spike 1992b, 'Transgressing Boundaries: Theories of Knowledge, Gender and International Relations', *Millennium*, vol. 21, no. 2, pp.183–206

Peterson, V. Spike 1994, 'Gendered Nationalism', *Peace Review*, vol. 6, no. 1, pp.77–83.

Peterson, V. Spike 1995, 'Reframing the Politics of Identity: Democracy, Globalisation and Gender', *Political Expressions*, vol. 1, no. 1, pp.1–16.

Peterson, V. Spike and Runyan, Anne Sisson eds 1993, *Global Gender Issues*, University of Minnesota Press, Minneapolis.

Petras, James and Wongchaisuwan, Tienchai 1993, 'Free Markets, AIDS and Child Prostitution', *Economic and Political Weekly*, 13 March, pp.440–2.

Pettman, Jan 1992a, *Living in the Margins: Racism, Sexism and Feminism in Australia*, Allen & Unwin, Sydney.

Pettman, Jan 1992b, 'A Feminist Perspective on Peace and Security', *Interdisciplinary Peace Research*, vol. 4, no. 2, pp.59–71.

Pettman, Jan 1992c, 'Gendered Knowledges: Aboriginal Women and the Politics of Feminism', *Journal of Australian Studies*, no. 35, pp.120–31

Pettman, Jan 1992d, 'National Identity and Security' *Threats Without Enemies*, eds G. Smith and St J. Kettle, Pluto, Sydney.

Pettman, Jan Jindy 1992e, 'Women, Nationalism and the State', Gender Studies Occasional Paper no. 4, Asian Institute of Technology, Bangkok.

Pettman, Jan Jindy 1993, 'Gendering International Relations', *Australian Journal of International Affairs*, vol. 47, no. 1, pp.47–62.

Pettman, Jan Jindy 1995a, 'Border Crossings/Shifting Identities' in *Territorial Identities and Global Flows*, eds M. Shapiro and H. Alker, University of Minnesota Press, Minneapolis.

Pettman, Jan Jindy 1995b 'Gender, Ethnicity, Race and Class in Australia' in *Unsettling Settler Societies*, eds D. Stasiulis and N.Yuval-Davis, Sage, London.

Pettman, Jan Jindy 1996a, 'Second Class Citizens? Nationalism, Identity and Difference in Australia', in *Governing Gender: Sex, Politics and Citizenship in the 1990s*, eds B. Sullivan and G. Whitehouse, University of New South Wales Press, Sydney.

Pettman, Jan Jindy 1996b, 'An International Political Economy of Sex?' in *Globalization: Theory and Practice*, eds E. Kofman and G. Youngs, Pinter, London.

Pettman, Jan Jindy 1996c, 'Boundary Politics: Women, Nationalism and Danger', in *Women's Studies in National and International Contexts*, eds J. Purvis and M. Maynard, The Falmer Press, London.

Pettman, Ralph 1991, *International Politics*, Longman Cheshire, Melbourne; Lynne Reinner, Boulder.

Phare, Jane 1993, 'Women at War', *New Zealand Defence Quarterly,* no. 2, Spring, pp.2–7.

Phillips, Anne 1993, *Democracy and Difference*, Pennsylvania State University Press, University Park, Pennsylvania.

Pierson, Ruth Roach ed. 1987, *Women and Peace: Theoretical, Historical and Practical Perspectives,* Croom Helm, London.

Pietila, H. and Vickers, Jean 1990, *Making Women Matter: the Role of the United Nations,* Zed Books, London.

Pittaway, Eileen, 1991, 'Refugee Women—the Neglected Majority?', *Migration Action*, vol. 14, no. 3, 44–8.

Piquero-Ballescas, Rosario 1993, 'The Various Contexts of Filipino Labor Migration to Japan', *Kasarinlan,* vol. 8, no. 4, pp.124–45.

Plumwood, Val 1991, 'Rethinking Ecofeminist Politics', *Refractory Girl*, no. 41, pp.44–6.

Plumwood, Val 1992, 'Feminism and Ecofeminism: beyond the Dualist Assumptions of Women, Men and Nature', *The Ecologist*, vol. 22, no. 1, pp.8–13.

Poole, Ross 1985, 'Gender and National Identity', *Intervention*, no. 19, pp.71–80.

Poonacha, Veena 1993, 'On the Edge of Silence: Gender within Human Rights Discourse', *Economic and Political Weekly*, 9 October, pp.2192–4.

Potts, Lydia 1990, *The World Labour Market: A History of Migration*, Zed Books, London.

Poya, Maryam 1992, 'Double Exile: Iranian Women and Islamic Fundamentalism', in *Refusing Holy Orders: Women and Fundamentalism*, eds G. Sahgal and N. Yuval-Davis, Virago, London.

Pratt, Mary Louise 1992, *Imperial Eyes: Travel Writing and Transculturation*, Routledge, London and New York.

Price, Charles, 1990, *Ethnic Groups in Australia*, Australian Immigration Research Centre, Canberra.

Price, Susanna 1993, 'Politics and Practice of Gender Analysis in Development', *Development Bulletin*, no. 26, pp.5–9.

Przeworski, Adam 1991, *Democracy and the Market: Political and Economic Reforms in Eastern Europe and Latin America*, Cambridge University Press, Cambridge.

Puka, Bill 1993, 'The Liberation of Caring: a Different Voice for Gilligan's "Different Voice" ' in *An Ethic of Care*, ed M. Larrabee, Routledge, New York.

Quijano, Anibal and Wallerstein, Immanuel 1991, 'Americanity as a Concept, or the Americas in the Modern World-Systems', *International Social Science Journal*, vol. 4, no. 134, pp.549–57.

Radcliffe, Sarah and Westwood, Sallie eds 1993, *'Viva': Women and Popular Protest in Latin America*, Routledge, London.

Radhakrishnan, A. 1992, 'Nationalism, Gender and the Narrative of Identity', in *Nationalisms and Sexualities*, eds A. Parker, M. Russo, D. Sommer and P. Yaeger, Routledge, London.

Rai, Shirin, Pilkington, Hilary and Phizacklea, Annie eds 1992, *Women in the Face of Change: the Soviet Union, Eastern Europe and China*, Routledge, London.

Ralston, Carolyn 1990, 'Deceptive Dichotomies: Private/Public and Nature/Culture, Gender Relations in Tonga in the Early Contact Period', *Australian Feminist Studies*, no.12, pp.65–82.

Ram, Kalpana 1989, 'The Ideology of Femininity and Women's work in a Fishing Community of South India', in *Women, Poverty and Ideology in Asia*, eds H. Afshar and B. Agarwal, Macmillan, London.

Ram, Kalpana 1993, 'Too "Traditional" Once Again: Some Poststructuralists on the Aspirations of the Immigrant/Third World Female Subject', *Australian Feminist Studies*, no. 17, pp.5–28.

Ramusack, Barbara 1990, 'Cultural Missionaries, Maternal Imperialists, Feminist Allies: British Activists in India, 1865–1945', *Women's Studies International Forum*, vol. 13, no. 4, pp.309–21.

Randall, Melanie 1988, 'Feminists and the State: Questions for Theory and Practice', *Resources for Feminist Research*, vol. 17, no. 3, pp.10–16.

Randall, Vicky 1987, *Women and Politics: International Perspectives*, 2nd edn, Macmillan, London.

Razack, Sherene 1994, 'What Is to Be Gained by Looking White People in the Eye? Culture, Race and Gender in Cases of Sexual Violence', *Signs*, vol. 19, no. 4, pp.894–922.

Reanda, Laura 1991, 'Prostitution as a Human Rights Question: Problems and Prospects for United Nations Actions', *Human Rights Quarterly*, vol. 13, no. 2, pp.202–28.

Reardon, Betty 1985, *Sexism and the War System*, Teachers College Press, New York.

Rees, Matthew 1992, 'Black and Green: The Birth of "Eco-Racism"', *New Republic*, 2 March, pp.15–18

Renteln, Alison 1992, 'Sex Selection and Reproductive Freedom', *Women's Studies International Forum*, vol. 15, no. 3, pp.405–26.

Review of Radical Political Economics 1991, special issue on Women in the International Political Economy, vol. 23, nos. 3 and 4.

Rhode, Deborah 1992, 'The politics of paradigms: gender difference and gender disadvantage', in *Beyond Equality and Difference: Citizenship, Feminist Politics and Female Subjectivity*, eds G. Bock and S. James, Routledge, London.

Rhoodie, Eschel 1989, *Discrimination Against Women: a Global Survey of the Economic, Social and Political Status of Women*, McFarland, Jefferson, DC.

Rich, Adrienne 1986, *Blood, Bread and Poetry: Selected Prose, 1979–1985*, Norton, New York.

Richardson, Jo and Howes, Ruth 1993, 'How Three Female National Leaders Have Used the Military', in *Women and the Use of Military Force*, eds R. Howes and M. Stevenson, Lynne Rienner, Boulder.

Ridd, Rosemary and Callaway, Helen eds 1987, *Women and Political Conflict*, University Press, New York.

Roa, Aruna ed. 1991, *Women's Studies International: Nairobi and Beyond*, Feminist Press, New York.

Roberts, Barbara 1984, 'The Death of Machothink: Feminist Research and the Transformation of Peace Studies', *Women's Studies International Forum*, vol. 7, no. 4, pp.195–200

Robertson, Roland 1992, *Globalization: Social Theory and Global Culture*, Sage, London.

Robinson, Lillian 1993, 'The Penile Colony: Touring Thailand's Sex Industry', *The Nation*, vol. 275, no. 14, pp.492–7.

Robson, Angela 1993 'Rape: Weapon of War', *New Internationalist and Amnesty*, June, pp.13–14.

Rodda, Annabel 1991, *Women and the Environment*, Zed Books , London.

Rogers, Barbara 1981, *The Domestication of Women: Discrimination in Developing Societies*, Tavistock Press, London.

Rollins, Judith 1985, *Between Women: Domestics and their Employers*, Temple University Press, Philadelphia.

Rose, Ellen Cronan 1991, 'The Good Mother: from Gaia to Gilead', *Frontiers*, vol. 12, no. 1, pp.77–93.

Rose, Kalima 1992, *Where Women Are Leaders: the SEWA Movement in India*, Zed Books, London.

Rosen, Jeffrey 1993, 'Good Help: Race, Immigration and Nannies', *New Republic*, 15 February, pp.12–15.

Rosen, Justin 1990, 'A Non-Realist Theory of Sovereignty', *Millenium*, vol. 19, no. 2, pp.249–59.

Rosser, Sue 1991, 'Eco-Feminism: Lessons for Feminism from Ecology', *Women's Studies International Forum,* vol. 14, no. 3, pp.143–51.

Rowbotham, Sheila and Mitter, Swasti eds 1994, *Dignity and Daily Bread: New Forms of Economic Organizing among Poor Women in the Third World and the First,* Routledge, New York,

Rowse, Tim 1993, 'Mabo and Moral Anxiety', *Meanjin,* vol. 52, no. 2, pp.229–52.

Rozario, Santi 1992, *Purity and Communal Boundaries: Women and Social Change in a Bangladeshi Village,* Zed Books, London.

Rubin, Gayle 1975, 'The Traffic in Women: Notes on the Political Economy of Sex', *Towards an Anthropology of Women,* ed. R. Reiter, Monthly Review Press, New York.

Rubin, Gayle 1984, 'Thinking Sex: Notes towards a Radical Theory of the Politics of Sexuality', *Pleasure and Danger: Exploring Female Sexuality,* ed. C. Vance, Routledge and Kegan Paul, Boston.

Ruddick, Sara 1983, 'Pacifying the Forces: Drafting Women in the Interests of Peace', *Signs,* vol. 8, no. 3, pp.471–89.

Ruddick, Sara 1989, *Maternal Thinking: Toward a Politics of Peace,* Beacon Press, Boston.

Ruddick, Sara 1992, 'From Maternal Thinking to Peace Politics' in *Explorations in Feminist Ethics,* eds E. Cole and S. Coultran-McQuinn, Indiana University Press, Bloomington.

Ruddick, Sara 1993, 'Notes towards a Feminist Peace Politics' in *Gendering War Talk,* eds M. Cooke and A. Woollacott, Princeton University Press, Princeton.

Runyan, Anne Sisson 1990, 'Gender Relations and the Politics of Protection', *Peace Review,* vol. 2, no. 4, Fall, pp.28–31.

Runyan, Anne Sisson 1996, 'Trading Places: Globalisation, Regionalisation and Internationalized Feminism' eds E. Kofman and G. Youngs *Globalization: Theory and Practice,* Polity Press, London.

Runyan, Anne Sisson and Peterson, V. Spike 1991, 'The Radical Future of Realism—Feminist Subversions of International Relations Theory', *Alternatives,* vol.16, pp.67–106.

Russell, Diana ed. 1989, *Exposing Nuclear Phallacies,* Pergamon, New York.

Rutherford, Jonathan ed 1990, *Identity: Community, Culture, Difference,* Lawrence and Wishart, London.

Rutter, Itala 1990, 'Feminist Theory as Practice: Italian Feminism and the Work of Teresa de Lauretis and Dacia Maraini', *Women's Studies International Forum,* vol. 13, no. 6, pp.565–75.

Ryan, Lyndall 1986, 'Aboriginal Women and Agency in the Process of Conquest: a review of some recent work', *Australian Feminist Studies,* no. 2, pp.35–43.

Ryan, Michael and Gordon, Avery eds 1994, *Body Politics: Disease, Desire, and the Family,* Westview, Boulder.

Sahgal, Gita 1992, 'Secular Spaces: The Experience of Asian Women

Organising' in *Refusing Holy Orders: Women and Fundamentalism*, eds G. Sahgal and N. Yuval-Davis, Virago, London.

Sahgal, Gita and Yuval-Davis, Nira eds 1992, *Refusing Holy Orders: Women and Fundamentalism*, Virago, London,

Said, Edward 1978, *Orientalism*, Routledge and Kegan Paul, London.

Salleh, Ariel 1992, 'The Ecofeminism/Deep Ecology Debate: a Reply to Patriarchal Reason', *Environmental Ethics*, vol. 14, no. 3, pp.195–216.

Salleh, Ariel 1993, 'Class, Race, and Gender Discourse in the Ecofeminism/Deep Ecology Debate', *Enviromental Ethics*, vol. 15, no. 3, pp.225–44.

Sanchez, Laura 1993, 'Women's Power and the Gendered Division of Domestic Labor in the Third World', *Gender & Society*, vol. 7, no. 3, pp.434–59.

Sander Rajan, Rafeswari 1993, *Real and Imagined Women: Gender, Culture and Postcolonialism*, Routledge, London and New York.

Sangari, Kumkum and Vaid, Sudesh eds 1990, *Recasting Women: Essays in Indian Colonial History*, Rutgers University Press, New Jersey.

Sangari, Kumkum 1993, 'Consent, agency and Rhetorics of Incitement' *Economic and Political Weekly*, 1 May, pp.867–82.

Sardar, Ziauddin 1992, 'When Dracula Meets the "Other": Europe, Columbus and the Columbian Legacy', *Alternatives*, vol. 17, no. 4, pp.493–517.

Sassen-Koob, Saskia 1983, 'Labour Migration and the New Industrial Division of Labour' in *Women, Men and the International Division of Labour*, eds J. Nash & P. Fernandez-Kelly, State University of New York Press, Albany.

Sassoon, Anne S. ed. 1987, *Women and the State*, Hutchinson, London.

Saunders, Kay and Bolton, Geoffrey 1992, 'Girdled for War: Women's Mobilisation in World War 2' in *Gender Relations in Australia: Domination and Negotiation*, eds K. Saunders and R. Evans, Harcourt Brace Jovanovich, Sydney.

Saunders, Kay and Evans, Raymond eds 1992, *Gender Relations in Australia: Domination and Negotiation*, Harcourt Brace Jovanovich, Sydney.

Saunders, Malcolm 1991, 'Are Women More Peaceful than Men? WILPF in Australia 1915–45', *Interdisciplinary Peace Research*, vol. 3, no. 1, pp.45–61.

Sawer, Marion 1994, 'Reclaiming the State: Feminism, Liberalism and Social Liberalism', *Australian Journal of Politics and History*, vol. 40, Special Issue pp.159–72.

Scarry, Elaine 1985, *The Body in Pain*, Oxford University Press, Oxford.

Schick, Irvin Cemil 1990, 'Representing Middle Eastern Women: Feminism and Colonial Discourse: Review Essay', *Feminist Studies*, vol. 16, no. 2, pp.345–80.

Seager, Joni 1993, *Earth Follies: Ecofeminism, Politics and the Environment*, Earthscan, London.

Seager, Joni and Olson, Ann 1986, *Women in the World: an International Atlas*, Simon and Schuster, New York.

Segal, Lynne 1987, *Is the Future Female? Troubled Thoughts on Contemporary Feminism,* Virago, London.

Segal, Lynne 1993, 'Changing Men: Masculinities in Context', *Theory and Society,* vol. 22, no. 5, pp.225–42.

Segal, Lynne and McIntosh, Mary eds 1992, *Sex Exposed: Sexuality and the Pornography Debate,* Rutgers University Press, New Brunswick.

Segal, Mandy 1992, 'The Role of Women: the Evidence', in *Women and the Use of Military Force,* eds R. Howes and M. Stevenson, Lynne Rienner, Boulder.

Seidel, Gill 1993, 'Women at Risk: Gender and AIDS in Africa', *Disasters,* vol. 17, no. 2, pp.133–42.

Seidel, Helen 1993, *The Comfort Women Challenge Realism,* Honours thesis, Political Science Department, Australian National University, Canberra.

Seidler, Victor 1989, *Rediscovering Masculinity: Reason, Language and Sexuality,* Routledge, London.

Seitz, Barbara 1992, 'Women under Chamorro's Regime', *Against the Current,* January/February, pp.9–12.

Selig, Michael 1993, 'Genre, Gender, and the Discourse of War: the A/Historical and Vietnam Films,' *Screen,* vol. 34, no. 1, pp.1–18.

Sen, Gita and Grown, Caren 1987, *Development, Crises and Alternative Visions: Third World Women's Perspectives,* Monthly Review Press, New York.

Sen, Gita, Germain, Adrienne and Chen, Lincoln eds 1994, *Population Policies Reconsidered: Health, Empowerment, and Rights,* Harvard University Press, Boston.

Seth, Sanjay 1993, 'Political Theory in the Age of Nationalism,' State in Transition conference paper, La Trobe University, Melbourne.

Shah, Fabia 1994, *Gender and Development: a Bibliographical Guide,* Gender Relations Project, Australian National University, Canberra.

Shah, Nasra, Al-Qudsi, Sulayman and Shah, Makhdoom 1991, 'Asian Women Workers in Kuwait', *International Migration Review,* vol. 25, no. 3, pp.464–87.

Shaheed, Farida 1989, 'Purdah and Poverty in Pakistan' in *Women, Poverty and Ideology in Asia,* eds H. Afshar and B. Agarwal, Macmillan, London.

Shaheed, Farida 1994, 'Controlled or Autonomous: Identity and the Experience of the Network, Living under Muslim Law', *Signs,* vol. 19, no. 4, pp.997–1019

Sharoni, Simona 1993, 'Middle East Struggles Through Feminist Lenses', *Alternatives,* vol. 18, no. 1, pp.5–28.

Sharoni, Simona 1995, *Gender and the Israeli–Palestinian Conflict: the Politics of Women's Resistance,* Syracuse University Press, Syracuse.

Sharpe, Jenny 1991, 'The Unspeakable Limits of Rape: Colonial Violence and Counter Insurgency', *Genders,* no. 10, pp.25–46.

Sharpe, Jenny 1993, *Allegories of Empire: the Figure of Woman in the Colonial Text,* University of Minnesota Press, Minneapolis.

Shilts, Randy 1993, *Conduct Unbecoming: Lesbians and Gays in the US Military, Vietnam to the Persian Gulf*, St Martin's Press, New York.

Shiva, Vandana 1989, *Staying Alive: Women, Ecology and Development*, Zed Books, London.

Shklar, Judith 1991, *American Citizenship: the Quest for Inclusion*, Harvard University Press, Cambridge.

Shrage, Laurie 1994, *Moral Dilemmas of Feminism: Prostitution Adultery and Abortion*, Routledge, London and New York.

Shukla, Vibha 1991, 'Victims of the State: Yayavar Women Describe Government Oppression', *Manushi*, no. 66, pp.3–7.

Signs 1991, special issue on Women, Family, State and Economy in Africa, vol.16, no.4.

Siim, Birte 1994, 'Gender, Power and Citizenship', International Political Science Association congress paper, Berlin.

Silverberg, Helene 1990, 'What Happened to the Feminist Revolution in Political Science? *Western Political Quarterly*, vol. 43, no. 4, pp.887–903.

Silverblatt, Irene 1988, 'Women in States', *Annual Review of Anthropology*, vol. 17, pp.427–60.

Sivanandan, A. 1982, 'From Resistance to Rebellion: Asian and Afro-Caribbean Struggles in Britain', *Race and Class*, vol. 23, no. 2–3, pp.111–52.

Sivanandan, A. 1989, 'New Circuits of Imperialism', *Race and Class*, vol. 15, no. 2, pp.1–12.

Smith, Bernard 1981, *The Spectre of Truganini*, Australian Broadcasting Commission, Sydney.

Smith, Hugh and McAllister, Ian 1991, 'The Changing Military Profession: Integrating Women into the Australian Defence Force', *Australian and New Zealand Journal of Sociology*, vol. 27, no. 3, pp.369–90.

Smith, Joan and Wallerstein, Immanuel 1992, *Creating and Transforming Households in the World Economy*, Cambridge University Press, Cambridge and New York.

Smith, Steve 1993, 'Unacceptable Conclusions for Whom? Feminism, Masculinity and the Study of International Relations', International Studies Association conference paper, Acapulco.

Smith, Tim, 1984, 'The Polls: Gender and Attitudes towards Violence', *Public Opinion Quarterly*, vol. 48, no. 3, pp.384–96.

Snitow, Ann 1989, 'Pages from a Gender Diary: Basic Divisions in Feminism', *Dissent*, vol. 36, Spring, pp.205–224.

Souter, Fenella, 1992, 'The Bad Man of Bangkok?', *HQ*, Autumn, 110–14.

Spain, Daphne, 1993, 'Gendered Spaces and Women's Status', *Sociological Theory*, vol. 11, no. 2, pp.137–49.

Spelman, Elizabeth 1988, *Inessential Woman: Problems of Exclusion in Feminist Thought*, Beacon Press, Boston.

Spivak, Gayatri 1985, 'The Rani of Sirmur: An Essay in Reading the Archives', *History and Theory*, vol. 24, no. 3, pp.247–72.

Spivak, Gayatri 1987, *In Other Worlds: Essays in Cultural Politics*, Methuen, New York and London.

Spivak, Gayatri 1989, 'In a Word: Interview', *Differences*, vol. 1, no. 2, pp.124–56.

Spretnak, Charlene 1984, 'Naming the Cultural Forces That Push Us towards War' in *Nuclear Strategy and the Code of the Warrior*, eds R. Grossinger and L. Hough, North Atlantic Books, Berkeley.

Squier, Susan 1993, ' "The [Impregnable] Mother of All Battles": War, Reproduction, and Visualisation Technology', *Meridian*, vol. 12, no. 1, pp.3–18.

Stabile, Carol 1994, ' "A Garden Inclosed Is My Sister": Ecofeminism and Eco-Valences', *Cultural Studies*, vol. 8, no. 1, pp.56–73.

Stack, Carol 1993, 'The Culture of Gender: Women and Men of Colour' in *An Ethic of Care*, ed. M. Larrabee, Routledge, New York.

Staeheli, Lynn 1994, 'Empowering Women's Citizenship', *Political Geography*, vol. 13, no. 5, pp.443–60.

Standing, Guy 1992, Global Feminization through Flexible Labour' in *The Political Economy of Development and Underdevelopment*, eds C. Wilber and K. Jameson, McGraw Hill, New York.

Stasiulis, Daiva and Yuval-Davis, Nira eds 1995, *Unsettling Settler Societies*, Sage, London.

Staudt, Kathleen ed. 1990, *Women, International Development and Politics: the Bureaucratic Mire*, Temple University Press, Philadelphia.

Staunton, Irene 1991, *Mothers of the Revolution: the War Experiences of Thirty Zimbabwean Women*, Indiana University Press, Bloomington.

Stead, Mary 1987, 'Women, War and Underdevelopment in Nicaragua' in *Women, State and Ideology—Studies from Africa and Asia*, ed. H. Afshar, State University of New York Press, Albany.

Steady, Filomina ed. 1993, *Women and Children First: Environment, Poverty and Sustainable Development*, Schenkman Books, Rochester.

Stiehm, Judith ed. 1984, *Women and Men's Wars*, Pergamon Press, Oxford.

Stiehm, Judith ed. 1984, *Women's Views of the Political World of Men*, Transnational Publishers, Dobbs Ferry, New York.

Stiehm, Judith 1989, *Arms and the Enlisted Woman*, Temple University Press, Philadelphia.

Stimpson, David, Jensen, Larry and Neff, Wayne 1992, 'Cross-Cultural Gender Differences in Preference for a Caring Morality', *Journal of Social Psychology*, vol. 132, no. 3, pp.317–22.

Stoler, Ann 1991, 'Carnal Knowledge and Imperial Power: Gender, Race and Morality in Colonial Asia' in *Gender at the Crossroads of Knowledge*, ed. M. di Leonardo, University of California Press, Berkeley.

Stone, Robert 1993, 'Uncle Sam Doesn't Want You', *The New York Review of Books,* 23 September, pp.18–23.

Strange, Carolyn 1990, 'Mothers on the March: Maternalism in Women's Protests for Peace: North America and Western Europe 1900–1985' in *Women and Social Protest*, eds G. West & R. L. Blumberg, Oxford University Press, New York.

Strobel, Margaret 1991, *European Women and the Second British Empire*, Indiana University Press, Bloomington.

Stoltzfus, Brenda 1990, 'Do Prostitutes Have Human Rights?' in *And She Said No! Human Rights, Women's Identities and Struggles*, eds L. Bautidta and E. Rifareal, National Council of Churches in the Philippines, Quezon City.

Sturdevant, Sandra and Stoltzfus, Brenda 1993, *Let the Good Times Roll: Prostitution and the US Military in Asia*, New Press, New York.

Suganami, Hidemi 1990, 'Bringing Order to the Causes of War Debate', *Millennium*, vol. 19, no. 1, pp.19–35.

Sunstein, Cass ed. 1990, *Feminism and Political Theory*, University of Chicago Press, Chicago.

Sylvester, Christine 1987, 'Some Dangers in Merging Feminist and Peace Projects', *Alternatives*, no. 12, pp.493–509.

Sylvester, Christine 1989a, 'The Emperors' Theories and Transformations: Looking at the Field Through Feminist Lenses' in *Transformations in the Global Political Economy*, eds D. Pirages and C. Sylvester, Macmillan, London.

Sylvester, Christine 1989b, 'Patriarchy, Peace and Women Warriors' in *Peace: Meanings, Politics, Strategies*, ed. L. R. Forcey, Praeger, New York.

Sylvester, Christine 1991, 'Urban Women Cooperators, Progress and African Feminism in Zimbabwe', *Differences*, vol. 3, no. 1, pp.39–62.

Sylvester, Christine 1992, 'Feminists and Realists View Autonomy and Obligation in International Relations', in *Gendered States: Feminist (Re)Visions of International Relations*, ed. V. S. Peterson, Lynne Rienner, Boulder.

Sylvester, Christine, 1993 'Feminists Write International Relations', *Alternatives*, vol. 18, no. 1, pp.1–4.

Sylvester, Christine 1994a, *Feminist Theory and International Relations in a Postmodern Era*, Cambridge University Press, Cambridge.

Sylvester, Christine 1994b, 'Empathetic Cooperation: a Feminist Method for International Relations', *Millenium*, vol.23, no. 1, pp.407–24.

Taussig, Michael 1992, 'The Magic of the State', *Public Culture*, vol. 5, no. 1, pp.63–6.

Taylor, Diana 1993, 'Spectacular Bodies: Gender, Terror and Argentina's "Dirty War"', in *Gendering War Talk*, eds M. Cooke and A. Woollacott, Princeton University Press, Princeton.

Tetreault, Mary Ann ed. 1994, *Women and Revolution in Africa, Asia and the New World*, University of South Carolina Press, Columbia.

Tetreault, Mary Ann 1995, 'Accountability or Justice? Rape as a War Crime', International Studies Association conference paper, Chicago.

Theweleit, Klaus 1993, 'The Bomb's Womb and the Genders of War' in *Gendering War Talk*, eds M. Cooke and A. Woollacott, Princeton University Press, Princeton.

Thiam, Awa 1986, *Black Sisters, Speak Out: Feminism and Oppression in Black Africa*, Pluto, London.

Third World Quarterly 1989, special issue on Ethnicity and World Politics, vol.11, no.4.

Thompson, Dorothy ed. 1983, *Over Our Dead Bodies: Women against the Bomb*, Virago, London.

Thompson, Janna 1991, 'Women and War', *Women's Studies International Forum*, vol. 14, no. 1/2, pp.63–75.

Tickner, J. Ann 1991, 'On the Fringes of the World Economy: a Feminist Perspective', in *The New International Political Economy,* eds C. Murphy and R. Tooze, Lynne Rienner, Boulder.

Tickner, J. Ann 1992, *Gender in International Relations*, Columbia University Press, New York.

Tilly, Charles 1985 'War Making and State Making as Organised Crime' in *Bringing the State Back In*, ed. P. Evans, Cambridge University Press, New York.

Tinker, Irene ed. 1989, *Persistent Inequalities: Women and World development*, Oxford University Press, New York.

Tinsman, Heidi 1992, 'The Indispensible Service of Sisters: Considering Domestic Service in Latin America and United States Studies', *Journal of Women's History*, vol. 4, no. 1, pp.37–59.

Togeby, Lise 1994, 'The Gender Gap in Foreign Policy Attitudes' *Journal of Peace Research*, vol. 31, no. 4, pp.375–92.

Tohidi, Nayereh 1994, 'Modernity, Islamization, and Women in Iran', in *Gender and National Identity: Women and Politics in Muslim Societies,* ed. V. Moghadam, Zed Books, London.

Tong, Rosemarie 1989, *Feminist Thought: A Comprehensive Introduction*, Unwin Hyman, London.

Tonkinson, Myrna 1988, 'Sisterhood or Aboriginal Servitude? Black Women and White Women on the Australian Frontier', *Aboriginal History*, vol. 12, nos. 1/2, pp.27–39.

Trinh, Minh-ha 1989, *Woman, Native, Other: Writing Postcoloniality and Feminism*, Indiana University Press, Bloomington, Indiana.

Tronto, Joan C. 1987, 'Beyond Gender Differences to a Theory of Care', *Signs*, vol. 12, no. 4, pp.644–64.

True, Jackie 1994 'Gendered Citzenship: East and West Compared' International Political Science Association conference paper, Berlin.

Truong, Thanh-Dam 1990, *Sex, Money and Morality: Prostitution and Tourism in South-East Asia*, Zed Books, London.

Tsolidis, Georgina 1993, 'Revisioning Multiculturalism within a Feminist Framework', *Journal of Intercultural Studies*, vol. 14, no. 2, pp.1–12.

Tucker, Margaret 1987, *If Everyone Cared: an Autobiography*, Grosvenor, Melbourne.

Turner, Bryan 1990, 'Outline of a Theory of Citizenship', *Sociology*, vol. 24, no. 2, pp.189–217.

Turshen, Meredeth ed. 1991, *Women and Health in Africa*, Africa World Press, Trenton NJ.

Turshen, Meredeth and Holcomb, Briavel eds 1993, *Women's Lives and*

Public Policy: the International Experience, Greenwood Press, Westport.

Tylee, Claire 1990, *The Great War and Women's Consciousness: Images of Militarism and Womanhood in Women's Writings, 1914–64*, University of Iowa Press, Iowa City.

United Nations 1994, *Final Report of the Commission of Experts Established Pursuant to Security Council Resolution 780 (1992)*, S/11941 674, United Nations, New York.

United Nations Development Program 1993, *Human Development Report* Oxford University Press, New York.

United Nations Development Programme 1995, *Human Development Report*, Oxford University Press, New York.

UNICEF 1995, *The State of the World's Children*, Oxford University Press, Oxford.

Valenzuela, Luisa 1991, 'Symmetries', *Arena*, no. 96, pp.38–46.

Valenzuela, Maria Elena 1989, 'Women and Peace Report', *International Peace Research Newsletter*, no. 28, 4, pp.11–13.

Valenzuela, Maria Elena 1990, 'Gender Issues in Chilean Politics', *Peace Review*, vol. 2, no. 4, Fall, pp.24–7.

Valleroy, Linda, Harns, Jeffrey and Way, Peter 1993, 'The Consequences of HIV/AIDS in Eastern Africa on Mothers, Children and Orphans', *Population and Environment*, vol. 14, no. 3, pp.301–6

Vance, Carole ed. 1984, *Pleasure and Danger: Exploring Female Sexuality*, Routledge and Kegan Paul, Boston.

Vasta, Ellie 1993a, 'Immigrant Women and the Politics of Resistance', *Australian Feminist Studies*, no. 18, pp.3–23.

Vasta, Ellie 1993b, 'Multiculturalism and Ethnic Identity', *ANZ Journal of Sociology*, vol. 29, no. 2, pp.209–25.

Vellacott, Jo 1987, 'Feminist Consciousness and the First World War' in *Women and Peace: Theoretical, Historical and Practical Perspectives*, ed. R. Pierson, Croom Helm, London.

Vickers, Jeanne 1990, *Women in the World Economic Crisis*, Zed Books, London.

Vickers, Jeanne 1993, *Women and War*, Zed Books, London.

Voet, Rian 1994, 'Women as Citizens: a Feminist Debate', *Australian Feminist Studies*, no. 19, 61–77.

Walby, Sylvia 1989, 'Theorising Patriarchy', *Sociology*, vol. 23, no. 2, pp.213–34.

Walker, Alice 1982, 'Advancing Luna—and Ida B. Wells' in *You Can't Keep a Good Woman Down*, The Women's Press, London.

Walker, Rob 1988, *One World/Many Worlds*, Lynne Rienner, Boulder.

Walker, Rob 1993a, 'Excluded Subjectivities: Gender, International Relations, World Politics', International Studies Association conference paper, Acapulco.

Walker, Rob 1993b, *Inside/Outside: International Relations as Political Theory* Cambridge University Press, Cambridge and New York.

Wallerstein, Immanuel 1974, *The Modern World System*, Academic Press, New York.

Waltz, Kenneth 1959, *Man, the State and War: a Theoretical Analysis*, Columbia University Press, New York.

Waltzer, Michael 1977, *Just and Unjust Wars*, Basic Books, New York.

Ward, Anna, Gregory, Jeanne and Yuval-Davis, Nira eds 1993 *Women and Citizenship in Europe*, Trentham Books and European Forum of Socialist Feminists, Oakhill.

Ward, Glenys 1988, *Wandering Girl*, Magabala Books, Broome.

Ward, Kathryn B. 1988, 'Women in the Global Economy' in *Women and Work: an Annual Review*, vol. 3, eds B. Gutek, A. Stromberg and L. Larwood, Sage, Newbury Park.

Ward, Kathryn B. 1990, *Women Workers and Global Restructuring*, ILR Press, Ithaca, NY.

Ward, Kathryn 1993, 'Reconceptualising World System Theory to Include Women' in *Theory of Gender/Feminism on Theory*, ed. Paula England, Walter de Gruyler, New York.

Ware, Vron 1983/4, 'Imperialism, Racism and Violence against Women', *Emergency*, no. 1, pp.25–30.

Ware, Vron 1992, *Beyond the Pale: White Women, Racism and History,* Verso, London.

Waring, Marilyn 1988, *Counting for Nothing*, Allen & Unwin, Wellington.

Waters, Malcolm 1989, Citizenship and the Constitution of Structured Social Inequality', *International Journal of Comparative Sociology*, vol. 30, nos. 3/4, pp.159–80.

Watson, Irene 1993, 'Has Mabo Turned the Tide for Justice?', *Social Alternatives*, vol. 12, no. 1, pp.5–8.

Watson, Peggy 1993, 'The Rise of Masculinism in Eastern Europe' *New Left Review*, no. 198, pp.71–80.

Watson, Sophie ed. 1990, *Playing the State, Australian Feminist Interventions*, Allen & Unwin, Sydney.

Waylen, Georgina 1994, 'Gender, Adjustment and Democratization', International Political Science Association conference, Berlin.

Weber, Cindy 1994, 'Good Girls, Little Girls and Bad Girls: Male Paranoia in Robert Keohane's Critique of Feminist International Relations', *Millennium*, vol. 23, no. 1, pp.377–49.

Weber, Cynthia 1992, 'Reconsidering Statehood: Examining the Sovereignty/Intervention Boundary', *Review of International Studies*, vol. 18, no. 3, pp.199–216.

Weed, Elizabeth ed., 1992, *Coming to Terms: Feminism, Theory, Politics*, Routledge, New York.

Welling Hall, Barbara 1994, 'Is There Room in the Universe for Gender?', *Mershon International Studies Review*, vol. 38, supp. 2, pp.253–9.

West, Guilda and Blumberg, Rhoda Lois eds 1990, *Women and Social Protest*, Oxford University Press, New York.

West, Lois 1992, 'Feminist Nationalist Social Movements: beyond

Universalism towards a Gendered Cultural Relativism', *Women's Studies International Forum*, vol. 15, no. 5/6, pp.563–81.

White, Sarah 1992, *Arguing with the Crocodile: Gender and Class in Bangladesh*, Zed Books, London.

Whitworth, Sandra 1989, 'Gender and the Inter Paradigm Debate', *Millennium*, vol. 18, no. 2, pp.265–72.

Whitworth, Sandra 1994, *Feminism and International Relations*, St Martin's Press, New York.

Wickham, Gary and Kendall, Gavin 1992, 'Civic Centre', *Australian Left Review*, no. 143, pp.20–3.

Wiegman, Robyn 1993, 'The Anatomy of Lynching', *Journal of the History of Sexuality* , vol. 3, no. 3, pp.445–67.

Williams, Christine 1989, *Gender Differences at Work*, University of California Press, Berkeley.

Williams, Louise 1993, 'Domestic Bliss: the Asian Advantage', *Sydney Morning Herald*, 9 March, p.8.

Wiltshire, Anne 1985, *Most Dangerous Women: Feminist Peace Campaigners of the Great War*, Pandora, London.

WING (Women, Immigration and Nationality Group) 1985, *Worlds Apart: Women Under Immigration and Nationality Law*, Pluto, London.

Winter, Bronwyn 1994, 'Women, the Law, and Cultural Relativism in France: the Case of Excision', *Signs*, vol. 19, no. 4, pp.939–74

Women Working Worldwide 1990, *Common Interests: Women Organising in Global Electronics*, WWW, London.

Women's Studies International Forum 1989, special issue: In a Great Company of Women: Non-Violent Direct Action, vol. 12, no. 1.

Women's Studies International Forum 1991, special issue on Reaching for Global Feminism, vol. 14, no. 4.

Wong, Diana 1994, 'Refuge and Women: Flight as a Biographical Theme', Linking Our Histories conference paper, University of Melbourne, Melbourne.

Woolf, Virginia (1993) [1938] *A Room of Her Own* and *Three Guineas*, ed. Michele Barrett, Penguin, London.

Wright, Shelley 1993 'Human Rights and Women's Rights', *Alternative Law Journal*, vol. 18, no. 3, pp.113–17.

Wrigley, Julia 1991, Feminists and Domestic Workers' *Feminist Studies*, vol. 17, no. 2, pp.317–29.

Yeatman, Anna, 1990, *Bureaucrats, Technocrats, Femocrats: Essays on the Contemporary Australian State*, Allen & Unwin, Sydney.

Yeatman, Anna 1993, 'Voice and Representation in the Politics of Difference' in *Feminism and the Politics of Difference*, eds S. Gunew and A. Yeatman, Allen & Unwin, Sydney.

Youngs, Gillian 1996, 'Dangers of Discourse: the Case of Globalisation', in *Globalization: Theory and Practice*, eds E. Kofman and G. Youngs.

Yuval-Davis, Nira 1985, 'Front and Rear: The Sexual Division of Labour in the Israeli Army', *Feminist Studies*, vol. 11, no. 3, pp.649–75.

Yuval-Davis, Nira 1991, 'The Citizenship Debate: Women, Ethnicity and the State', *Feminist Review,* no. 39, pp.58–68.

Yuval-Davis, Nira 1993, 'Gender and Nation', *Ethnic and Racial Studies,* vol. 16, no. 4, pp.623–32.

Yuval-Davis, Nira and Anthias, Floya eds, 1989, *Woman–Nation–State,* Macmillan, London.

Zak, Michele Wender and Moots, Patricia A. eds 1983, *Women and the Politics of Culture: Studies in the Sexual Economy,* Longman, New York.

Zalewski, Marysia 1994, 'The Women/"Women" Question in International Relations', *Millennium,* vol. 23, no. 1, pp.407–27.

Zalewski, Marysia and Parpart, Jane eds 1996, *The Man Question in International Relations,* Westview, Boulder.

Zegeye, Abebe and Ishemo, Shubi eds 1989, *Forced Labour and Migration: Patterns of Movement within Africa,* H. Zell, London and New York.

Zlotnik, Hania 1990, 'International Migration Policies and the Status of Female Migrants', *International Migration Review,* vol. 24, no. 2, pp.372–81.

Zohar, N. 1993, 'Collective War and Individualistic Ethics—Against the Conscription of Self-Defence', *Political Theory,* vol. 21, no. 4, pp.606–22.

Zolberg, Ariste 1989, 'The Next Waves: Migration Theory for a Changing World', *International Migration Review,* vol. 23, no. 3, pp.403–30.

Index